TOO OLWELL

Inglemoor High School and Beyond

Robert L Olwell with David H Olwell and Timothy P Olwell
2/16/2014

The absurd reality that surrounds the Family Olwell is portrayed in this second installment. The antics and adventures continue.

CONTENTS:

Preface

      Too Olwell: Inglemoor High School and Beyond focuses on Robert's brothers and sisters antics in High School. From 1969 to 1984, Inglemoor High School was represented by at least one Olwell. In 1975, Dianne, Tim and Tom all were enrolled there making it the highlight of Mr. Rumpee's(the Vice Principal at Inglemoor High School) career.

      Too Olwell takes a look at Tim's Air Force Academy days. His experiences were vastly different than Robert's at Washington State University described in **Growing Up Olwell**.

      Travel has been an integral part of the Olwell family. Some of Robert's adventures as a group Tour Escort for his mother's travel agency are described in humorous detail. From Robert's first trip he escorted to Hong Kong to his being chastised by the group in Spain, the stories will make you glad you travelled alone.

      Most chapters are introduced by a family member or friend with knowledge of the actual events from the story. This allows other perspectives into **Too Olwell**. Later in the book, you will be introduced to Robert's friend, Scott. Scott has a completely different take on the 'events' in some of the stories and is not shy about pointing out the discrepancies in his own style.

      This compilation of stories continues what **Growing Up Olwell** started.

Acknowledgements:

I would like to acknowledge my brother Dave. He was the one who suggested that I compile my short stories about the family into book form. **Growing Up Olwell** and **Too Olwell** are the direct result of his confidence in my writing. So in a way, he is also to blame.

As Dave commented in my first book, **Growing Up Olwell**, contained many stories that were 'Robert-centric'. In **Too Olwell**, I attempted to remedy this by including stories about my brother, Tim, and my sister, Allison. Both reviewed the stories and offered suggestions. Tim critiqued many of these stories in early form and also took the time to write many of the intros.

My brother, Tom, still has small children and has been adamant about minimizing his presence in any of my stories. For the most part, I have honored that request. By the way, 'For the most part' equals loop hole.

Special thanks to Jon Edwards and Megan Johnson Aumiller. Both reviewed the book in draft form and made suggestions that improved the content. These two made my high school days memorable and their willingness to assist all these years later was much appreciated.

The intros at the beginning of most chapters were written by friends and family. All of whom took the time to review the particular story and added to its value of it by offering their remarks. I truly believe the book is more fun as a result.

Many of the adventures include my wife, Cheryl, who has made life fun and exciting. Her love and support means everything to me.

No acknowledgement would be complete without thanking my folks who raised seven kids the best they could. At least they have said they 'did their best'. It could be that by the time I was a teen, their best was a little tired after raising my five older siblings. Nevertheless, I am what I am because of my parents and step parents, so in a way they too share the blame with Dave for this book.

PART I

HIGH SCHOOL TIMES

During my first week of High School at Inglemoor, "Robert Olwell to Mr. Rumpee's Office" was announced over the PA system . I had no idea why. My classmates looked at me with either glee or concern depending how they thought of me as I got up from my desk and left Ms. Fry's French class.

Mr. Rumpee pointed to the middle chair across from his desk and said I could sit in Dianne's chair. He laughed when he said it but I did not get the joke. He looked at me for a few minutes without saying anything.

When I took out my box of Junior Mints and started tossing them in my mouth, he shook his head. He told me not to eat in his office. I complied as I had finished the box anyway.

He then asked about Dianne, Tim and Tom. He commented on how wonderful Veronica was and that he was sorry she transferred schools. The last thing I wanted to hear was how great my older sister was. I looked at the clock on the wall and told him if there wasn't anything important to discuss I needed to head to my next class.

He rubbed his eyes and muttered, "That's all I needed to know," and dismissed me.

My friends asked about the encounter. When I explained it was no big deal, they did not understand. Most of them had never been to the Principal's Office before. I had been sent to the Principal's office numerous times dating back to the second grade. It wasn't until many years later I understood the underlying reason for this meeting though.

CHAPTER **1**

Tom Meets Mr. Rumpee

Tim: "This takes place my junior year. I am not sure some of the details are perfect, but Dianne did almost start the riot. Tom and I did start together in the victory over Bothell. I had been to the office several times and usually knew ahead of time why I had been summoned. This was one time I did not have any inkling why I was there. Dianne had a way of sucking Tom and me into her web of antics and grief. She would claim she was including us." Circa 1974.

"Why are you wearing my jersey?" Tim asked his older sister as he entered the office at Ingelmoor.

"I am so proud of you. I just had to wear it," Dianne answered.

It was said in a tone that made Tim wonder if she was screwing with him or actually being serious. He never liked not knowing. Not with anyone but especially not with Dianne. He decided he needed to strengthen his poker face. This was going to be the first time he was called to the Vice Principal's office without any ability to create an alibi or cover story mainly because he was unaware of the reason for the summons. He was going to have to be on his toes to cover himself.

"Tom? What are you doing here?" Dianne asked as Tom joined them in the office.

Tim started to wonder about the game that night. What if he and Tom were both in trouble? What was going on?

"I don't know. The teacher got a note to send me to the Principal," Tom replied, "I would rather be here than Algebra 2."

"The Vice Principal will see you now," the office secretary announced with a disapproving look.

The three Olwells entered the office. Dianne knew to shut the door from the many times she had visited the Vice Principal over the past three years. She threw the secretary a glare as she shut the door. Dianne didn't feel intimidated by a mere secretary.

Tom sat down.

"Move over, that's Dianne's chair," Tim said.

Tom scowled but moved a chair to the left.

"One more, that's my chair," Tim directed.

Dianne sat down and placed her purse over the back of the chair. The purse clanked when it hit the chair. She cringed at the thought she had left her pipe in it. Even with the cork handle it made a big noise. She hoped the Principal didn't hear it.

"You two have assigned chairs in the Principal's Office?" Tom asked in a voice that sounded kind of impressed.

"Someday I am sure you will, too," Tim laughed.

Mr. Rumpee looked up from his desk at the sound of laughter. He frowned.

"The Olwells, oh it is that meeting. When are you guys going to give a poor Vice Principal a break?" he asked rhetorically shaking his head.

"I can give you a break right now and go back to class," Tim offered and started to stand. Tim was hoping to get out before he had to come up with some story without knowing why they were there.

"Sit back down, Tim," he said again shaking his head.

He just looked at the three of them. He opened his top desk drawer and took out a bottle of aspirin. He counted out two and took them with a drink from his water glass.

"Guess who I got a call from during lunch?" he finally asked.

"Based on the aspirin, I am thinking your wife?" Tim offered without thinking. He was determined to keep a straight face.

Dianne whipped her head around and looked at Tim. She saw his straight face and smiled barely perceptibly. Tom burst out laughing. Both Tim and Dianne glared at him. Tom should have known that is not the way this is played.

"Ha, Ha, Tim, if you weren't starting against Bothell tonight, that would have cost you. I'll tolerate no more of that," he lectured. "Dianne, were either of your brothers aware of the stunt you pulled at lunch?"

"What stunt would that be Mr. Rumpee? It was a busy lunch today. I am afraid you will have to be more specific," Dianne replied.

Tom really looked at his older sister. It was like seeing her for the first time and he was impressed. He still didn't know what was going on but was awed that his sister didn't seem concerned at all.

"The Bothell Principal called about you walking through their cafeteria yelling 'Inglemoor is going to kick your butts because my two brothers are starting on defense', does that ring a bell?" he clarified.

"You didn't do that? Did you? I have to play them tonight!" Tim asked his sister.

"Of course I did, I wanted to warn them you are going to kick their butts," Dianne told Tim.

"You did that in my jersey? You might as well have just painted a bull's eye on my back," Tim said shaking his head.

"You'll be fine. You are tougher than any of those bum Bothell players," Dianne said reassuring him.

"The Principal said there were two other young ladies with you. We were only able to identify you because you were and are still wearing Tim's jersey. Who else was with you?" Rumpee asked picking up a pen preparing to write.

"You should know by now I am not going to help you," Dianne said and crossed her arms in front of her. Tom whipped his head around again at his sister's obvious ongoing defiance.

"Listen, Dianne, this is serious. The Bothell Principal called the District Superintendant and then they got me on a conference call. The Bothell Principal is livid. He convinced the District Superintendant that you were the ring leader. The District Superintendant wants you expelled for at least a month. Based on the fact the police had to come and arrived just in time to keep a riot from occurring I am not sure it isn't justified. Someone is in a lot of trouble for this and it might go easier on you if I can tell the Superintendant you were cooperative," he explained.

"I guess the Superintendant has never heard of the First Amendment," Dianne replied.

Mr. Rumpee put down the pen, took off his glasses and rubbed his eyes. He put the glasses back on.

"Tom, I am convinced you were not involved. You may return to class," he directed.

Tom looked disappointed but left the office. He was learning a lot more here than he would in math class. He was pretty sure he knew who Dianne's accomplices were and was glad he hadn't been asked. He

11

knew not to volunteer information, not to lie, and to be silent from dealing with his Dad for years with his brother and sister.

"Dianne, listen I am on your side this time. I know there wasn't anything damaging or malicious in your stunt. But it did nearly cause a riot, so much so the police were called. I don't know why the county police arrived first; they didn't even get your accomplices' names. Deputy Lyons seemed to think it was no big deal. It is a good thing he got there before the Bothell Police, you might have gone to jail otherwise," he said scratching the side of his head. Tim smiled at the mention of Jay Lyons. He had busted the Olwells for years and always punished them himself rather than arrest them. It was nice to be on the good side of his policing for once. Jay didn't like the Bothell team either.

"Do what you need to do. I am not ratting on my friends," Dianne said wondering if Mr. Rumpee could bar her from the game.

"Dianne, I will do my best. Leave my office," he told her and she left.

Tim was there all alone. Mr. Rumpee made a big deal of rubbing his head.

"Tell me, Tim, can we win tonight?" Mr. Rumpee asked.

"Yes, Sir. Coach Durst has us really well prepared and we have a great game plan. I feel really good about it. I will tell you they won't run to our side with me and Tom in there. That I can promise. They can't win if they can't run the ball. Their O-line is terrible at pass blocking."

"I hope you are right. Listen, I understand you getting dragged in all the time because of your sister. I hope you can be a better example for Tom," Rumpee said in a serious tone.

"What do you mean? Dianne has been a great example for me," Tim said defending his sister.

Mr. Rumpee just stared at him.

"Okay, I get your point," Tim laughed finally realizing he was going to be able to play that night.

Mr. Rumpee walked Tim out of his office. There he found Tom and Dianne, "Didn't I tell you two to go back to class?"

"You didn't say which class," Tom said.

"I wrote a note dismissing me for the rest of the day," Dianne stated.

Rumpee looked at the three Olwells and was exasperated, "Dianne, take off Tim's jersey and get out." As she made an attempt to take off the jersey, the secretary gasped as it became apparent Dianne wasn't wearing anything under the jersey. "Leave the jersey on and just leave!" an exasperated Mr. Rumpee said.

At the Bothell-Inglemoor Football game that night tension was high. On the first down from scrimmage when Tim and Tom were on defense, the Bothell quarterback yelled, "Hey Olwell, we're coming your direction."

"Your sister has a big mouth!" the Bothell running back yelled.

The ball was hiked. It was handed to the running back. Tim came up to make the play when he was chop blocked at the knees by the guard. As the running back darted to the outside, Tom avoided the fullback's lead block and crushed the ball carrier. He literally picked him off his feet and buried him into the turf on his back.

As Tom got up, he pushed off the running back's helmet and said, "My sister does have a big mouth. So do you! But I can shut yours. See you soon!"

The announcer said, "Tackle by Olwell." Bothell tried running the ball to the right twice more and each time the announcer repeated, "Tackle by Olwell." Bothell punted on fourth down and the game settled into a real battle. They didn't run much to the right side of the defensive line the remainder of the half. Inglemoor went into halftime leading 7-6.

During halftime, Coach Durst announced that he was going to rotate Tim and Tom from right to left side together and separately to screw up the Bothell offensive line. Turns out Inglemoor defeated Bothell, 28-6. After the game, the stands went crazy. It was the first time Inglemoor had beaten the cross town rivals in three years. Dianne and her two friends were being rewarded with praise and attention. Mr. Rumpee pretended not to notice who Dianne was parading with. He smiled as he walked towards the parking lot to supervise the cars leaving. There had been trouble with cars squealing tires and other pranks in the past after big victories.

Monday morning Dianne was again summoned to the Vice Principal's office. This time they used the school loud speaker to summon her which was unusual. She smiled knowing the entire school now knew of her prank. She stood tall during her walk of shame. She wondered how long she would be out of school.

"Dianne, you are on a one month in-school suspension," Mr. Rumpee told her.

"What does that mean?" she asked.

"It means you're in big trouble Miss but with no real consequences. I bet the Bothell Principal that if we lost you would be suspended for a month. If we won, you would not actually be suspended. Thank your brothers!" he added as he silently hoped the District Superintendent didn't follow up on her punishment. "By the way, did I see you in your car smoking before school again this morning?"

"How would I know what you saw?" Dianne answered.

"Really? Didn't I tell you that I didn't want to see you smoking on school grounds anymore?" he persisted.

"I believe I suggested that if you didn't want to see me smoking you should avoid the parking lot before school or during lunch," Dianne said with a look.

"Go back to class! Oh, and no notes excusing yourself from class for the duration of your suspension!"

"When exactly is that?" she asked.

"As the day is mostly over, it will run from tomorrow for thirty days. No shenanigans during the whole time or else!" he threatened. With that Dianne left his office.

He shook his head after her. He looked at the football schedule on his desk. Now if we can only beat Issaquah, we would make the playoffs, he thought.

He suddenly picked up the phone and called the attendance office, "Hi Joan, is Dianne Olwell at your desk?"

"Why yes she is. She just gave me a note excusing herself for the rest of the day. How did you know?" she asked.

"Tell her to go back to class and Joan let all the staff know that Dianne cannot write any notes for the next thirty days." He hung up the phone satisfied that he was starting to figure out the Olwells.

Note: Jay Lyons, a King County Deputy, was our neighbor's son. He always seemed to respond to police calls when we were involved. He handled the situations usually without notifying our parents and always "off the record." He displayed tough love on more than one occasion.

CHAPTER **2**

Tim's Advocate

> *Tim: "Dianne, Tom, Veronica and I got tickets at this neighborhood speed trap. Our parents were not sympathetic until one day when our mother got a ticket there. She came home and complained of the 'Speed Trap'. I never had to pay Mom back the twenty. If asked whether I would rather of had my dad get me out of trouble or had my stepdad teach me responsibility, I would have said, "Taking responsibility is overrated." Circa 1975.*

"Gordy will go with you," my mother insisted.

My brother Tim started to protest but knew when our Mom had made the final decision.

"Why do I have to go?" our stepfather protested.

My mother just looked at him and pursed her lips. All discussion ended on the subject. The discussion ended but that didn't keep Gordy from talking to himself as he left the kitchen and wandered down the hall.

"Thanks for taking me," Tim said on the drive to the Municipal Court.

"No problem, where did you get this ticket?" Gordy inquired.

"Right up here," Tim said, "I put my car in neutral and coasted home. I was doing 35 at the bottom of this hill. I was in the house for twenty minutes and when I came out the cop was sitting in the street blocking my car with his lights on. He was hiding in the vacant lot when I went by. I got a 35mph in a 25mph."

"Why are we going to court? Just pay the fine," Gordy said.

"I can beat this," Tim said and silence followed.

"Tim Olwell," the bailiff called.

"Here," Tim said. Gordy and he approached the table in front of the judge.

"Olwell? Any relation to Dave Olwell?" the judge asked.

"He is my father your honor," Tim answered.

"I went to law school with your Dad. How is he doing?"

"He's good your honor," Tim responded feeling pretty good about his chances.

"Well before I decide whether I need to recuse myself, who is this person with you?" the judge questioned.

"I am his stepfather, Gordon Swanson, your honor," Gordy announced.

"Well do you have anything to offer?" the judge inquired.

"Tim is an idiot. He is guilty. I would suggest jail time," Gordy offered.

The judge laughed a bit then realized Gordy was serious. "What is the minimum fine for ten miles over in a residential area?" the judge asked the bailiff.

"Twenty dollars your honor," the bailiff said after referring to his notes.

"Okay, I won't recuse myself and make you come back another time to see a different judge if you plead guilty. The fine would be twenty dollars. What do you say Mr. Olwell?" the judge asked.

"Guilty," Tim plead and looked disappointed.

"Twenty dollar fine, see the bailiff to pay the fine," the judge said banging the gavel, "say 'hi' to your Dad for me."

"Thank you your honor, and I will," Tim smiled.

Gordy and Tim went to the bailiff who asked for the twenty dollars.

"I didn't bring any money. I was going to beat this. I would have until you announced I was guilty," Tim said.

The bailiff looked at my stepdad. Gordy looked startled and looked at Tim then back to the bailiff. Finally, he reached into his wallet and paid the fine.

The drive home was quiet. About a block from the house, Gordy asked, "When are you going to pay me back?"

"My Dad would have gotten me off," Tim said flatly.

"You were guilty. You told me you were speeding. I was teaching you responsibility," Gordy said, "so when are you going to pay me back?"

"Soon," Tim said.

Later that evening, Tim asked Mom for twenty dollars. She looked in her purse and did not have enough cash. "Can I write you a check?"

"No, I need cash," Tim insisted.

"Just a second," our Mom said and went down the hall and got the money from our stepdad.

"Thanks," Tim said.

Tim waited about ten minutes then went down the hall and gave the twenty to my stepdad, "There you go."

Gordy was trying to figure out what happened when my brother went out the front door. Tim made it to his car before he started laughing. Gordy angrily explained the situation to my Mom. She started laughing. The more annoyed he got the funnier our Mom thought it was.

Note: By the time I started driving, a house had been built in the vacant lot previously used as the speed trap in this story. Otherwise, I may have had to borrow money from my mom to pay my stepdad back as well. Interestingly enough, my first speeding ticket was enroute back to WSU after spring break in 1982. The fine was $71. Dad sent me a check for $100 to cover it. Mom only sent me $71. I never asked her if she got it from Gordy. In case you are wondering, I did make a $100 off that ticket.

Family Picture with Gordy

CHAPTER **3**

Inglewood Country Club

Tim: "When we moved from Capitol Hill in Seattle to the suburbs in 1968, there were only two good points that we saw right away. One was our proximity to Lake Washington and the other was Inglewood Golf Course. We played golf, snow skied and sledded on the steep 4th hole, cut across it to get places, and caddied. Tim, Tom and Robert all participated in the economic engine for large teenage boys who could carry an overstuffed golf bag for four hours on Saturday or Sunday morning. We were paid cash after the round and we didn't need a car to get there . You could caddy as young as fourteen." Circa 1975.

"Robert what was your first job?" Tim asked me.

"My first real job? I worked at Inglewood Country Club," I replied.

"As a caddy?" Tim asked.

"I caddied before but I worked for the Pro Shop picking up the balls from the driving range, cleaning and storing member's clubs, and putting away the rental carts," I recalled.

"I used to make good money caddying. The going rate was seven dollars and I usually got a three dollar tip. Not too bad for a few hours on a Saturday morning," Tim recollected.

"I had a good gig when it came to caddying. Rick Adele, the Club Pro, would call me on short notice and I would go down and caddy for him. He would just add my time to the hours at the Pro Shop so I was getting $3.35 an hour. Also before the back nine, he bought me lunch at the food shack. I usually made fifteen bucks plus lunch," I smiled.

"That's pretty good," Tim acknowledged.

"Hey, I was caddying once when a friend of Rick's asked me if I was related to you. He recognized our last name."

"Really, how did he know me," Tim asked.

"Apparently, he was in a foursome where you caddied for one of the other guys - Hap Lightfoot's brother, I think he said. Anyway, on the eighteenth green when Lightfoot was putting, the clubs you were handling accidently fell into the sand trap and he missed his putt. He said Lightfoot went berserk on you. Rick and he discussed and laughed about it for three holes after that. Then this guy tipped me twenty bucks just for being your brother."

"Oh my God, I forgot about that. Lightfoot did go wild. But it served him right," Tim laughed.

"What does that mean?" I asked.

"The guy was a jerk. I had worked really hard to help him the whole round. I mean I improved his lie, I pretended not to notice lousy shots he didn't count on his score card, and once I even dropped a ball for him as he couldn't find his drive. What I didn't know was he was playing the other guys for big money. Otherwise, I wouldn't have done it," Tim said looking serious as he said it.

"Really, the guy was cheating when money was involved?" I asked incredulously.

"Yes, his best club was his size 10 1/2 foot wedge. He was cheating the entire round. Then on the seventeenth hole he pressed the bets," Tim said with a nod.

"What does that mean?"

"It means he doubled the amounts they were betting. Then he made a big putt on the seventeenth green so he pressed the bets again on the eighteenth before his drive. He would either break even or lose $400.00. He teed up the ball. His drive was long but faded into the trees. Then he started yelling at me saying I gave him a dirty club and that's why he sliced it," Tim recalled.

"A dirty club wouldn't cause that!" I protested.

"I know - so did the other three guys - but Lightfoot kept yelling at me and telling me he was going to complain to the Pro, he wasn't going to pay me, and he was going to make sure I would never caddy again. Anyway, his ball had careened off a tree and was barely in the fairway. He hit a long second shot and a beautiful third. He had a four foot putt for a birdie. If he made it he would win all the bets and survive. I figured everything was cool but when I handed him the putter he sneered he still wasn't going to pay me," Tim continued.

"What an ass. What did you say?" I asked.

"Nothing, what could I say? Anyway, you know the sand traps next to the elevated green on eighteenth? They are really deep. I set his clubs right on the edge of the green precariously close to the trap. I waited until the back swing of his putt then I nudged the golf bag with my heel and it fell into the trap creating a racket just as he hit the ball. The putter took a divot and the ball flew across the green," Tim said and he was laughing pretty hard reliving the event.

"You didn't?" I was aghast. Caddies never made any noise when someone was hitting.

"Oh hell yes I did. Well he started screaming at me. I was acting all apologetic. I was telling him I didn't know how it could have possibly happened. It was so hard keeping a straight face. Then he lifted his hand as if to strike me. I just smiled at that point and moved closer just inches away from his face. I told him if he touched me they would be pulling golf clubs out of his ass for weeks," Tim stopped laughing and looked pretty serious saying that.

"What did he say?"

"Nothing, he could tell I was serious and I wasn't afraid of him. He just put his head down and went to complain to the Pro. While he was doing that, the other three golfers came over and each gave me twenty bucks. Apparently, the bets were pretty large. We had to clear the green for the next foursome. I was standing by the caddy shack wondering what to do with Lightfoot's clubs when I saw the Pro approaching me with a very stern face. I thought I was through caddying and it bummed me because I needed the cash money. It was instant gratification. Get up early, carry a twenty pound bag for a few hours and get paid cash.

The Pro came up to me and told me not to worry about it and gave me ten bucks. He made Lightfoot pay me for being his caddy including a tip. The Pro never even asked if I had done it on purpose. One of the other golfers in the round vouched that it was an accident. He told the Pro he saw me set it down and he should have warned me about the positioning of it. I made seventy bucks that round," Tim laughed, "the Pro did suggest I stay away from Lightfoot. He insisted that I never threaten a member again though. Then he looked really serious and asked if I really told Lightfoot they would be pulling clubs out of his ass for weeks. When I said yes, he just walked away laughing and muttering about what it would look like with an oversized driver."

"I bet you didn't caddy much after that," I suggested.

"Think again, all the guys that didn't like Lightfoot's brother made sure I had a job anytime I went down to the golf course and there were a lot of guys that didn't like Lightfoot. Then I started working at Herfy's and I didn't caddy as much."

"How did you know you were getting work from guys who didn't like him?"

"I could tell because I always got a bigger tip and they usually said that was for Lightfoot when they gave it to me. I was making about twenty bucks a round for six months after that. They always told me how much he yelled and screamed like a little baby when the other three guys made him pay off his bets. There were a lot of members at the poker table in the men's locker room when he paid up. You could hear him complaining all over the club house. Everyone knew the story before I could walk home. Mr. Lightfoot, our neighbor, never mentioned it to me."

Inglewood Country Club, Kenmore, WA

Note: Caddying for the Club Pro, Rick Adele, was a good gig. He was a good golfer so I was walking the shortest distance possible and the round went by faster. Occasionally, when he was golfing with ladies, he would decide I needed to carry their clubs as well. Eighteen holes carrying three or four bags wasn't fun. Then the ladies would tip me a dollar. If Rick was paying attention, he would supplement their tip. If he was busy, I was just out of luck that day.

I thought these were great opportunities to practice my charms on a whole variety of people. Heck, they were basically a captive audience for four hours. Rick suggested I would get tipped better if I kept my mouth shut. I never thought I was charming while miming.

CHAPTER 4

That's My Boy!

Tim: *"Dianne was a senior, I was a junior and Tom was a sophomore in this story. Tom played football well but was not as dedicated as others after his junior year. He was a good athlete. As his friends quit playing, Tom fell away from sports. He could have started his entire senior year but decided not to play. It is still a fond memory of having Tom's tackles added into my tackle count at the end of the game. Tom could be stubborn and this story relates one of those incidents."* Circa 1974.

"Robert, do you want a soda or a hot dog?" Dad asked me.

"Sure! Both!" I answered and we walked over to the concession stand under the main bleachers. There was a noticeable buzz from the crowd as we waited for the game to begin in about fifteen minutes. Hope springs eternal at the start of every sporting season. This one was different though, for the first time in years, Inglemoor had depth at every position.

Dad ordered the food and we headed to the stands at Pop Keeney Field in Bothell. It was Inglemoor's first game of the season and Tim was starting at inside linebacker. Tom had also suited up with the Varsity. He had done extremely well during the two a day practices over the summer. Tom had picked up the 4-3 defensive scheme easily. Tim said he had a good chance for playing time as a sophomore. Dad explained to me how impressive that would be and how long Tom's arms were.

"Did you play football Dad?" I asked.

"I was the manager for Seattle Prep's Team. When I graduated high school, I was six foot one and weighted one hundred and one pounds. I was too thin to play, son, but I was there every game to support the team," he said while putting the mustard on the hot dog.

I laughed.

"What are you laughing about?" Dad asked feigning annoyance.

"I already weigh a hundred pounds and I am in the 7th grade," I told him.

"Shut up and eat your hot dog!" he laughed and shook his head at the mustard on his shirt.

The game started and Dad explained what was going on. The announcer would call out the yardage and the offensive and defensive players of note for each play.

"Tackle by Olwell," The PA would blare fairly often.

"That's my boy!" Dad would yell each time.

The other Inglemoor players' dads nearby would wave each time. Dad would acknowledge the other dads when their son's names were called. Mr. Metzger, Mr. Goodman, and Mr. Brossman were busy with Dad during half time congratulating each other for their sons' performance.

"Connie must have been some athlete," Mr. Metzger said to Dad.

"Nice one," Dad replied and just laughed it off.

The game started to come under control by the middle of the fourth quarter. Inglemoor had reached a fourteen point lead with a few minutes left.

"Olwell in for Fulmer!" Assistant Coach Yonk yelled.

"Olwell's already in coach!" Robert Jackson pointed out.

"Not Tim, Tom Olwell in for Fulmer!" he yelled again.

"Fulmer is an inside linebacker, I play defensive end Coach Yonk," Tom said as he approached the coach.

"Hey Dave! They're calling Tom in!" Mr. Metzger yelled. He pointed to Tom next to Coach Yonk. Mr. Metzger was nodding his head in approval.

"That's my boy!" Dad yelled.

Meanwhile, "Have Williams move to the inside for Fulmer and you take his position right end," Yonk explained.

"No," Tom said.

"No what?" Coach Yonk asked turning face to face with my brother.

"I'm not going in," Tom stated flatly.

"What do you mean you're not going in?" the Coach yelled.

"The last few minutes are for the scrub players and I am not a scrub. If you want me to play, I'll start next week. But I am not going in at the end of this game when we have already won," Tom told him.

Coach Yonk grabbed Tom by the face mask and pulled him closer, "You get your butt on the field right now, mister!"

"What's going on down there Dave? Yonk's got your son by the face mask and is pushing him around," Mr. Goodman asked.

"That's Connie's boy!" Dad yelled and shrugged his shoulders at me.

For the next few plays, nobody watched the game even though the defense held and the offence was back on the field. Everyone was watching Coach Yonk and Tom being separated by the other coaches and players. Finally, Coach Durst sent them both to the locker room.

After the game, Tim and Tom came over to us.

"Great game, Tim!" Dad said proudly.

"Tom, what was that all about?" I asked.

"I had a disagreement with Coach Yonk. He wanted me to mop things up out there. I told him only the scrubs went in at the end of the game and I wasn't a scrub," Tom told us with his hands folded across his chest.

"Yonk is pissed. Durst laughed and told him that he better work harder if he was going to start on this team," Tim said while looking at his brother with disapproval.

Coach Yonk wanted Tom thrown off the team for insubordination. Yonk was even madder when Tom asked what insubordination was. Coach Durst did not want to lose Tom for this season or his junior and senior years. Inglemoor had the smallest enrollment in the league. Durst convinced Yonk to keep him on the team and take his frustration out on Tom during practices.

"I will be starting by mid season," Tom declared.

"That's my boy," Dad laughed.

"I thought you said he was Mom's boy?" I said to Dad, and then turned to Tim, "Mr. Metzger said you played like Mom out there."

Tim looked at me funny then towards Mr. Metzger.

"He was making fun of me, Tim, not you," Dad told him smacking me in the back of the head, "When you were arguing with the Coach, I said you looked like your mother," he told Tom and Tim smacked me on the back of the head. "That's enough out of you," he said to me and Tom smacked me on the back of the head.

25

"Okay, that makes sense. Come on, Tom, we've got to catch the bus back to school. Bye, Dad," Tim said and they left.

"You want some ice cream?" Dad asked.

"Sure," I said rubbing my head.

"That's my boy," he said patting me on the shoulder.

Note: I wrestled and played football at Kenmore Junior High. I lettered but did not excel in either sport. I started playing lacrosse my senior year at Inglemoor. I took to the sport and I was a starting defenseman for WSU's Lacrosse Club for my junior and senior years there.

Seattle Prep Football Team: Dad is Top Right

CHAPTER 5

My Dad's A Lawyer!

Tim: "Dad was not living with us by the time this story takes place. He still got calls to help us out but usually without our Mom's knowledge. He had stopped drinking and had become extremely active in AA. He helped save the careers of many police officers and other lawyers. Karen knew how to get in trouble all by herself, but if she was with Dianne, it was always Dianne's idea that would be at fault. I can attest to that. When I was involved, it was always Dianne's fault! High school was a colorful time in the Arrowhead subdivision!" Circa 1975.

The sudden knock on the driver's side window startled Dianne and Karen. It had been very peaceful at Golden Gardens looking out onto Puget Sound. Dianne turned to see the nightstick tap her window again through the smoke. As she rolled down the window, she noticed the baggie of marijuana they had left on the dashboard. She reached out to grab it.

"You can leave that right where it is young lady," the Officer commanded, "and turn the radio down."

"Yes Sir," Dianne said with a deflated voice. Karen reached to turn the rock and roll station, KJR 95, off.

"License and registration please, and I will need to see your identification as well," he said to Karen. He reached in and took the marijuana off the dash board. He was trying to do it without getting pot smoke all over his newly pressed uniform.

Dianne handed over the licenses, "I don't think you had probable cause to disturb us. Her brother is a King County Deputy and my Dad is an attorney!"

KLANG, was the sound of the cell door shutting behind Dianne and Karen. Dianne was trying to figure out how the Officer had handcuffed them, put them in the patrol car and got them to the Ballard

Precinct office so fast. To say her head was spinning would be an understatement. She thought she might be sick.

Karen wasn't saying much. She just sat in the corner and prayed.

"Afternoon ladies, I am Sergeant Hanrahan. I am the Duty Supervisor. I have spoken to Officer Novak. So, who would you like me to call for you: the County Deputy or the Lawyer?" he said with his hands on his hips. He wasn't smiling.

Clearly this wasn't going well, Dianne thought. "Sergeant Hanrahan, please call my father," Dianne offered with Dad's phone number. She decided to hope Dad could handle it better than she had to this point.

About an hour later, Dad walked into the Precinct. He had his 'I'm not amused' look on his face until he saw the desk sergeant.

"Hi Dennis," he said to Sergeant Hanrahan, "How the hell are ya?"

"I'm great Dave; it is good to see you. I am sorry to bring you down here but with drug charges pending and your daughter throwing your name around, I thought you should be involved," he explained.

"No Dennis, I appreciated the call. Drug charges? Marijuana?" Dad asked. Now his 'I'm not amused face' turned to his 'who am I going to kill' look.

"Yes Dave, by my calculation two ounces. I am sure it is for personal use, since she and her friend were smoking it when Officer Novak walked up to them in the parking lot. They didn't even notice his approach. Even through the haze, the drugs were visible on the dashboard. He didn't have a lot of latitude as they were so brazen about it," Hanrahan explained.

"I see. Where are the little criminals?" Dad asked and was taken back to a meeting room.

Dianne and Karen were relieved to see him. The room had stopped spinning and both Dianne and Karen were coming down from being high in the jailhouse. It was a terrible way to quit being high.

"Marijuana? And in public? What were you two thinking?" Dad asked.

"Everyone's doing it Dad!" Dianne blurted.

"They are Mr. Olwell," Karen confirmed.

"Really? Everyone? That's hard to believe as you are the only two pot smokers in jail at this Precinct. So either everyone is not doing it or everyone else has more brains than the two of you. Which do you think it is?" Dad asked displaying his annoyance. He looked at one then the other in the eye and didn't like the glazed looks he got back in return.

Neither of them responded. They had seen this look before from Dad and knew silence was always the best way to handle that look.

"Sergeant Hanrahan, may I see the confiscated drugs please?" Dad asked.

"Sure thing Dave, I will have Officer Novak bring the evidence in," The Sergeant replied.

"Why aren't you two in school?" Dad asked still wondering why he had to respond to Ballard during the school day when these girls should be in high school thirty miles away.

"I wrote a note excusing us," Dianne answered and then explained since she was eighteen, she could write her own notes.

A few minutes later, Dianne and Karen were sitting at the table with the marijuana on it. Across from them were Dad, Hanrahan and Novak.

The girls started to sweat as none of the men were talking. Dad and the Officers just scowled at them and waited them out.

"Okay, I am sorry! We shouldn't have been smoking marijuana in public and we shouldn't have told you my Dad was an attorney and her brother was a cop," Dianne said meekly. She folded her hands in front of her and looked down at the table.

"Mr. Olwell, may I have a word?" Sergeant Hanrahan asked.

Dad and the Sergeant left the room. Officer Novak watched Dianne and Karen with his hands folded across his chest. He gave them his best 'you are so busted' look.

"How do you want to handle this Dave?" Dennis asked.

"I would really like you to leave me alone with the girls and the pot for a few minutes. Does the bathroom work in the adjoining room?" Dad asked sending a clear message to the Sergeant what he had in mind.

Sergeant Hanrahan smiled then they stepped back into the meeting room. He asked Officer Novak to step out. Officer Novak reached for the evidence.

"Leave it," the Sergeant told him.

Officer Novak gave him a questioning glare but complied. The desk Sergeant could handle this anyway he wanted. Novak was not senior enough to even question him out loud.

After the Officers left the room, Dad picked up the baggie and went and flushed it down the toilet.

"Who's going to pay for that?" Dianne demanded.

"Really? I'll tell you what. You tell your Mom and Gordy about this. I am sure they will be happy to reimburse you," Dad lectured as he took off his glasses and rubbed his eyes. He paced a few steps then settled down a bit.

Dad knocked on the door and the Officers returned. Both looked surprised that the marijuana was missing. They even pretended to look for it.

"Well without the evidence, I guess you ladies can go. Understand though, I have been at this Precinct for eighteen years and I have another twelve before I retire. If either of you two comes before me again, it will not end well. Do you understand?" Sergeant Hanrahan asked menacingly.

Officer Novak did not understand why his evidence had been allowed to disappear and was sincerely looking pissed at the two teenagers. He was going to lose two busts towards his monthly quota.

"Yes sir," both girls answered.

Dad drove Karen and Dianne back to Golden Gardens where their car was. It was a silent drive.

"Hey Dad, can you buy us dinner? We are hungry," Dianne asked. She may have come down a lot but she still had a serious case of the munchies to deal with.

"No. Go Home!"

"Mr. Olwell, are you going to tell my Dad?" Karen asked.

"No, but you should probably discuss it with him. I don't know if Hanrahan called or not," Dad said.

"Mr. Olwell, thank you," Karen said sincerely, "I should have known better than to listen to Dianne about it being okay to smoke here."

"Yeah thanks Dad," Dianne said although she was glaring at Karen when she said it.

Dad was still shaking his head as the girls drove away. He hoped they would call Jay Lyons, the deputy sheriff, next time.

CHAPTER 6

Brilliant Friends

Tim: "Fred and his brother, Ron, were the only boys Tom and my age when we moved into the neighborhood. His stepdad, Bob Alamo, worked for the national gas company. He was a big man and pitched for a men's slow pitch softball team. Fred and Ron were loyal and fun to hang around with. We drifted apart as we grew older and our circle of friends grew beyond three blocks." Circa 1974.

Fred was a friend to my brothers Tim and Tom. My mother never considered Fred too swift. As a matter of fact, one day while being quite annoyed by him, she exclaimed, "Fred, you have an I.Q. of 16!"

Fred was very pleased and stated. "That's pretty good, I'm only 15 years old!"

My mother just rolled her eyes and shook her head.

"Do you think I should tell him an IQ of 100 is average and anything below 80 is considered retarded?" Tim asked her.

"No, he looks so happy. Just let him be," she laughed.

This was not the only opportunity Fred allowed for us to witness his intellectual prowess. One Friday evening in the early 1970's, there was a get together at our house. In the downstairs rec room, there were around ten of Tim and Tom's friends. During the evening, Fred was in full bravado.

"I'll bet you $5.00; you can't knock me out with one punch!" Fred challenged Tom.

At first Tom was feeling challenged. He could knock out Fred with one punch. Then he was beside himself in glee. Here was an opportunity to hit Fred as hard as he could with no chance of retaliation. He could just swing away. A nose could be broken, teeth wrecked, or eyes closed. There was no downside to this. Heck, if he hit him hard enough, Fred would actually pay him to do it!

If you knew Fred at all, you would be glad to have an opportunity to punch him. He was the type who just needed to be punched and often.

The problem was Tom did not have the $5.00 in the event he lost. There was a big scuffle around the basement looking for $5.00. But no one would give Tom the money.

"Lend me $5.00," Tom asked Tim.

"No," Tim refused.

My brother Tim had $5.00 but for some reason would not give it to Tom. Tim has regretted little of his actions in life, but he admits this was a possible poor choice.

Sadly enough, we will never know if Fred could have been knocked out. I think it goes without saying that had he been hit, little or no damage would have been done to him intellectually.

I often though Fred would make a good proofreader at the M&M factory. No, he would probably just get fired for stopping the factory because he saw a W!

Many years later I asked Tim why he didn't give Tom the five bucks.

"I had been trying to knock Tom out with one punch for years and no one ever gave me five dollars!" he laughed.

Note: At this party, someone bet Tim he couldn't do a hand stand. He tried and fell over putting his foot through my fish tank. That was the end of my guppies. By the way, Fred had four younger siblings. Three of them made him look like a genius!

CHAPTER **7**

Repeated Invitations To The Principal's Office

Tim: "Inglemoor was our high school. Between Dianne, Tim and Tom, we had all the groups and cliques covered from athletic, academic, clubs, and even the parking lot crowd. Still, all the groups would come together to pull stunts if the dreaded Bothell High School was the target of the prank. We pulled two really great stunts and several smaller, mostly unnoticed ones. Since it was a rivalry and we didn't vandalize the buildings, we were questioned but not overly critically. At our five year reunion, Mr. Rumpee declared all statute of limitations had expired and we talked openly about our shenanigans. This was my senior year." Circa 1976.

"You three in and shut the door," Vice Principal Rumpee stated firmly.

Tom started to sit.

"That's my chair," Tim said.

Without a question, Tom slid over one chair. Robert Jackson took the chair on the end.

Tim just smiled a little and was seated.

The Vice Principal just glared at the three of them while tapping his pencil on the table. If he thought this would unnerve an Olwell, clearly he was mistaken. Olwells have faced down priests, nuns, and even our parents on occasion.

Tim elbowed Tom and jerked his head towards Robert Jackson. Apparently it was working on him. Robert was turning red and sweating profusely. He was a virgin to the Principal's office for an inquisition.

Finally, Mr. Rumpee broke the silence, "After your sister graduated, I expected to see less of you in my office, Tim."

Tom laughed.

"Do you think this is funny, Mr. Olwell?" Mr. Rumpee glared then realized there were two Olwells before him, "Tom?"

"I do so far," Tom replied now starting to lean way back in his chair.

Even Tim looked a little shocked at that response.

"Maybe I should just call your father," Rumpee threatened while leaning over and spinning his rolodex for effect.

"Say 'Hi' for me," Tom said, "hand me the phone, I'll dial it for you."

"Do you think this is appropriate behavior Mr. Olwell, Tom?"

"Mr. Rumpee, I have not done anything wrong and I don't even know why I am here. If you think you and your office scares me, you are sadly mistaken!" Tom rocked forward in his chair slamming the legs down to emphasize his point. "So tell me why I am here or I am leaving."

"Just get out of my office," Mr. Rumpee seethed.

With that Tom got up and left.

Tim and Robert Jackson had remained quiet throughout the exchange. Tim was laughing on the inside where it counted and Robert looked horrified. Mr. Rumpee was trying to hold his composure.

"I am starting to miss your sister Dianne, Tim," Rumpee finally said, "Your brother is going to be a pain in my ass like you have been, isn't he."

"Looks like it to me!" Tim said and laughed.

Mr. Rumpee even laughed and that broke the tension.

Robert Jackson was speechless. He had never seen or even heard about an exchange with a Principal like what he was witnessing.

"What is this about?" Tim asked.

"I just got off the phone from the Principal from Bothell High School. They started classes two hours late today. It seems someone cemented a couple of toilets in the street blocking the entrance of the school. The busses were lined up for a half mile waiting to pull onto campus. What do you have to say about that?"

"I would say that they are a bunch of idiots, it wouldn't take two hours for Inglemoor students to get off the bus a block from school and get to class," Tim said.

Robert nodded in agreement.

"That's not what I meant! Were you involved in this?" The Vice Principal asked directly.

"Mr. Rumpee, you have been cool to me for the last three years so I won't lie to you," Tim said.

"So what are you telling me?"

"I am not going to say anything else. Otherwise, I would probably have to lie," Tim said.

Mr. Rumpee leaned down and banged his head on the desk several times.

"After Tom, how many more are there?"

"How many more what?" Tim asked.

"Olwells?"

"Three more after Tom," Tim answered now laughing into his hand.

"Off the record, pretty funny stuff as no damage was done. On the record, get out of my office." Mr. Rumpee was remembering the riot Diane had started in the Bothell high school cafeteria the week Tim and Tom both started on defense for that game. That had been impossible to settle down since Inglemoor and Bothell Highs were in the same district. Even district personnel wanted Dianne suspended or expelled. He had protected her from that and had managed an in school suspension. Dianne had been a good sport and even pretended to obey it.

"What were you thinking?" Tim asked Tom.

"Just setting the tone, I can't have the Principals thinking I scare easy, I got another year with him after you." Tom answered.

"You two are crazy. I am glad I was in there with you. I would have never believed it. He never even asked me a question," Robert Jackson commented. Robert's parents responded to calls from the Principal with grave concern and he was pretty sure Vice Principal Rumpee would not remember he had been part of the meeting at all.

He finally had been part of one of the Olwell escapades that he had heard about since Arrowhead Elementary! He had been Tim's friend since 4th grade there. Everyone would know he was involved in the prank because he had been called on to the carpet with them. He walked off whistling wondering how this would improve his homecoming date status. Then he thought he better warn his brother, Alan, he was in the same year as the next Olwell brother, Robert.

35

Five years later, it was just one of the many conversations Tim had at the class reunion with school staff that wanted to know the logistics of that and other pranks.

Note: Alan Jackson and I were pretty good friends all throughout school. We played lacrosse at Inglemoor together. During our college years at WSU, we often ran across each other. He even worked for my mother's travel agency and escorted tours with me.

Although, I did visit Mr. Rumpee's office occasionally, Alan was never involved.

CHAPTER 8

Wrestling Toward A Basketball Letter

Tim: "I was a hard working athlete. Not big as some but big enough for high school football. I was successful largely because of those around me. Wrestling, though a team sport, is a one on one endeavor during your time on the mat. I was not very good at takedowns but was able to make up the loss of those points quickly. I was 6-2 and about 185 during football and dropped to 169 to wrestle. I was a horrible basketball shot and didn't play subtle defense. No blood, no foul was the way we played pickup basketball. Even with that rule, I got called for fouling a lot! This story really happened. I enjoyed punishing other team's tough guys. Some of my teammates on the basketball squad were on my side about lettering!" Circa 1976.

With great anticipation, Tim arrived at the Kenmore Junior High gym for basketball tryouts. Now that football season was over, he was excited about the opportunity to play basketball. The coach called the practice to order.

"All right all you newbies, watch the eighth and ninth graders do the drill first then you join them" Coach Devere yelled. Then he blew his whistle and the older players started running the drills.

Within a few minutes, some of the seventh graders started joining them. A few minutes after that, Tim stepped up and joined the drills. He was trying really hard when Coach Devere came up to him, "Olwell, come with me."

Tim complied. Mr. Devere led Tim through the locker room, past the gymnastics room, down the stairs, past the building heater and hot water room and into where the wrestling team was practicing.

"Cowles, I have a wrestler for you," Coach Devere said.

Mr. Cowles came over and looked at Tim, "I am Coach Cowles, let me see you do fifty pushups."

Coach Devere and Coach Cowles chatted while Tim dropped to the mat and started doing pushups. The other wrestlers stopped what they were doing and started betting on whether Tim could actually do fifty. Obviously, they had never been a smart aleck in Mr. Schoenfelder's 6th grade class before. If they had, they would have known that you learned how to do lots of pushups in his class.

By the time Tim reached fifty, Coach Devere had left. Coach Cowles was smiling as Tim had made it to fifty without even breaking a sweat.

"Let's see what you are made of young man!" he said. He pointed to an older and bigger student and pointed to the center of the mat.

The rest of the wrestling team made a circle and Tim faced off against the bigger kid. After a few minutes, Tim had held his own to the surprise of everyone in the room.

"Is that all you got? My sister, Dianne, could take you," Tim sneered.

"What's your name? Is it Olwell?" Coach Cowles asked.

"Yeah, Tim Olwell."

"I know Dianne. She might be able to take him but save the trash talk for the other schools. We are a team in here. I think you are going to be a fine wrestler as soon as I teach you a few moves," the coach smiled.

Tim's wrestling career had begun.

A few years later, Tim was practicing with the Varsity wrestling team at Inglemoor High School. As a junior, he had placed fourth in the regional and qualified for state as the 16th seed. He lost his first match against the number one seed. As a senior, he was expected to win the Kingco Division title. He was on pace to achieve that when one practice, the Basketball Coach, Mr. Pressey interrupted.

"Coach Golberg, may I borrow Olwell for a few minutes," he asked.

"Certainly, Coach Pressey. Olwell, with Pressey. The rest of you back to work," Coach Golberg directed.

Tim followed Coach Pressey out of the wrestling room as Coach Yonk, the assistant wrestling coach, looked on smiling.

"How would you like to suit up Friday night with the Varsity Basketball team?" Coach Pressey asked.

"Sure Coach, I've got moves!" Tim laughed, "Seriously, what's up?"

"First, as to your moves, I don't want you dribbling the ball or shooting the ball. I may not even need you on the court but Issaquah's Number 15 has been hammering the other teams of the league. I mean he is super physical to the point of playing dirty and I don't have any big players. You know what I mean, big strong tough players."

"I got it Coach. Just tell me when and where," Tim agreed, "It can't interfere with wrestling though, I am going to win Kingco."

"No problem Olwell, I don't need you at any of the practices, only for game time."

The Basketball team did not know what to think when Tim got on the bus in uniform. It seems Pressey never told them what was up. No one talked to him on the drive to Issaquah. Tim did not participate in the pregame drills. In fact, Coach Pressey had to tell him to stop talking to the girls in the stands and go back and sit on the bench.

Tim was watching the game with mild interest when a few minutes into the game, Issaquah's Number 15, hammered Jack Brossman going up for a lay in. Jack had been intentionally fouled to make a point not to drive the lane. It was a dirty play but Jack got up and shook it off. Jack was tough and didn't show how much it had hurt.

"Olwell, you're in for Renneker," Coach Pressey yelled.

Tim stripped off his sweats and went to the scorer's table.

"Don't shoot or dribble. Hell, don't touch the ball if you can avoid it," Pressey told him. "A rebound would be enough."

Tim jogged up to the lane and stood next to Number 15.

"Sorry," Tim said to him.

"What for?" Number 15 asked.

Tim smiled. Jack Brossman threw up his foul shot. He missed it on purpose. Tim stepped on 15's foot to keep him from jumping then elbowed him in the throat disguised as a weak attempt to get the rebound.

Number 15 crumpled to the court gasping for air. Tim thought the Issaquah player was overdoing it.

Tweet. The ref blew a foul on Tim.

"Good call ref. I was a little wild. I have got to work on that," Tim said and held his hand up to recognize the foul to the scoring table. As the ref went by assigning the foul to him, Tim bent down to help

Number 15 from the floor, "I have four more fouls. You better stop that cheap stuff."

Number 15 just glared at him and refused to take the helping hand up.

Immediately, another Inglemoor player came into replace Tim.

Even before he reached the sideline, Pressey was on him, "Olwell you can't play like that. Keep your hands up for the rebound. Sit down!"

"Sorry Coach, I know you have been working on my control," Tim said hanging his head low pretending to be sad.

"Nice job," Coach said quietly as he passed.

For the rest of the game, any time Number 15 even played one of Tim's team mates tough, Tim yelled, "Put me in Coach!"

Number 15 played the rest of the game straight in his team's losing effort.

On the bus ride back to Inglemoor, Jack sat next to Tim, "Thanks, Tim." Tim and Jack had been football teammates since 7th grade.

"Any time Jack, I was hoping to get more playing time though, I've been working on my layups in case I actually got a rebound!" Tim laughed.

Pressey came back and gave the game ball to Jack. Jack tried to give it to Tim but Pressey wasn't allowing it.

When Coach Pressey returned to his seat on the bus, Robert Jackson asked, "How do I count Olwell's time on the court?"

"Why?"

"He was only in the game for a free throw and the clock wasn't running," Robert pointed out.

"Mark it a zero seconds playing time, one foul," Pressey laughed.

When they arrived back at the school, Coach Pressey pulled Tim aside, "Thanks Tim, you really did make a difference. In two weeks, we have Mercer Island at home, want to suit up?"

"Sure thing," Tim laughed.

In addition to the Issaquah away game, Tim suited up for the two Mercer Island games and the home game against Issaquah. On each occasion, he went in and punished any opponent for playing dirty against his team. He would always get called for a foul. Tim would tell the ref it was a good call and then Pressey would yell at him. At the end of the Issaquah home game, Robert Jackson told him as he had played in eight quarters in Varsity games he only needed to play in two more to letter in Basketball.

The following Friday without being asked, Tim suited up for the Bothell home game.

"What are you doing here?" Coach Pressey asked seeing him on the bench before the game.

"I'm just here to help," Tim smiled.

"We don't need you tonight Tim," he said.

"You never know," Tim said.

"Olwell, what is going on?" the coach finally asked.

"I only need to play in two more quarters and I will have earned a basketball letter," Tim informed him.

"Olwell, I appreciate your help but there is no way in hell you are going to letter on this team. No one ever letters in wrestling and basketball at the same time," Pressey said.

"I can be the first."

"Listen, you can sit there on the bench but I am not putting you in the game. Is that understood?"

"Kill joy," Tim said smiling at the nearest cheerleader. It was Connie, Jack's girlfriend.

He decided to stay and watch the game from the bench. He kept offering to go in but Pressey didn't call his name. At halftime, the coach told him not to huddle with the team during time outs. At the end of the game, Tim left the bench and went to shower up. As soon as he had taken off his uniform, Coach Pressey appeared and held out his hand. Tim went to shake it but Pressey said, "No, Olwell, I don't want to shake your hand. Give me your uniform. Your season is over."

Tim responded, "But Coach, what about the playoffs?"

The coach laughed as he walked off without dignifying Tim's question with a response. Jack told him later that Issaquah hadn't qualified for the playoffs.

Tim's stats for the season were: Played in 4 games, 8 Quarters, about 6 minutes, 1 rebound, 1 turnover, no points, and 13 fouls. His shortest stint was no seconds played as the clock doesn't run during foul shots. Tim is still mad he didn't get a high school varsity basketball letter.

Note: He came in second on the voting for team MVP though. Brossman won with 11 votes. Tim had the only other vote, Jack's. Pressey had to invite Tim to the Award's Banquet because of the vote.

Tim said he wouldn't go unless he received a basketball letter. Jack told him he missed a nice dinner.

Principal Rumpee is in the middle. Please note the inscription from my 1981 yearbook.

"You're graduating and my nightmare is over with your departure."

CHAPTER 9

The Usual Suspects

Tim: "In case it doesn't come through clear enough, we had great teachers, coaches, staff, counselors and principals at Inglemoor. We tested all of them often. The Vice Principal got to deal with all of us often as issues usually ended in his office. The time he spent with us prepared him for his posting to Principal a few years later. I'm surprised they didn't have an Olwell wing!" Circa 1976.

"Why does Rumpee want to talk to us?" Jack Brossman asked.

"Probably for the prank we pulled on Bothell High School last night," Tim answered.

Robert Jackson and Tom just smiled a bit.

"What prank?" Jack asked.

"Mr. Rumpee will see you now," the office secretary said looking up.

Jack looked around for the right office.

When the secretary saw that, she added sarcastically, "The Olwells know the way."

"What prank? You'll find out soon enough Jack," Tim laughed leading the way into the vice principal's office. Tom closed the door.

The four students walked into Mr. Rumpee's office. Jack started to be seated.

"That's Tim's chair," Tom said patting Jack on the shoulder.

Jack looked at Robert. He just nodded. Jack moved one chair to the left.

"That's my chair," Tom said claiming his Olwell rite of passage.

Jack looked at Robert Jackson who just shrugged. Jack moved left one more time. This time prior to seating he looked to Tom first. Tom nodded and he was seated.

Mr. Rumpee started speaking without really looking at them, "The reason I called you three to my office is to try to get to the bottom of what happened at Bothell High School last night."

Jack held up three fingers to Tim with a question in his eyes.

Tim just shrugged.

"It seems someone placed sixty or so used tires from the base of their flag pole to the top. They were unable to put their flag up this morning. IHS was spray painted on the tires in Gold paint. The Bothell Principal took that to mean students from Inglemoor did this. He also said that their janitor tried to cut through the tires with a chainsaw but every third tire was a steel belted radial. They have had to call in a crane to remove the tires. The Principal is curious as to just how this stunt was accomplished. Frankly, I am curious too, that pole must be twenty feet in front of the nearest building," he said, "Why don't we try this the easy way first, do you three know anything about this?"

He looked up from his desk into four faces. Tim smiled at him. Robert avoided making eye contact. Jack was reading his Calculus book. Tom was blowing a bubble with his gum.

"Olwell, what are you doing in my office?" Rumpee asked.

"I was called here," Tim answered.

"Not you! Tom, what are you doing here?" Rumpee clarified.

"It was either this or Spanish class. I thought this would be more fun," Tom replied. Tom always learned more from visiting with Mr. Rumpee than any other teacher in school.

Mr. Rumpee rubbed his eyes then said, "Go back to class."

"Okay, by the way, my Dad says 'hi'," Tom said as he was getting up from his chair. He had been part of the prank but didn't want to admit to it at this point. It was easier to wait outside the office and let his brother, Tim, handle it.

Mr. Rumpee did not like that much at all. The last time he threatened to call the Olwells' father, Tom had offered to dial the phone.

"Get out of my office!" Rumpee yelled.

"See you guys when the clock turns in our favor," Tom said and left the office. He purposely left the door open.

"Brossman, close the door," Rumpee said shaking his head, "And what does that mean, 'when the clock turns in our favor'?"

"It means after the last school bell of the day; when our life is our own again," Tim said, "my sister, Dianne, started that."

"Did I tell you lately that I miss her?" Rumpee asked sarcastically.

"Really?" Robert asked.

"No! Let's try and get back on track. Jack, were you involved in any prank at Bothell last night?" he asked.

"No, I wasn't," Jack answered.

"You can go back to class," Rumpee said dismissing him.

Tim then Robert Jackson also got up to leave.

"Where do you think you two are going?" the Vice Principal asked.

"You told us we could go back to class," Tim said with a straight face. He had practiced this many times before. While Rumpee examined his expression for any sign of amusement, Tim wondered how Jack could get off so easy. Did other students just get to come in and say they weren't involved in something and the Principal believed them? One day, he thought he would find out. The only problem is that Rumpee had never on those numerous occasions called Tim to the office when he hadn't been involved.

Mr. Rumpee looked to see if Tim was serious or just screwing with him. He had an idea but wasn't sure, "I meant Jack. Now Robert, what do you know about what happened?"

"I heard someone placed a bunch of tires over Bothell High's flag pole. They painted them our school colors and included some steel belted radials so they could not be cut through," Robert Jackson answered.

Tim glared at Robert. Mr. Rumpee caught the glare.

"Good, now we are getting somewhere. Who told you that?" Mr. Rumpee said hopefully.

"You did a few minutes ago," Robert answered. He too had a straight face.

Tim started laughing as that was nicely done.

Rumpee got mad, "What are you laughing about Olwell?"

"That was the greatest answer I have ever heard. I have no idea if he was being straight or screwing with you. Robert, you just earned this chair, move over and sit down next to me," Tim laughed.

"Thanks Tim," Robert replied while moving seats. He was genuinely touched by the gesture. He was going to be famous by the end of the day if it got out he now had a designated chair next to Tim's.

"That is enough you two! Olwell were you involved?" Rumpee sighed.

"On the record or off the record?" Tim asked.

"Really?" Rumpee said with exasperation.

"I have an appointment to the Air Force Academy, I am not screwing that up by being honest with you now," Tim said with conviction.

"I've been around you Olwells too long because that sort of makes sense. Mr. Jackson, go can back to class."

When Robert left, Mr. Rumpee just stared at Tim for a while.

"We are alone so off the record what happened at Bothell last night?" Rumpee asked.

"I was involved. It was awesome. You would have been so proud. No damage was done to their school. Any paint was on the tires we provided. It was truly a harmless prank," Tim said leaning forward in his chair.

"No damage, they are bringing in a crane to remove the tires. Who is going to pay for that?" Mr. Rumpee asked.

"If they are too stupid to get the tires off without a crane, then they can pay for it. We didn't use a crane," Tim said with contempt in his voice.

"Okay then but how did you do it?" Rumpee asked with a small smile developing.

"I am sworn to secrecy on that. I respect you enough to tell you I was involved off the record but I can't really tell you anything else. You will have to wait for the five year reunion for that," Tim said.

"Other than the IHS paint is there any way it can be traced back to any student in this school?" Rumpee asked.

"I really don't think so, but you figured out I was involved?" Tim said.

"In the last four years, how many decent pranks were pulled off without you, or Dianne before you, being involved?" he asked.

"Decent pranks? I see your point," Tim laughed.

"By the way, was Tom involved?" Rumpee asked.

"Off the record?" Tim asked back.

"Just get out!" Rumpee said.

Tim left the Vice Principal's office. He wrote a note excusing himself from the last two classes of the day. He handed it to the office secretary.

"What's this?" she asked.

"The clock turned in my favor early today," he said and left.

The secretary brought the note into Mr. Rumpee. Tim caught up with Robert and Tom outside. Jack had actually gone back to class.

"Tim's old enough to write his own notes and his mother gave him permission. Mark his absences for sixth and seventh period as excused. Please close my door and see that I am not disturbed for at least an hour," Mr. Rumpee asked her while muttering about the continuing Olwell Nightmare.

She stood outside the closed door for a moment after closing it. It sounded like someone banging their head on the desk. She was sure she was mistaken as she went back to her desk.

About an hour later, Mr. Rumpee came out of his office, "Get one of the Principals of Kenmore Junior High on the phone."

"Mr. Rasmussen speaking," Kenmore's Vice Principal answered.

"Dave Rumpee here, listen do you have any Olwells enrolled?"

"Yes, Veronica's in eighth grade and Robert is in seventh?" he replied.

"Any problems?"

"Veronica is pretty sharp but that Robert is a handful already. They have another sister still in elementary school though. I think she is in 4th grade. Why?" Mr. Rasmussen asked.

"I just figured out that it will be eight more years before I have a break from that family and I wanted to see the lay of the land," Mr. Rumpee said and thanked him.

"Well, if it helps at all. I'm glad you have Tim and Tom now. Don't bother calling their Dad though. He has a great sense of humor and seems to be laughing each time he leaves the office. Besides, he is one of the best attorneys in Seattle and doesn't take threats well at all," Mr. Rasmussen said, " I am sure glad that Veronica is so nice."

"What about Robert Jackson's siblings?"

"He has a brother Alan in seventh grade. No problems out of him," the Kenmore Vice Principal reflected.

Mr. Rumpee thanked him and hung up as he wrote 1984 on his pad next to Allison's name; the youngest Olwell child. He circled the year twice then left the office to take his mind off it. He wondered how he could get the clock to turn early in his favor.

Note: Senior year at Inglemoor : Greg Bergmann, John Hoskins, Jeff Dyson, Jon Edwards and I played a minor prank in the middle of the night at Bothell High School. We thought it was pretty cleaver but it was fairly minor compared to what my older siblings pulled off. I won't go into the details at this time as it may end up in another story. I will tell you it involved twenty five pounds of lard and that I had to drive across town to pick up Jon Edwards and return him home safely afterwards.

Bothell High School

CHAPTER **10**

The Day Before: Operation Goodyear

Tim: "This story is very true. The logistics of getting 50 tires onto a flag pole in the middle of an open u shaped court yard at the front of the high school entrance along one of the busiest streets in Bothell were complex. I had spent some serious time planning it and needed help from my friends, acquaintances, my brother, Tom's friends, and some other willing accomplices. We kept the group as small as possible to ensure secrecy and success. The key was Eric and his climbing ability. The rival high school had to rent a crane to undo our handiwork. That is part of another story though." Circa 1976.

"Who is bringing the rope?" Tim asked.

"I got the rope," Robert Jackson replied.

"And the tires?" Tim asked. When no one initially responded, he looked up from his list, "Hey, focus up people. Who is getting the tires?"

"Sorry, Kirk and I will bring them. Fifty right?" Mark answered.

"Just put as many in the trucks as you can. Remember we need a steel belted tire for every four bias ply tires. Do you need any money?" Tim asked.

"No, my buddy works at Fitz Auto Wrecking and he said I could have as many as we needed."

"Eric, do you need anything?" Tim continued referring to the list.

"I'm good but what about the grease?"

"I've got a twenty pound block of shortening from work," Ron chimed in.

"That will do."

"We need six guys in the trees, four guys on the roof with me, two guys on the roof with Robert, four as look outs, and someone spotting Eric. That's twenty," Tim counted.

Robert Jackson started counting heads, "We have twenty two."

"Okay, Tom and Mark; take those five guys and you are responsible for getting the tires to the base of the building. Kirk and you three will be on the near roof with me. Robert, you take those two, and you will run the rope from our building to yours. That leaves Terry with Eric, do what you need to do. Okay, any questions?"

"What time are we meeting?"

"Midnight at the backside of Bothell High School on the road behind the wooded area,"

"What about us?" Ron asked, referring the three guys with him.

"Oh right, you're..." Tim hesitated referring to his list.

"Lookouts?" Robert asked.

"Right, lookouts. You need to come up with six walkie talkies,"

"I've got that covered," Bill said.

"Any questions?"

"I need a ride," one of the guys stated.

"Okay, let's meet at Inglemoor at 11:30 and we can carpool from there."

With that everyone dispersed leaving Tim, Robert, Tom, Bill and Kirk. They went over the plan again and discussed logistics. Before heading out, Tim pulled Becky and Bill aside for a moment.

Later that night, when they arrived behind the woods at Bothell High School, everyone quickly went into action. Kirk and Ron headed across the field with the ladder.

"Tom, tell your guys to carry the tires. I don't want to see anyone rolling them to the building," Tim said sternly.

"Why?" Tom challenged.

"I don't have time to do this now! Just trust me," Tim said softening his tone.

"Whatever," dismissed Tom.

Tim looked like he was going to punch Tom but then Mark came up and said, "Tim, we should tell everyone to carry the tires. With the slope of the field, if one got away it would be hell catching up with it."

Tom looked annoyed.

"Yeah, good idea," Tim said to Mark while glaring at his brother. "Mark, which ones are the steel belted ones?"

"See the ones with the duct tape wrapped around them? Those are the steel ones," Mark said pointing to the tires.

"What's the deal with the steel belted tires?" Tom asked.

"I didn't know this until Mark told me, but you can cut a bias ply tire with a chainsaw. But you can't do that to a tire with a steel belt," Tim explained.

"Right on," Tom said nodding his head understanding the difficulty of removing the tires if they were successful

Mark and Tom pulled their guys together and started giving directions. Tim left them to it.

After climbing the extension ladder, Tim arrived on top of the near building. Kirk had the ropes secured and dropped to the ground where Tom had arrived with two tires. Tom tied the first tire and Kirk directed the guys to pull it up. Kirk and Tim walked to the atrium side. There the ropes had been run across the atrium and Robert was pulling it up to the top of his building. He was across from them with the flagpole in between.

Terry was helping Eric at the flagpole. Eric had his safety gear to help secure him to the flagpole once he got to the top but climbing the pole was all on him. Tim was impressed at the apparent ease at which Eric scaled the pole. When he reached the top, he secured his two harnesses and leaned back into them and signaled that he was ready.

While Robert and Kirk pulled the atrium ropes tight and aligned them with Eric, Ron and Bill flashed their lights up to Tim showing where they were guarding from.

The first tires started arriving to Kirk and were piled next to where he secured the ropes.

"Hey, put the ones with the duct tape in a pile right here. Pass that on to the others," Tim directed, "Kirk every fourth tire needs to be one of the tires with duct tape."

"Got it. Don't you have someone else to bother?" Kirk asked.

Robert signaled he was ready.

"This is going to work!" Kirk smiled tying a tire to the atrium ropes.

"VIKING, VIKING, VIKING," came suddenly over the radio followed by silence. Tim looked around to see everyone drop to the roof. He waved to Robert who had also dropped to his knees. Tim and Kirk scurried to the other side of the building and saw Mark slip back into the woods. He whispered to Kirk to quietly pull up the ropes. Tom and another quietly lowered the ladder and set it against the base of the building and then raced across the field for cover.

Tim moved back to the side of the building facing the parking lot. He looked over the side of the building in time to see a police car cruise in front of the school. From his viewpoint, he could see several of the guys hiding in the bushes below. Tim held his breath as the cruiser shined the spot light on the building. He hoped his backup plan would work.

Then the cruiser turned on his lights. Tim held his breath but was quickly relieved to see the police car tear out of the parking lot and headed toward town.

"CLEAR, CLEAR, CLEAR," the radio sounded.

Tim walked back over to Kirk. He had just lifted the tire over the side of the building. He signaled Robert. The tire was pulled across the atrium to the flagpole. Eric untied the tire and held it over the top of the flagpole. Then he released one of his safety harnesses and cleared the tire. He reattached the harness. Then he unclasped the other side of his harness clearing the tire which dropped straight down to the ground with a WHOMP sound.

Tim flinched at the sound. He hoped no one heard that. Kirk just smiled and started tying the next tire to the rope he had retrieved. He signaled Robert and the second tire went across the atrium to Eric. He repeated the process by maneuvering the tire through the safety harnesses and dropping it. This time the tire landed on the first tire and the sound was much less.

With each following tire, Eric was getting quicker with the tire. Over the next two hours, the process continued without interruption. When the tires were eight feet from the top of the pole, Terry signaled that it was enough. He jerked the line to Eric. Eric started pulling up the grease.

Kirk signaled Robert to start pulling in the atrium ropes. Then he told the roof guys to retrieve and lower the extra tires before dropping the ropes. Tom and Mark directed the remaining tires back into Mark's truck.

Tim did a quick last check. He waved to Eric who had just finished greasing the top eight feet of the pole and began his climb down the tires.

When the roof was clear, Tim climbed from the roof. Kirk helped him take down the ladder and they headed across the field and through the woods to the cars.

Eric and Terry were the last to make it back.

"That was awesome!" Robert said.

"What took you guys so long?" Tim asked.

"Have you ever tried to climb down a stack of tires around a flag pole? I thought I was going to fall on three different occasions," Eric said seriously, "Besides I had to wait for Terry."

"Why did he have to wait for you," Tom asked.

Terry held up a can of gold paint. "I had to let them know we were here," Terry laughed.

"We said no vandalism or damage," Tim said confronting Terry.

"What? No, I painted HIS on the tires. It looks sweet," Terry responded.

"It does look good," Eric confirmed.

Bill and Ron came over. "We need to get out of here before the cops come back around. It sure was lucky the cop left when he did. He was about to shine his light where I was," Ron said.

"Luck had nothing to do with it," Bill said and he and Tim high-fived each other.

"What?" Terry asked.

"When Ron called VIKING, VIKING, VIKING, I was at the payphone where Tim had me stationed. I called his girlfriend Becky. She then called in to the police there was a suspicious person walking around cars in the Safeway parking lot. It worked."

"Good thinking!" Eric said.

"Let's get out of here, I have class in a couple of hours," Tim said and they all laughed.

A half hour later, Tim turned off the car and coasted down 64th and turned onto our street coming to a quiet stop in front of the house. My brothers snuck into the house.

Upstairs, our stepfather, Gordy, shook his head at the clock which read 3:52am.

Our stepdad awoke Tim and Tom, "Come on, I need your help."

"We have school today," Tim said.

"I will have you two back in time for first class. Now get up. We are leaving in five minutes," he directed.

Five minutes later, Tim and Tom were dressed and in the car. As Gordy, pulled onto Juanita Drive, Tim noticed the clock: 4:20am. He just laughed to himself.

Gordy drove them around making a few stops and got them back to the house by 7:00am. Tim and Tom never had to get out of the car but were kept awake the whole time by Gordy's talking.

"Why did he need us?" Tom asked getting in Tim's car.

"I don't know. But I am sure glad we got home before he got up!"

"Yeah, he would have been mad if he had caught us," Tom said and gave his brother a high-five.

"What were you doing with the boys this morning," Mom asked.

"Teaching them a lesson, they were out all night again. I made sure they didn't get any sleep," Gordy said.

Note: When Olwell's pulled 'all nighters' studying was never involved! Our stepdad awoke me on numerous occasions after coming home way too late. Like my older brothers, I never made the connection that he was 'teaching me a lesson.' We always thought we snuck back in. Therefore, waking us early was never a deterrent and our behavior continued.

Lawn Jockey

CHAPTER 11

Jockeys: Tidy Whitey

Annie emailed: "Let me get back to you, I have to verify that the police even came." (She never followed up with me. I take that as confirmation of this story!) Circa 1977.

"But Connie, I was just horrified when the police showed up," Jeannie explained.

"It's not that big of a deal," my Mom consoled.

"That's easy for you to say. It happens all the time at your house," Jeannie said too quickly, "you know what I mean."

"No offence taken," my Mom assured her. The police did show up a lot.

"What are the neighbors going to think?"

"Well they can move away like the ones before them is what I say," Mom encouraged.

"Oh Connie!"

Jeannie was one of my mother's closest friends. She lived on Mercer Island with her husband Bob and four kids. They were very close in age to us and we got along pretty well. I should point out that they lived on the poor side of Mercer Island but that is like saying you lived in the poor side of Beverly Hills.

Mercer Island is located in the middle of Lake Washington about five miles from downtown Seattle. Much of the island was populated with huge homes and spacious yards. It was not uncommon to drive down a street and see long driveways with manicured lawns and gardens adjoining it.

In the 1970's, it was also a common sight to see a "Lawn Jockey" out front. This is a statue about three feet tall. It was a man with white pants, a brightly colored shirt, and a white hat. His arm would be extended holding a ring. The ring was to tie your horse to if you had one I guess. They were all in black face.

After one mischievous night, many of the residents of Mercer Island awoke to find their lawn art spray painted white.

The police were called to investigate.

"Hello?" Bob said opening the front door.

"Good morning sir," the officer started. He then proceeded to explain the situation to Bob with Jeanine standing alongside. "You don't know anything about this do you?" the officer asked.

"No, I don't, which leads me to ask why you are here at our house," Bob responded politely.

"My kids were here all night! I do not understand why you are here accusing us!" Jeannie started.

The officer held up his hand then motioned as if to say, be quiet and follow me. He led them off the front porch and down their driveway. When he arrived out by his patrol car, he turned and pointed to their yard.

In the grass was the painted white outline of fifteen statues in the grass from the overspray of the cans of spray paint.

Bob looked down and then looked at Jeannie. Then they both looked at the house just in time to see the front curtains closing rapidly.

Jeannie started to apologize when the officer stopped her.

"I don't think I have my camera in the car. I probably will be back in say a half hour to take pictures of this evidence, if it is still here," he smiled then got in his car and left.

When he returned, the lawn was being mowed and one of the kids was raking leaves from the flower beds onto the grass. The cop just laughed and waved to the kids as he approached the parents.

Annie, the youngest, waved back. He laughed again as her index finger was covered in white paint.

"You might tell your little crime syndicate to use the backyard next time," he said shaking his head.

Just then, James walked by pulling the garbage can that was clanking from all the empty spray cans in it.

With that the officer laughed then left the scene.

Bob turned to Jeanine and said, "It looks like they were caught white handed."

She laughed and they went into finish breakfast leaving the kids to the yard work.

CHAPTER **12**

Night Of The Living Dead

Megan chides: "I cried when I read this. Cried in shame that anyone, anywhere would think that Robert and I had personality traits in common. Later, after the hysterics stopped, I realized that anyone who knows Robert would realize that it simply isn't possible for someone else to be "the same" as he was. Other than that, I think it's sweet that Robert assumes I enjoyed sitting with him at the movie. But seriously folks, Robert really did have friends everywhere, probably because he stuck around and pestered people enough that it wasn't worth the energy to make him go away. It's fun to see the past through Robert's eyes." Circa 1981.

"Hey," I said.

"Hey, Little Bobby Olwell," Megan replied with a smile and a laugh.

"Anyone sitting here," I asked pointing to the seat next to her.

She stopped laughing at that and looked a little apprehensive but after what I thought was way too long of a pause she finally reached over and removed her jacket from the seat. I took that as a gracious invitation to sit next to her.

As far as women in high school, that was about all I could have expected. As we were about to graduate, I had high hopes for college gals. My problem at the time was I did not realize how good looking, smart, and athletic I was; so I lacked confidence. What? Hey, it's my story so that's how I am writing it. Truth be damned.

Anyway, I sat down and didn't say much for a moment as I reflected on the previous years of Junior High and High School interactions with Megan. We had dated, once. I was still at that stage in life where first dates were difficult to get and second dates were? Well, when I get one I will let you know.

As the movie was not going to start for a while, I decided I would rivet her with conversation.

"Hey," I started. You had to start somewhere right?

"What's up with your idiot friends?" she asked.

"I think you will need to be more specific," I pointed out.

"I guess you have a lot of idiot friends now don't you?"

"Are you patronizing me?" I feigned shock.

"Russell and Rudy, you know you three who smacked me on the ass every time you saw me for years," she clarified.

"Well it was 'Spank a Megan' time," I replied lamely.
Somewhere I had got the idea to grab her ass at Kenmore Junior High. It was in eighth grade. She asked me why I touched her butt and 'Spank a Megan day' was all I could come up with. Rudy and Russell were there and if it was good enough for me, it was good enough for them and they started spanking her. Then 'Spank a Megan day' turned into 'week' then 'month' then 'year'. Only problem for Megan was they spanked her and spanked her hard. I had just tried to grab her.

"Rudy and Russell are good. I talked to them in the last week. They asked about you," I added for good measure.

"Really?" she wasn't buying it.

"Oh yeah, anyway Russell is going to Redmond and Rudy is at Mossyrock down toward White Pass. As I look back on it, I do feel bad about you getting smacked all the time," I apologized.

She started to say something. Almost like admitting to liking the attention but let the sentence and thought drift away. She just smiled and shook her head.

"I'm still confused why Jon Edwards and you kidnapped me from the Bothell football game," she commented.

Jon and I had grabbed a cheerleader, Camille Bailey, one game and Megan during a different game and carried them off and out of the stadium. It seemed like the thing to do. The fans cheered us for doing it. The problem was that once we got them to my car, we had no plan. So after a couple of minutes, we all just walked back to the game. You would have thought after Camille, we would have come up with a plan. Anyway our friends, players on the football team, were annoyed Jon and I always sat with their girlfriends. When we started abducting them, we were informed we should stop it or face dire consequences. I stopped for Jon's sake.

"Yeah, we really didn't think that through too well, but we did pick you over all the other women. I'm sure that raised your status," I said hopefully.

"Yeah it was a regular dream moment!" she announced sarcastically. We both laughed at that.

The movie started then. It was 'Night of the Living Dead.' The plot was a radioactive meteor came too near the planet and all the dead came back as zombies killing humans. It was in black and white and very campy.

During the scary parts, I leaned toward Megan to offer support. Okay, okay, I may have been scared. Anyway she let me lean closer.

When a little girl who had died came back to life and started stabbing her Mom with a trowel, we were counting the stabbings out loud. Megan and I were laughing when it ended at sixteen.

We hung out for a few minutes when the movie ended. It dawned on me that she was just like me. We were so similar in personality. The problem was there was only enough oxygen in the room for one of us. We had fun but opposites attract.

I said as much.

"If opposites attract, boy am I glad I am like you! Didn't think I would ever say that out loud," she laughed.

I open my arms for a hug and she gave a friendly hug.

"See you around, Little Bobby Olwell!"

I swatted her as she turned. Not hard, just enough to make us both laugh at how ridiculous the situation was.

She did not look back as she left.

I looked after her for a while. I wondered when we would see each other as she was going to Western and I was going to Washington State. I put the thought away and just shook my head at what an idiot I had been with her over the years. I must have been growing up because I started to realize what an idiot I was.

Note: Megan and Camille, the Cheerleader, were the only girls I got into the backseat of my car in high school. As previously stated, I had no plan once they got there. I figured it out about my Junior year at WSU. Mostly, the women had other ideas though.

Also, Megan could have just used *'It's fun to see the past through Robert's eyes,'* as her intro. The rest was rather hurtful although very amusing. Furthermore, **Night of the Living Dead** was the name of the movie not a description of a date with me!

Megan Johnson

She was just like me!

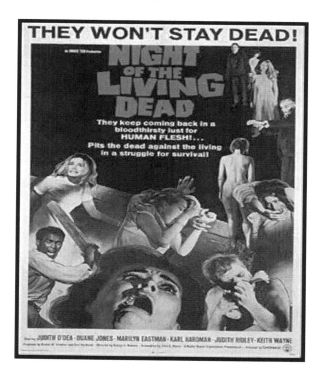

We counted as she stabbed her Mom 16 times.

Allison, the youngest Olwell child, is three years younger than me. I was never really interested in what she was doing. I spent more time and energy trying to keep up with my older siblings to worry much about her. I have always considered her a terrible driver. Although she may have improved over the years, my experience is limited to her younger days. She was the first Olwell child to scare Mom out of the car. After nearly running over Karen Lyons at Lake Cushman when driving with her, Mom vowed never to drive with her again. Mom often exaggerated so I don't know if she did or not.

I did give her my Ford Fairlane after my Freshman year at WSU. I believe it was her first car. It may have been one of the few nice things I did for her.

The following few stories about her driving are true and although some literary license was permitted, the pertinent facts are accurate.

Family picture at Lake Cushman around the time Allison got her driver's license.

CHAPTER **13**

First Lesson

Allison contends: "The events portrayed about this weekend are a saner version of the truth. Gordy Jr. actually received three DUIs and Sandee and I went to jail with him until they released him to my custody. You will have to buy me a glass of wine for the rest of those details. Although incomplete, this story has way more than the two required facts. I was more like Robert than Sandee was, heck I had fifteen marriage proposals and couldn't cook. Remember I was the Olwell in this story. Oh, and I hit the garbage cans with the car not Sandee." Circa 1981.

"Are you sure Allison will be okay?" Mom asked. She was obviously worried. Since I had gone off to WSU, she had to rely on my older stepbrother to watch after Allison. Allison had just turned fifteen so the need for her to be watched was minimizing but you know how moms can be.

"She will be fine. I talked to Gordon and he says he will be very aware of what Allison is doing," Gordy assured her.

Although still a little apprehensive, they left for Canada where she was to receive an award from the Tourism Board.

Later that night Gordy Jr. rear ended a Metro Bus with his van. He aggravated an existing knee injury and was cited for DUI. He was released on his own recognicence in time to watch Allison some more, she needed watching! I'm not sure who was watching him though.

Friday was uneventful as Gordy Jr. spent most of the day with his leg up taking prescription pain killers. On Saturday, he was feeling better and offered to take Allison and her friend, Sandee, to the movies.

"Okay, have fun! I will be back in two hours to pick you guys up. I will expect to find you right here," he explained and gave them a few dollars.

"Got it, we will be right here at 4:00pm waiting," Allison answered after looking at her watch.

Sandee thanked him and they went to watch their movie.

"He's not coming back," Sandee said.

"He is just late. He will be here," Allison said confidently.

"Look it is 9:00pm; he is already five hours late. I think we should call my Mom," Sandee suggested.

"And just what will happen if your Mom comes and gets us?" Allison asked starting to think like an Olwell for the first time in her life.

"I see your point, I will never be allowed to stay with you again," Sandee considered.

"Besides, it will take them an hour to get here from Redmond. Let's give Gordy Jr. a few more minutes," she said. Sandee agreed.

Finally Gordy Jr. pulled up to the curb where they were sitting.

"Sorry, I lost track of time. It must be these pain killers," Gordy Jr. apologized.

"It's okay. It was only six hours," Sandee said sarcastically.

Allison shot her a glare and Sandee let it go.

"Damn, not again! " Gordy Jr. exclaimed looking in his rear view mirror for the first time in twenty minutes.

"What?" Allison asked.

"I'm getting pulled over. Put this under your seat," he said handing her a paper bag.

She complied as Gordy brought the car to a standstill. Gordy quickly surveyed the interior of the car for any other items to get out of sight. He knew how this game was played from previous experience. If the cops couldn't see it, he might be home free. He would never consent to a search. Only an idiot would agree to that.

Allison looked back to see the patrol car with its lights on. The Officer stepped out and walked up to their car cautiously. When he was assured of his safety, he approached the driver's side window.

"Good evening, license and registration please," he said flashing his light in and around the front seat of the car.

"Sure Officer," Gordy Jr. said. He started to reach for the glove box but remembered he should not open it in front of a cop. He knew that so he had put the registration in the sun visor. He retrieved the registration and took his driver's license from his wallet.

The Officer took the identification back to his car. He returned after a few minutes.

"Do you know why I pulled you over Mr. Swanson?" he asked.

"Why don't you know?" Gordy Jr. responded sarcastically.

"Seriously Sir, are you aware you crossed the yellow line several times in the last half mile?" the Officer asked.

"Really? No I was not aware of that," Gordy Jr. said.

"I have a report saying you were issued an infraction for driving under the influence two days ago. Have you been drinking tonight?"

"I have had one beer. That is all," Gordy Jr. responded.

"Step out of the vehicle."

Gordy complied.

"Sir, I am going to administer a field sobriety test. I would like you to follow my instructions very carefully. If you do not understand an instruction please ask for clarification. Other than one beer, have you had anything else to drink or are you on any medication?" the Officer asked.

"I am on prescription Percodan for the accident on Friday," Gordy Jr. said.

"Percodan is a controlled substance. It is pretty powerful pain killer. Are you aware you are not supposed to consume alcohol when taking that drug?" the Officer questioned.

"What are you a pharmacist or something? I had one friggin beer. So what?" Gordy Jr. snapped at the Officer.

"Sir, please check your tone," the Officer stated holding his twenty inch flashlight in his right hand.

Over the next few minutes, the Officer had Gordy Jr. lean back and touch his nose with each finger. Then he walked heel and toe over a line.

"Please say the alphabet," he instructed tapping his flashlight into his left hand.

"Forwards or backwards?" Gordy Jr. asked.

"Sir, I am issuing an infraction for driving under the influence. You have admitted to using alcohol and a controlled substance. You have marginally passed the field test but I feel based on your inability to keep the vehicle in your lane, your abilities have been compromised."

"Really? That's just great!" Gordy Jr. exclaimed.

The cop placed the three of them in the back seat of his squad car. Gordy Jr. was handcuffed. Sandee asked if they would turn on the sirens. Gordy Jr. asked if the officer would stop by 7-11 so he could pick up a beer and laughed. The Officer was not impressed with either of them.

"Are you able to make arrangements for your vehicle or do I need to have it impounded?" the Officer asked writing the ticket.

"Can't my sister drive me home? She hasn't been drinking nor has she taken any prescription drugs," Gordy Jr. pleaded.

The Officer shone the flashlight at Allison then into Sandee's face in the back. He returned the light to Allison's eyes, "Have you been drinking miss?"

"No sir." She lifted her hand to screen the light.

"Have you smoked or taken any drugs tonight?" he asked.

"No sir."

"What about you?" he turned to Sandee.

"I am only fifteen!" she answered and pretended to cry.

"If I release Mr. Swanson and this vehicle to your custody, will you see that they are taken straight home?"

"Yes sir," Allison answered wondering what this was all about.

With that the Officer had Gordy Jr. sign the ticket.

Allison got out of the squad car and climbed in the driver's seat. Gordy Jr. got in the passenger seat. Allison had to adjust the seat. She didn't know to adjust the mirrors.

"Okay Allison, just drive slowly until we get out of Mountlake Terrace. We will be in Lake Forest Park in a half mile and out of his jurisdiction," he advised.

"How do I start the car?" she asked while turning the steering wheel back and forth.

Sandee laughed nervously.

"What?" Gordy Jr. asked.

"This is the key right?" she asked playing with the key ring hanging from the steering wheel column.

"Wait a minute. You haven't driven before?" Gordy Jr. asked incredulously. He looked in his side mirror at the police car with the lights still on.

"No," she said.

"How old are you?"

"Fifteen," she said.

"And you haven't driven? My god girl, it is time you learned. Step on the brake; the big pedal then turn the key," Gordy Jr. instructed wondering how long the cop would stay behind them. He was still watching the side view mirror when the police car made a u-turn and sped off in the opposite direction.

Sandee was praying loudly in the back seat.

"That's distracting," Gordy Jr. told her.

They made it home alive.

"I don't think you should mention this to my mother," Sandee said pulling Allison aside.

"You really think that is necessary to tell me that?" Allison asked.

"You're not really very good at dealing with this kind of stuff. Your brother, Robert, handled this stuff like a pro. He kept Russell out of trouble all the time. You not so much."

"Who got Russell into all that trouble in the first place? Robert was a hack compared to Dianne, Tim and Tom but I get your point. Actually, you are more like Robert and I am more like Russell," Allison considered.

"Thanks," Sandee said, "Don't be so hard on yourself. No one is like my brother Russell."

"Come on," Gordy Jr. said getting back in the car.

"Where are we going?" Allison asked.

"I need beer and cigarettes. Drive me up to the 7-11," he told them.

"Drive yourself!"

"I have a suspended license. I can't drive. Besides, I am pretty wasted," he laughed.

"I don't have a license to even be suspended," Allison exclaimed.

"I'll drive if you teach me," Sandee said and climbed in the driver's seat of the car.

Allison decided to wait at the house until they made it back. About thirty minutes later, Sandee pulled the car into the driveway and knocked over the garbage cans.

"That was awesome," she said exiting the vehicle.

"You guys want a beer?" Gordy Jr. asked.

Sandee reached for the beer and Allison stopped her, "You are like Robert!"

"Thanks!" Sandee said.

"That wasn't a compliment. Let's go to bed, it is after midnight."

Gordy Jr. and Allison picked up the folks at the airport. Mom asked Allison how the weekend went. Allison told her it was great. Sandee and she had gone to the movies while he stayed at home and slept. She didn't tell Mom for four days that she had nearly been to jail.

Gordon Jr. finally had to tell his Dad that he had gotten the DUIs while they were out of town. As for Allison's driving, our mother often said she wished she was on drugs when Allison was learning to drive. If she only knew!

Note: As I was writing this story at Tim's, our mother, who was visiting, kept arguing some of the lesser facts but did not disagree with the main story. Two DUIs: she confirmed but suggested it was Lake Forest Park not Mountlake Terrace. As those cities adjoin, I figured it was close enough. She seems to have a vivid memory of our stepbrother's transgressions even if she has forgotten all of ours. Sandee and Allison both confirmed their parts.

Mountlake Terrace Police: Probably not the same cruiser.

CHAPTER **14**

Driver's Ed

Allison: "The issue was not that I was going to fail Driver's Ed but that I was going to pass. My teacher, Mr. Ristow, called the meeting. He did not want to pass me because he felt I would be an unsafe driver. My husband agrees with him by the way. Mom did insist on a passing grade because of my written test scores so I kept my 3.0. She then put Gordy Jr. in charge of my driving instruction. He would always have me drive to the 7-11 at the top of the hill first where he would buy enough gas and beer to make it through my lesson. Usually he would buy $2 of gas and $12 of beer." Circa 1982.

"May I help you?" the office secretary at Inglemoor asked Mom.

"I have an appointment with Mr. Ristow, the Driver's Ed Teacher," Mom said.

"I know what he teaches," the secretary said in a tone.

"Can you direct me to his classroom?" Mom responded curtly.

"And you are?" the secretary inquired.

"Connie Swanson, I am Allison's mother."

"Allison Swanson? I don't recall a student by that name," the secretary said scratching her head with a pencil.

"Allison Olwell is my daughter," Mom clarified.

The secretary gave her a funny look and gave her directions to Mr. Ristow's classroom. When Mom left the office, the secretary got up and raced into Principal Rumpee's office.

"You'll never guess who just came into the office," she said.

"Who's that?" Mr. Rumpee asked.

"Connie Swanson, the Olwells' mother," she said putting her hand on the side of her face when emphasizing the word Olwells, "she's here to see Mr. Ristow."

"I need to finally meet her!" he said. While quickly leaving his office, he wondered what she would be like and why would she come to the school after all these years.

Meanwhile, Mom found Mr. Ristow's classroom and introduced herself remembering to use both last names.

"My son, Rusty was a classmate with your son, Robert. I enjoyed him in my class. What can I do for you?" he asked.

"That's nice to hear about Robert and Rusty, but I am here to discuss Allison," Mom announced.

"What can I help you with?"

"She came home and told me she is failing your course."

"Well let me see," he said and opened his grade book after flipping a few pages, "oh here we are. Oh dear, oh that's not good, yes I remember that, wow! Yes, she is correct. She will fail the course."

"It is that bad?"

"Two of the instructors will not drive with her again. She has hit every cone in the parking lot training course. None of the other students will get in a car with her. She has passed the written portion of the class. Basically, she has no awareness of her surroundings when driving. It appears she is afraid of the car she is driving. In reality, everyone else should be afraid of a car she is driving,"' he finished with a laugh.

Mom didn't laugh.

"She needs a passing grade to keep her grade point at an acceptable level. I know she has struggled that is why I did not allow her to take the course until her junior year. What can be done for her to pass the class?" Mom asked.

"I don't know that she can," Mr. Ristow said.

"What if I promise I will not let her get a license until she is seventeen? That gives me another nine months to work with her driving skills," Mom suggested hopefully.

Mr. Ristow looked to be contemplating the suggestion when Mr. Rumpee came in the classroom.

"Dave?" Mr. Ristow acknowledged.

"Don't get up, I wanted to meet Mrs. Swanson," he said and turned to Mom extending his hand, "Hi, I am Dave Rumpee the Principal here at Inglemoor."

"There was a Vice Principal Rumpee that was here when my older children attended," Mom remembered taking his hand.

"Yes, that is me. I just wanted to say what a wonderful daughter you have," he smiled.

"Allison is very good," Mom acknowledged with a smile.

"Not Allison, Veronica. I have had one, two or three of your children here at Inglemoor for each of the last twelve years. I'm not sure which child was the worst although it was probably Dianne. The only year where an Olwell child was not a pain in my side or overly obnoxious was 1978, the year Veronica was a sophomore. Then of course, she transferred to another school as a junior and Robert showed up and the grief started all over again for another three years. Allison showed up last year and she has been kind of anticlimactic. I mean I have heard nothing from her or any of her teachers. It is like she is not even an Olwell," Mr. Rumpee recalled almost disappointed Allison wasn't more interesting.

Mr. Ristow moved away from the conversation. He had heard of the pranks that were perpetrated by the older Olwell children. He had not made the connection to the quiet and polite Allison.

"I am not sure what you are saying. I have seven wonderful children and for your information I can assure you Allison is an Olwell," Mom stated with pursed lips.

"I didn't mean to offend you. It's just that Dianne, Tim and Tom all had assigned chairs in my office. Robert was in the office everyday doing the announcements and pulling his stupid pranks and gags. But you should know this from all the notes I sent home. I always thought it was kind of rude that you never replied to any of them but that is water under the bridge," Rumpee continued.

"I have never received a letter from you and what are you talking about with assigned chairs?" Mom said standing up and facing the Principal. She was quickly getting annoyed.

"You never got any of my letters? Of course you didn't, that makes too much sense. Anyway, your older kids were in my office so often that they claimed and then designated chairs as their own. It was actually kind of funny when I got over the initial annoyance. But anyway, I wanted to say hello. I will let you two get back to your meeting," he said and made a quick exit. He now knew where the Olwell kids got there gumption and confidence. He wondered what Mr. Olwell was like. He was probably the most like Tom he decided as he went back into his office and closed the door behind him.

Mr. Ristow was left with Mom and she was not looking too pleased.

71

"I will give her a D if you promise not to let her drive. It was nice meeting you," Mr. Ristow said hoping to get out of the classroom in one piece. He hoped Allison would not be insured by his insurance company. He didn't want his rates to go up.

"Thank you," Mom said as she was too stunned to communicate any further.

"How did the meeting go at Inglemoor," our stepdad asked.

"Fine, Allison will pass. I met the Principal, Mr. Rumpee," Mom added.

"Why is his name familiar?"

"I don't know but he said nice things about Veronica," she recalled.

"Veronica? She was only there one year!"

"Maybe that's why," Mom answered and laughed.

Allison had to wait until she was seventeen to schedule her driver's test. In an ironic twist fate, it was scheduled when mom was magically out of the country. It had to be a coincidence, right?

Note: I had Mr. Ristow for Driver's Ed as well. His son, Rusty, was in my French class. Everyday Ms. Fry would call on him first and brutalize him over his incomplete homework. This allowed the rest of the class time to finish theirs. It was unfair and I would have said something but I was finishing my homework at the time.

Mr. Ristow, Inglemoor's Driving Ed Teacher.

CHAPTER **15**

Driver's License Test

Gordy Jr. says: "I don't readily recall this story, however I can say that Allison was easy to teach and did just fine."

Allison: "This is pretty close to the events of my driver's test. Gordon Jr. bought a six pack of beer and gave two beers to the mechanic that fixed my car along with the two bucks. He kept the other four for himself. After a few miles, he did let me drive home while he sat in the back seat and drank his beer. He laughed because as his license was suspended I could drive him around while he drank. He wouldn't get another DUI saying, "that ought to make the old man happy." Gordy Jr. was really good to me but he probably doesn't remember much of the 1980s." Circa 1983.

"We need to hurry," Allison told Gordy Jr. Allison had been ready for hours and thought the clock on the wall had stopped several times before lunch.

"Your appointment isn't until 2:00pm. I will have you there in plenty of time," Gordy Jr. promised. "You know I took my driver's test at the same DMV location when I was your age. Just remember to go a few miles slower than you think the speed limit is and use your blinkers."

"I know. I know. Just leave me alone. I am nervous enough," Allison replied, again looking at her watch.

"Did Tim ever tell you the story about his driving test? He said he was taking it in your Dad's old Cadillac. It was huge. When it came time to parallel park, he told the officer that he would spot him those points. When asked why, Tim explained his Dad made him promise never to parallel park the Cadillac. Your Dad insisted it was too big. The officer told Tim he had to try. So Tim tried with one back up, stopped looked at the officer, and asked if it was good enough. He lost those points but didn't hit anything then went on to pass the test. Remember, slow, use your blinkers, and don't hit anything," Gordy Jr. told Allison trying to ease her anxiety. He had been driving extra carefully as he got closer to the State Police office.

"See! Here we are and you are twenty minutes early. Go sign in," Gordy Jr. told her and walked over to the smoking area. Gordy Jr. was trying to blend into the crowd so as not to be recognized. He had been pulled over many times by the State Patrol and didn't want to be confronted. He was even fairly confident he didn't have any outstanding warrants at the time. He hoped that the officers pulling driver test duty had not been out on patrol recently.

Allison went into the DMV Office and signed in. Gordy Jr. lit up a cigarette and sat down back in a corner. He reached for the beer in his pocket but decided that might not be a good move.

A few minutes later, Allison came out of the office.

"You should wait inside until they call your name," he suggested.

"I already failed," she cried with her head down and lower lip trembling.

"What?"

"They called my name. I got in the car and the emergency brake didn't work so I failed! The next appointment isn't for three weeks," Allison said with tears streaming down her face.

"Here," he said handing her a dollar, "go get a Coke from the machine inside and come back and sit on this bench. I will be right back."

Gordy quickly looked up and down the street for something. He jumped in the car and raced out of the parking lot. He drove straight across the street to Ray's Garage. An old guy in a blue jump suit came out rubbing his back.

"I'm Ray, what can I do for you?" he asked.

"My little sister has a driver's test in," Gordy Jr. paused to look at his watch, "six minutes and the emergency brake cable needs to be tightened. She's across the street crying because they failed her. If you can fix it I will get them to retest her."

Ray looked at Gordy Jr. and then across the street at the DMV. He frowned then said, "I am on it!"

He grabbed a couple of wrenches from the tool drawer. Then he swung open the driver's door and climbed in under the steering wheel. He came out about ninety seconds later straightening up rubbing his back.

"Try it now!" Ray said.

Gordy Jr. jumped into the driver's seat. He started the car. He put it in gear and the car held in place with the emergency brake on.

"Awesome, how much do I owe you?"

"Two bucks," Ray said wiping his wrench off with the handkerchief he had in his pocket. He then used the same handkerchief to wipe his face.

"Okay, can I go get her test started and then come back and pay you?" Gordy Jr. asked.

"Just get your sister going - that will be fine," Ray smiled.

Gordy Jr. raced the car back across the street. He waved Allison over as he went into the DMV. He looked at his watch. It read 1:58.

"Hi, my sister is here for her driver's test," Gordy said at the desk.

"Hi, I am Officer Dirksen. Your sister had her test and failed. The next appointment is in three weeks. I already told her that," he said in a dismissive tone.

"No, she did not fail the test. The car failed the test. I had it fixed. The next appointment time is at 2:00pm which is her appointment. We are actually one minute early," Gordy Jr. said very respectfully and as forcefully as he dared. He didn't recognize Officer Dirksen but didn't want to press too hard.

Officer Dirksen looked at Gordy Jr., at the clock on the wall, and then Allison. He started to say something then stopped. Then he smiled, "Okay Allison, let's go check that emergency brake. If it is working, you can take your test."

"Thank you," Allison said with great relief. She looked at Gordy Jr. and patted his hand.

"Thanks," Gordy Jr. added now looking for a place to be invisible again.

The Officer had Allison get in the car. Once it was started he had her put the car in gear with the emergency brake engaged. The car held.

"Okay, let's proceed shall we?" he said.

He got into the car and took Allison over to the parallel parking area. Gordy Jr. watched as Allison tried and failed to get into the parking spot. However, she had not hit any of the cones so she would lose points but not an automatic fail. He nodded his head as Allison turned onto the road in front of the DMV. She signaled and he saw her check her blind spot. Maybe she would pass after all. He walked across the street and paid Ray.

About fifteen minutes later, Allison pulled the car back into the DMV. Officer Dirksen got out of the car and went into the office.

"How did it go?" Gordy Jr. asked.

"You saw my parallel parking," she laughed nervously, "and backing around the corner didn't go so well either. Other than that I think I did okay."

Officer Dirksen came out and asked, "How did you fix the emergency brake so fast?"

"Ray fixed it," Gordy Jr. said pointing across the street to his garage.

"Let me guess, he charged you two bucks?" Officer Dirksen laughed.

"How did you know that?" Gordy Jr. asked with a laugh.

"Ray's just like that. He seems to always charge two bucks. Anyway, you passed the test young lady with two points to spare. Congratulations!" the Officer said and handed her a temporary driver's license. "Drive safely!" He then went back into the DMV.

"Can I drive home?" Allison asked clutching her new license to freedom in her hand.

"NO!" Gordy Jr. said and got in the driver's seat. He wanted to get a few miles away as fast as he could. He wanted to be away from so many cops before he opened his beer.

Lake City DMV: I think all the Olwell children tested for their driver's licenses here.

PART II

TIM AT THE AIR FORCE ACADEMY

In the introduction of **_Growing Up Olwell,_** my brother Dave pointed out that only stories of my college years were included. Dave doesn't tell me any of his college stories for fear I will relay them. Dianne, Tom and Allison did not attend college until they were much older. All three graduated. My sister Veronica, spent more time berating my college than talking about hers. I am saddened with her passing, her stories may be lost. That leaves Tim and he still talks to me, so here is what I can offer.

Tim left for the Air Force Academy in June of 1976. In the many years since his graduation, I have only heard from him how poor he was during his college years. He was always broke and could never afford to return to Seattle on school breaks. He constantly reminded me the Academy was not a fun place like Washington State University.

He graduated as the Outstanding Law Student in 1980. Since Law was not an accredited Major, his diploma is for Bachelor of Science without a Major. He did, however, relay a few events which make up the following stories.

Do not feel sorry for Tim. After graduation, he spent a year in Lubbock, Texas attending flight school. That was the year he enjoyed the "College" experience. He doesn't whine about the time there. He actually speaks fondly of it.

The Air Force Academy, Colorado Springs

CHAPTER **16**

First Year Ends: Nowhere To Go But Up

Tim: "I really did have the lowest military ranking in my freshman group of the 30 cadets assigned to our squadron. The time at Keesler AFB, Biloxi, Mississippi convinced me I would not fail out of the Academy and I would not quit yet. If you fail out, the AF would make you honor your commitment as an enlisted man. I was convinced that would not be a good time." Circa 1977.

"Congratulations on your upcoming graduation and good luck at flight school," Tim said to Joe Burns.

Joe Burns was a Fourth year in Tim's squadron. Although, it was the Second Year Cadets who disciplined the First Year Cadets the Third and Fourth Year Cadets paid attention to a degree to what was going on.

"Thanks, Olwell, don't worry about this year. Next year you will be in a different squadron and no one will know what went on here. You will have a fresh start," Joe said.

"I'm not sure what that is supposed to mean," Tim said with a laugh.

"I saw your military score. You didn't do so well. Even with your academic score, you were not rated very high."

"Not very high?"

"Actually last," Joe laughed.

"By who? The Second Years? What a bunch of idiots. They never understood what we were doing," Tim said in disgust.

"Now I don't understand, what's up?" Joe asked with his interest piqued.

"We decided as a class we were not going to let anyone fail due to harassment. So Gregg, Larry and I watched out for the others. If they were being ganged up on in the hall, one of us would walk by and say hi," Tim told him.

"First Years are not allowed to speak in the hall way," Joe said.

"Exactly, so the Second Years would immediately stop abusing their victim and fly onto us and abuse us while the other cadet got away. You guys could yell at me all day, I didn't care. But it really affected some of the women and a few of the guys. We just gave them a break when it went on for more than ten minutes," Tim explained.

"That's what you were doing?"

"Yes," Tim went on, "We only dumped Martinez's room when he was going too far with Henderson and Gavin. If we felt the discipline was fair or justified we did not interfere."

"Wow, I didn't know. I really wish I did. That sucks for you," Joe was serious then laughed.

"What does that mean?"

"Summer assignments are based on Military Score and you three had the lowest scores in the squadron. You have one of the lowest in your cadet corps. They are already assigned. I am sorry there is nothing I can do at this time," he said and shook Tim's hand. "Best wishes."

"What are you doing for summer assignment?" Tim asked.

"I am spending three weeks in the Pentagon."

"I have three weeks at NATO head quarters in Belgium."

"I am spending my time in Honolulu."

"Tim, what are you doing?"

"I am stationed in Mississippi," he laughed.

His fellow cadets looked at him with concern and pity.

"I am sure it will be really nice," one suggested.

"Mississippi in the summer? Wow! You're in for a real treat," another said and they all laughed.

"Cadet Olwell reporting sir!"

"Sergeant, get Olwell suited up and explain his task," the Lieutenant said.

"Welcome Olwell, who did you piss off?" the Sergeant laughed. The sergeant knew that the task Tim had in front of him for three weeks could easily pass as the worst job in the entire Air Force.

"It is a long story, Sarg," Tim said, "What are we going to do?"

"We've got plenty of time for that story but in a nutshell, you will get in a full hazmat suit with oxygen tanks. Then you will go out there where it is ninety-five degrees with ninety percent humidity. The tarmac is one hundred twenty degrees in the shade. You will clean the underside of tanker planes by spraying caustic chemicals on them," he said pointing to the planes on the runway.

"Seriously?"

"Son, it is easily the worst job in the Air Force and for the next three weeks it is all yours," the Sergeant replied.

"Well, what are we waiting for then?" Tim said with determination.

"Good attitude son, but we need the MPs to bring the prisoners so they can suit up too," the Sergeant informed him.

"I am assigned duty usually tasked to military prisoners? I guess I really did piss someone off," he said with an incredulous laugh.

When the prisoners arrived and suited up, they went out in their hot suits onto an even hotter tarmac, each wearing a fifty pound breathing apparatus. They proceeded to spray nasty chemicals on the big planes. They had to have a break every forty-five minutes to avoid heat exhaustion. After a couple hours, they came back in to change oxygen tanks.

"How are you doing, Olwell?" the Lieutenant asked, "Miss the Academy yet?"

"Fine, sir!" was his answer but not what Tim was actually thinking.

When the Lieutenant was out of earshot, the Sergeant said, "Tell me your story."

Tim explained assisting the classmates from harassment and the conversation with Joe Burns.

After the Sarg stopped laughing, he said, "Do a good job on those planes for a week and I will get you reassigned to guard duty. Is that a deal?"

"That would be awesome," Tim said, "thanks."

"First time anyone thanked me in a hazmat suit."

Tim wondered what the Sergeant drank. Later that week, he found out.

Cleaning Planes

CHAPTER **17**

Olwell Tact

Tim: "My Dad married two wonderful women. His second wife was as much of a gem as my Mom and as loving as Gordy our stepfather. To marry anyone with seven kids, the father or mother, takes a strong person and giving endlessly. We were still very young when Dad and Susan married and it would be years until most of us moved away from Seattle. This story was one of the first grand dinners that Susan hosted. I don't like olives. And, I was always hungry as a freshman at the Academy, so was David. Veronica watched Susan cook, she did not cook. Veronica was famous for her effort at cooking dinner but the results always seemed to be burnt. Occasionally involving the fire department."

Cheryl: "Can someone please look-up the word 'oxymoron?'"
Circa 1977

The calm surrounding the holiday evening at my dad and stepmother, Susan's, home was short lived. The organized chaos that ensued whenever the Olwell children arrived always made an impression on the host or hostess, in this case Susan. With both Dave and Tim home from the Academies for break, all seven of her stepchildren descended on her home at the same time. The small nature of the Lakehill's house made our invasion even more impressive.

My stepbrother, Doug, kept closing the door as one of my siblings entered only to be stopped by the next one. He finally exclaimed, "How many of you are there?"

"Seven," I said as I took the door from him and closed it after Allison entered.

A few minutes later, the roar of the conversation became muted as everyone started settling in. Susan was busy in the kitchen where my sister, Veronica had joined her.

Dad directed Doug and me at setting the table properly. "Properly" meant we had to do it over.

"Why do we have to fold the napkins? We are just going to unfold them when we place them in our laps," Doug asked.

"Yeah, that is a good question. Why do we have to fold them, Dad?" I asked and nodded in solidarity toward Doug.

Dad reached over and smacked me on the back of the head. Doug started folding the napkins faster, so much for solidarity. I rubbed the back of my head and Dad shook his head and smiled at me.

When Doug and I finished, Susan and Veronica started placing food on the dining room table. Susan announced dinner was ready.

When we were all seated, we held hands and waited for Dad to say grace. He looked at all of us then bowed his head and said, "Good food, good meat, good God, let's eat!"

We all laughed and started handing the serving dishes around the table.

"The China setting is beautiful," Veronica said.

"Thank you, they were my grandmother's. She gave the China to my mother who gave the setting to me. I love this pattern. You can't find it anymore," Susan said with great pride.

Dad leaned down to Doug and me and said, "That means be careful and don't break anything." There was warning in his eyes.

The table chat was pleasant.

"May I have another helping," Tim asked.

The food was passed to him and the conversation continued around Dave at West Point and Tim at the Air Force Academy. Dianne talked about her plans to move to Hawaii and stay with Aunt Mary Jo.

"Pass the Spaghetti, please," Tim asked again.

Conversation turned to Veronica getting her driver's license.

Suddenly, Tim got real stiff and dropped his fork in the bowl and then said, "Are those black olives? I don't eat black olives."

Taken aback as Tim was on his third helping, Susan laughed then asked, "You ate three bowls before you noticed the olives?"

"Oh, I noticed the black specks. I thought you burnt the sauce but I was too polite to say anything."

"Oh, you're polite!" Dave chided.

Dad just took off his glasses and started rubbing his eyes. With that I grabbed Doug and we left the table.

"You've got all the tact of..." Dad started.

"Of your father!" Susan laughed and broke the tension.

Dad feigned annoyance then laughed out loud. Then he got up and announced, "Susan, I am going to do the dishes as you did such an amazing job on dinner. Tim, you can help me."

"Sure Dad," Tim said and got up and started clearing the dining room table.

About that time, Doug pulled me aside and asked, "Why did you pull me from the table a few minutes ago?"

"Did you see my dad take off his glasses and rub his eyes?" I asked.

"Yeah I saw David do that, so?"

"He does that right before he explodes in anger. That is his warning to you to get away while the getting is good," I explained.

"Wow, come to think of it, he does do that. Thanks for telling me," Doug smiled.

CRASH! The only thing that would make that noise was a dish breaking on the tiled kitchen floor.

"Oh no!" Susan said and rushed into the kitchen.

When she turned the corner into the kitchen, she saw my dad standing over a broken dish. It was not one of the pieces of fine china. It was an everyday dish. It was clear from my father's expression that he had broken it on purpose. Then he started laughing.

"That's not funny," Susan said after a pause, "Clean it up!"

My attention turned back to Doug. "Does your mom have any warning signs before she gets angry?" I asked.

"Come to think of it she does. She usually gets mad just after your dad says you're coming over," he said and laughed.

I laughed too, then stopped and looked at him.

He smiled and said, "Mostly kidding."

Note: Susan always treated me well. I have great admiration for her grace and patience when dealing with me and my siblings. Some of my fondest memories with her are of the discussions we held about my college Management Courses. Her management experience at the phone company added tremendous insight to what my professors were trying to teach me.

Note two: Tim, to this day, tells people he still has all the tact he was born with. He claims he is waiting for the right time to use up that limited amount of Olwell tact. I can attest, he has passed up some really good opportunities thus far. I guess he doesn't want to waste it on just any occasion.

CHAPTER **18**

Computer Science

Tim: "I intended to be a computer science major. It didn't work out and later caused me problems. For a few very tense moments, an academic major was not my concern. It was being expelled. General Beck stood by the window and directed the inquisition. He was better at it than Principal Rumpee!" Circa 1978.

Tim entered the Computer Science Building at the Air Force Academy to input his class work onto the main frame. When a terminal became available, he sat down and began entering the program he had written for the assignment. Upon completion, he attached it to the assignment data which he was processing and hit the ENTER button. Then he waited.

He looked around the lab and saw that was what most of the cadets were doing. The programs were entered and then the waiting began. Tim considered why it took so long. He began to notice some of the First Year Cadets were getting their reports faster than him. That was odd, so he started to investigate.

Tim wondered why he was summoned to the Academy Commandant's Office as he sat in the chair outside his office.

"The General will see you now Mr. Olwell," the secretary told him.

"Thank you," Tim said. He stood up went to the door, straightened his uniform, improved his shirt tuck, then opened the door and entered.

After returning Tim's salute, the Commandant, Brigadier General Beck, asked him to be seated at the conference table. "Cadet Olwell, allow me to introduce the others at the table. Dean of the Computer Science, Colonel White; Major Henabray from the JAG office;

you know your Computer Science Professor Major Grebe and Lieutenant Beane the Computer Lab Administrator."

Tim shook each of their hands in turn through the introduction. He made a mental note of the cool hand shake he received from Colonel White.

"I wanted to get everyone together to discuss a disturbing accusation that came across my desk this morning. It seems that you, Mr. Olwell, have been accused of, let me get this right," the General said as he reached for a document in front of him, "ah, Academic Theft of Computer Processing Time with a potential penalty of expulsion from this Academy." The General paused as he watched Tim's expression slowly register shock.

"General, I do not know what you are talking about," Tim finally responded.

"Well, let's see if we can get to the bottom of this then. Colonel White, you made the accusation. Please elaborate," the General said.

"Sir, I was approached by Lieutenant Beane. He stated that he witnessed Cadet Olwell on two separate occasions at the Computer Science Lab where Cadet Olwell's computer terminal was nearly instantaneously responding to his commands."

"So?" General Beck asked.

"If you will allow sir?" Lieutenant Beane asked.

"Proceed."

"As each terminal on campus is connected to the same main frame computer, processing requests have delays as the computer completes requests in order of priority and request sequence. In practical terms, as a Second Year Cadet, Mr. Olwell should have had to wait thirty minutes on average for his requests to be processed. On both occasions that I observed, his requests were processed in under a minute."

"I see. How would you explain the speed of processing his requests?" The General asked and no one responded, "Anyone?"

Colonel White finally broke the silence, "If I wrote a program and attached it to the main operating system I could do it. What do you think, Major Grebe?"

"Oh, given the proper time I could come up with something but why don't we just ask Cadet Olwell how he did it?" he suggested.

"I'm sorry to interrupt but does anyone know what he actually did before he was accused of this and threatened with expulsion?" Major Henabray asked.

"I'm sorry, I assumed that you had actually found what he had done," The General stated looking annoyed at the Colonel.

The Colonel looked annoyed at the Lieutenant.

"General, I spent a week searching and I cannot find his program," the Lieutenant admitted.

"Okay, let's get to it then. Cadet Olwell did you insert a program into the Academy Mainframe?"' The General asked.

"You don't have to answer that," Major Henabray advised.

"It's okay Major, No! I did not insert any program into the Academy Mainframe," Tim replied.

"Now he is lying, General!" Lieutenant Beane blurted out.

"Lieutenant, I would like to meet you outside to discuss that statement. Be prepared to defend yourself," Tim said leaning over the desk sneering at the Lieutenant.

No one expected that, least of all the Lieutenant, then all hell broke loose at the table as the officers started exchanging comments. Tim watched with mild amusement but he had serious doubt about how he was going to survive a meeting with the Commandant.

"That is enough!" the General commanded, "Cadet Olwell, did you do something to reprogram our mainframe?"

"That is an improper question sir," the Cadet answered.

"Excuse me?" the General asked.

"If I answer in the affirmative, I could incriminate myself and if I answer in the negative, I could potentially violate the honor code. Basically, you cannot use the honor code to make me admit any wrong doing," Tim replied.

Major Henabray and Major Grebe both laughed which was quickly suppressed by a glare from the General.

Major Henabray started to explain Tim was right and the Honor Code workings when the General cut him off with a hand.

"May I try, General?" Major Grebe asked. The General nodded. "Cadet Olwell, if someone was going to change the prioritizing of the operating software how would they do it?"

"Hypothetically?"'

"Hypothetically."

"Someone could do it with one line of code entered into the system," Tim suggested.

"They could not!" the Lieutenant stated.

Tim just smiled.

"Are you smiling Cadet? This is no joking matter," the General stated clearly annoyed.

"No one understands that more than me sir. I have been accused of stealing processing time. Even if what they accused me of is true, I would not have stolen any processing time. I would have only minimized waiting in line time. No one likes to wait in line sir," Tim said.

"We cannot allow people cutting in line Cadet," Colonel White inserted.

"Is it cutting in line if someone just goes and gets in a shorter line?"

"If it is true you just added one line of code, and you truly just shortened your wait time, I would be willing to drop the charges of Academic Theft," the General decided.

"I would take that deal," the Major from JAG suggested.

"Can you show us what you did?" Major Grebe asked.

"I think so if you give me a few minutes and a computer terminal," Tim said thinking he might survive after all.

"Use mine," the General said pointing to his desk.

Tim sat at his desk, "Comfy chair, sir."

"Really?" the General asked taking his glasses off and rubbing his eyes, "Really?"

"Sorry, sir," Tim answered realizing that was a little much, "My sign on will not work on this terminal."

"I deactivated your sign on this morning," Lieutenant Beane stated with a smug look on his face.

"Okay, I get that. General what is your password?" Tim asked ready to enter it.

"I am sorry, you really expect me to give someone accused of hacking the Academy mainframe my password, really? You do not get to pin a star on your uniform by giving your passwords to hackers, young man," the General stated and took his glasses off again. It was tough to tell if he was aggravated or amused.

"Here," Major Grebe said and leaned over and signed in the system.

The officers mostly just chatted over the next twenty minutes as Cadet Olwell played with the computer. Lieutenant Beane and Major Grebe watched intently though. It was clear that Tim was hacking through the prioritization firewall and searching for something that was well protected. Finally, Tim started nodding and it became apparent that he was in familiar territory. Major Grebe watched in awe as Tim navigated through the firewall, several restricted access layers, and finally found the prioritization list that the Major knew must exist but had never seen.

"Here it is," Tim announced.

"I'll be damned," Major Grebe said loud enough for the others to hear.

"What?" the General said as he turned from his window and walked over to behind his desk, "Just show me."

The General looked at the screen. It was clear it was a prioritization hierarchy. He was happy to see that after the Superintendant and a few others, he was at the top of the list: then Deans, then Professors, and inserted between Professors and teaching assistants was a line of code: User 128650(Cadet Olwell). His eyes grew larger as he read the line out loud for the others in the room.

"You signed your name? What an arrogant son of a bitch!" The General stifled a laugh and smiled, "Delete that line of code then wait outside my office."

Tim complied. Nervously he marched out of the office to the large, empty waiting room in front of the secretary's desk. He paced as he was too agitated to sit. After a long period of wearing a rut in the carpet, he heard, "You may go back in now Mr. Olwell," the secretary announced.

Tim again straightened his uniform and returned to the office. After exchanging salutes, he pulled out his chair to be seated.

"Cadet, you will stand at attention," Colonel White shouted showing his continued rage at the entire meeting.

"Sir," Tim said while instantly straightening up.

"Cadet, all charges have been dropped. There will be no further military investigation and the matter will not be turned over as a possible honor code violation. However, Colonel White has insisted that you be banned from all Computer Science buildings for the remainder of your stay at the Academy. I approved his request. He also insisted that you receive a failing grade for your current Computer Science course. Major Grebe found it to be ironic to fail you in a computer Science course for outsmarting the main frame at the Academy. I had to agree. Major Grebe has advised you currently have a score of 98% in his class. That is the grade you will receive for the semester but you will not attend his class again as it is in the Computer Science Building. Consider yourself lucky Mr. Olwell, that is all," the General said dismissing him looking stern.

Tim remained at attention.

"Cadet, you are dismissed," Colonel White almost shouted and shaking his head. Major Henabray started to get up but sat back down as it appeared this meeting had not ended yet.

Tim still remained at attention.

"Cadet is there something else?" The General asked.

"Thank you sir, I accept your judgment in this matter and I appreciate your understanding. I apologize for the time you have had to apply to this issue. However, Lieutenant Beane impugned my name by calling me a liar. He did so in the witness of all the officers in this room. I would ask if you, General, would be my second in this matter."

"We don't duel anymore son," the General replied obviously amused, "Lieutenant Beane; do you wish to apologize to the Cadet?"

Lieutenant Beane looked uncomfortable and shifted in his seat, "Sir?"

"Either I will arrange a little boxing match between the two of you or you can apologize," the General paused to let it sink in a moment, "what do you say Lieutenant?"

"Cadet Olwell, it was an unfortunate choice of words when clearly you only added a line of code and not a program. Semantically, I was mistaken."

"Rather lame apology but an apology none the less, don't you agree Cadet," The General asked but it really wasn't a question.

"Yes sir, thank you sir," Tim replied, "Sirs." With that he saluted, spun around neatly and left the office before anything else could be said.

"So why did you have to go to the Commandant's Office," Tim's roommate asked.

"I got an A in Computer Science and I don't have to finish the class," Tim summarized.

"You don't have to take the final? Awesome," his roommate smiled

"It is, come to think of it, it is awesome. I hate finals." Guess I'll have to come up with a new academic major, Tim thought.

He hoped to someday hear about the entire meeting from someone in the Commandant's office that day but never did. The closest Tim got was a handshake and warm smile he received from

General Beck when he awarded Tim his boxing medal for coming in second in the wing open light heavyweight championship.

Tim later became friends with Major Henabray but the JAG never revealed 'behind doors conversations' and didn't fill Tim in. He would laugh like hell anytime anyone else brought it up. He did however teach Tim to drink Scotch neat and drink real ale.

Note: I went to Tim's graduation at the Air Force Academy in 1980. There was an audio visual presentation at the ceremony that included pictures from Tim's boxing match in the Open Wing Championship.   I would like to say the other guy's face looked worse than his but …

Portugal

CHAPTER **19**

Olwell Diplomacy

Tim: "I went from last in the military ranking as a first year to climb up to near the top of my class. I always was told not to volunteer for anything by my Dad and brother, David. I made an exception in this story and had a great three weeks. About six months after my trip, my Mom and Stepfather, Gordy, toured Portugal with a group. They took a care package to one of the helicopter pilots I had met. His wife had delivered a baby and he could not find cloth diapers in Portugal." Circa 1979.

"They are considering the value of a Military Academy. The purpose of the visit is to discuss your experiences here. Also, you can experience their Military Traditions. I think it will be very positive. The US State Department has asked for Air Force Academy Cadets. You three are my first choice, so what do you say?" Colonel Gendron asked.

Tim had just arrived and did not hear who or where but understood a free trip when he heard one. "I'm in. When do we leave?"

"Good man Olwell, we leave on the 15th. What about you two?" he asked.

The others agreed as well. After the meeting, Tim stayed behind to talk with the Colonel.

"I apologize for my late arrival," Tim said.

"That's fine Cadet."

"Sir?"

"What is it Cadet?" Gendron asked.

"What is it that I signed up for?" Tim inquired.

The Colonel looked up from his desk, took his glasses off then asked, "You volunteered without knowing what you volunteered for Cadet?"

"It sounded like some kind of a tour," Tim smiled hoping it wasn't going to be lame.

"One week traveling back and forth, a couple days in Spain and the remainder exploring Portugal. I hope that will be an acceptable summer diversion. If not, I can see if there is an opening in Mississippi. From your file, it appears you quite enjoyed that summer," the Colonel laughed. He was surprised that a cadet that had done so abysmally as a freshman had risen to such rank as a new senior to qualify for this trip.

"Yes sir, ah no sir. Anyway I am pleased to join your group Sir," Tim said and was dismissed.

"Portugal for three weeks? That's sweet, they make great wine and cheese there," Tim's roommate Bootsy said. Bootsy was a big wine drinker.

"I think so. Where are you off to?"

"Down to the atrium for a haircut," Bootsy replied.

"Will you drop this in the mail for me?" Tim asked handing an envelope.

"Sure," he said accepting the envelope. He looked at the envelope, "What's this? 'Do you still wet the bed?' written on the outside?" Bootsy laughed.

"Turn it over," Tim smiled.

"Cadet David H. Olwell USMA, you're sending that to your brother at West Point? But so what, he will just get it in his mail box and throw it away," Bootsy asked mystified.

"At West Point, the First Year Cadets deliver the mail to their rooms. Dave's underclassmen are going to read that and get a good laugh at his expense," Tim explained and laughed.

"Don't send me any mail in the future! You got that!" Bootsy ordered, "When do you leave for Europe?"

"Saturday."

"Cool, see you later," he said and left for the barber.

The flight to Portugal started with a commercial flight to JFK in New York City. There they boarded a military bus to Dover, Delaware. At Dover, they flew out on a military flight to a US Air Base called Torrejon in Madrid, Spain. The group couldn't fly the C-5 into Portugal because it took special support equipment and there was only five in the group so they didn't rate the trouble. Since the Portuguese and Spanish were quarreling over something at the time, getting through

Portuguese customs was a little difficult until our State Department representative showed up with a military escort. Otherwise the trip was uneventful.

When they arrived Colonel Gendron was met by his Portuguese counterpart. The itinerary was planned. Basically, the Cadets were to tour all of the Military bases in Portugal - all five of them. The bases were named: base 1, base 2, base 3, base 4, and you guessed it, base 5. Then, they would stay a few days at the proposed academy site giving suggestions.

There were morning tours, lunch, afternoon discussions and then dinner. At each meal, Colonel Gendron would sit at the table of honor with the Portuguese Brass. The Cadet's would sit at nearby tables with junior officers from Portugal. Most of them were combat experienced helicopter pilots. They had received commissions but couldn't remain on active duty unless they earned a bachelor degree. There were so many of them, the Portuguese Air Force had asked the US State Department to help investigate how to set up an academy for them. The US doesn't have an academy for married junior officers, but in the interest of diplomacy, it was decided to send over four cadets to look at the proposed facility and academic program. The State Department was funding the trip but their per diem was only $3.00 per day since room and meals were being covered.

The group stayed in a renovated Playboy club that was high on a hill overlooking Lisbon. The previous government had confiscated it and the military junta had turned it into a General Officers visiting quarters. Each had a single room and continental breakfast was provided since a group of five didn't merit opening the kitchen. Each morning they would dress and meet at the bar. The breakfast consisted of coffee, cheese, hard rolls and Aguardiente. Aguardiente is a distilled alcohol that has a nickname that translates into fire water. It was the staple of a traditional Portuguese breakfast. In the older times, farm hands and laborers would pour a shot, throw it into their mouths, swish it around, and then swallow. As their mouths caught fire and salivated in defense, they would chew the hard roll on the way to work. They might carry a cup of coffee with them but the distilled alcohol would keep their mouth salivating long enough to moisten the roll. The Generals insisted on keeping the tradition alive. Others thought it was an excuse for a hair of the dog each morning.

Tim learned that he had one tee-totaler, one lightweight and one Baptist among the other three cadets. So, he was the only one that had the fire water for breakfast. The bartender got paid by what he served and always poured four shots. The first day, Tim only drank one but the group got such grief from the escorting party, Tim started each day with all four shots, a hard roll, and a nap. After the third breakfast, Tim made a deal with the bartender to pour smaller shots and keep the difference.

Typically, Tim napped on the bus drive to the base they were going to tour. After arrival, there would be a meet and greet with the local commanders and a few of the helicopter pilots that needed to earn a degree. Each day, they would have a nice lunch. The seating would be: brass at the head table and four tables with one cadet each. Tim always sat at the table farthest from the head table where the drinking would take place. You see, each base inevitably had a couple helicopter pilots that wanted to enjoy the free alcohol available and attempt to get the cadets drunk. Tim always sat with that group.

The Portuguese Officers made sure there were plenty of refreshments at the table. They made sure there were lots of toasts and that Tim drank with them. The Colonel noticed this and the fact Tim was sleeping on the bus trips and tours. Tim always had a belly full of Port wine, Aguardiente, or other specialty drinks from the area they were in. He slept continuously on bus rides.

"Cadet Olwell, Tim, I am worried about you," the Colonel started.

"Sir?" Tim asked.

"How long have you had this drinking problem?" he asked.

"Drinking problem, Sir?" Tim looked puzzled.

"With the exception of the first two days, at every meal on this tour I have witnessed you drinking excessively," he clarified.

"I know! I could use a little help here. Maybe you could have one of the other Cadets sit with the party group of officers once in a while. I just felt it was rude that the other cadets wouldn't sit at the table at the rear of the hall. Those helo pilots are a blast and very interesting. The whole point of this exchange was for them to see what our cadet system is all about. We have had great conversations about the Academy at every meal, but that table always gets the leftover alcohol from the others and has more toasts than any," Tim blurted, "but anyway, can you assign one of the other Cadets to eat with them for a day or two? I really need the break. I just didn't want to be rude."

"That's what you were doing? You thought you were being a polite guest by eating and drinking with them and covering your classmates?" the Colonel considered.

"Yes, someone had to represent at that table and I think I'm the only drinker of the bunch," Tim answered.

"That's good to know. I was about to send you home. Now, I will see that the other Cadets eat meals with those officers to give you a break," he promised, "and thanks, I think what you did was right under the circumstances."

Tim was dismissed. He smiled all the way to his seat at the back of the bus. As it turned out, the other cadets asked Tim to continue covering for their sobriety. However, they in turn started to cover for his lack of attention in briefings and sleeping on the bus trips. It was a win-win situation. Tim had never slept so well as he did on that trip. It must have been the mattresses the government bought for the Generals. At the farewell luncheon, the helo pilots let on that they had wanted to have fun but after a day or two they realized Tim was the only drinker. So they were trying to see how much they could get into him. The word passed from base to base through combat friends what was being done. Colonel Gendron was glad that it was all in fun and no one was upset by his lack of participation in any way except meal time.

When Tim arrived back at the Academy, he received an accommodation from the Colonel for Service Above and Beyond. He got the highest marks possible for his academy military ranking for the three week summer period. Colonel Gendron laughed as he realized he was still helping Tim dig out of his freshman hole in that regard. Tim also received a letter from Dave at West Point. On the outside was written something pithy designed to cause ruinous harm that only fizzled as Tim was the only one to see it.

Air Force Academy Cadets

CHAPTER **20**

Making The Grade

Tim: "I spent the entire class trying to write programs without being able to troubleshoot the code in the computer labs. My teammate did great work with the iterations necessary to fix any of my mistakes. I enjoyed the class immensely but never intended to do the extra work required to excel. If the minimum was acceptable, anything more would have been wasted effort. So I used the extra study time for my other subject." Circa 1980.

Near the end of third year, Major Stevens entered Tim's Statistics class and asked the Professor if he could address the class. The Professor agreed.

"Good morning gentleman, my name is Major Stevens and I am preparing a class for fall semester. The course content will join statistical averages and management ideals with computer science technology. As computers become more prevalent in our society, I am convinced that the next wave of applications will be in this area. As it is a new course, I am required to have at least ten students to develop the class. As an incentive for trying a new class, anyone taking the class will be guaranteed a grade of B or better. I will be outside in the atrium following your class if you have any questions. The class will be called Econometrics 400. Thank you for your time."

After class, Tim stopped by to see the Major. He was addressing a few of his classmates.

"You will be in teams of two designing programs to analyze data and presenting the data in format easily understood by management decision makers," Major Stevens explained.

"Major, will this class be held in the Computer Science or Economics building?" Tim asked.

"All class activities will be in the economics area and the computer work will be in the main lab or on an auxiliary computer terminal."

"And everyone will get at least a B?" Tim continued.

"Yes, on my honor as an officer, the lowest grade will be a B," the Major replied.

"Where do I sign up?" Tim asked in front of the small group.

"Good man!" the Major said and handed him the application and course summary. Others soon followed in asking for applications.

"Welcome to the Econometrics final gentleman. I hope you found this course as exciting and informative as I did. You all did an extraordinary job on your programming. I was especially impressed with Mr. Morris and Mr. Olwell's presentation of cost/value asset planning.

Anyway, here is the final. You have four hours to complete it. Although you worked in teams this semester, the final will be an individual effort. If you have any questions, come up and I will try to clarify what I am asking for in a particular question. Good luck." With that, Major Stevens counted out the tests and handed them to each row. Then he went and sat at his desk.

Tim wrote his name and the date on the test. He then got up and went to the Major's desk.

"Already have a question?" the Major asked.

"No, I am finished," Tim answered handing him the test.

All the other Cadets looked up when he said that.

The Major looked at the test seeing only where Tim had placed his name and date, "I don't understand?"

"Major, I take you for a man of your word," Tim said.

"Thank you," the Major answered.

"When you introduced this class at the end of last semester, you guaranteed everyone a grade of at least a B," Tim reminded.

"I did. So finish your test and see if you can do better," he replied extending the test back toward Tim.

"I guess you don't understand. I will take the B. I did not study for this exam as I have spent the time studying for my other subjects. A B is good enough for me, thank you," Tim said and turned and left the class.

That afternoon Tim ran into his partner Cadet Morris, "Hey Steve."

"That was the gutsiest move I've ever seen," Steve laughed.

"You think?"

"When you turned and walked out, we all started laughing and then the Major went nuts. I swear we all stopped breathing at once. You should have heard Stevens after you left. He totally lost his composure. He was ranting for about fifteen minutes then he announced everyone in the class was going to get an A and you were the only one who was going to get a B. He felt he really showed you," Steve was laughing about the whole thing.

"I don't care what grade you guys get, I just wanted the B he promised."

"Well thanks; I can really use the A. Oh after the exam, he pulled me aside and asked about your participation in the assignments. I told him you wrote most of the programs but never went to the computer lab," Steve explained.

"He asked why you didn't go to the lab and I told him I didn't know. Anyway all the guys in the class want to buy you a drink. We owe you."

"Great, tell them I drink straight Scotch, single malt, neat, and two finger pours," and he turned to walk away smiling that he had helped his classmates. Cooperate and Graduate!

When the grades came out, Tim received a B. The other nineteen cadets all received As. After Christmas break, they made good on their promise and bought Tim several good glasses of Glen Marangie, a twelve year old scotch that was Tim's favorite at the time. It was a great evening of storytelling and reliving not having to take the final. What his friend had failed to tell him was after about thirty minutes, no one could really concentrate and they all turned their exams in since the Major had said they would receive As. They felt that qualified them for some of the glory in the overall story.

A few months later, Tim ran into Major Stevens in the courtyard.

"Mr. Olwell," he said returning the salute.

"Major," Tim acknowledged and stopped since the Major looked like he was going to say something further.

"I ran into Major Grebe. I vented about your escapade finals week. He told me your story. I am not mad anymore," he laughed, "Did you really tell the General his seat was comfy when you asked for his password?"

"Yes on both points, sir," Tim smiled.

"One more thing, you didn't really ask the General to be you're second in a fight with Lieutenant Beane, did you?"

"Let me put it this way, if you had not given me my B, I would have asked the General to be my second in a fight with you," Tim smiled, saluted smartly and walked away.

Major Stevens laughed but it was uncomfortable. Major Grebe had also told him Tim was the second best light heavyweight boxer at the Academy and not to be trifled with in or around a boxing ring.   He was still shaking his head as Tim entered the nearby building.

Tim walked on thinking it was the only grade less than an A he had gotten that semester. I wonder what that makes my Major GPA, he thought to himself.

Gordy, Tim and me: Air Force Academy Graduation '80

Note: After graduation, I drove back to Seattle via Reno and Bakersfield with Tim. In California, Tim tackled me in the front yard of his friend's house and gave me a haircut. Cheryl agrees with Tim about my hair. Looking at the picture, I am starting to agree as well.

CHAPTER **21**

Dave Corrects A Paper

Tim: "Dave visited Colorado our senior year. I went to West Point, New York to watch the rivalry game the year before. Gregg Royer really did hook me up for the weekend. I was invited to keep his girlfriend's sister busy. Dave really did correct the paper. He caused me some trouble but he also met the Department Head of the Legal Studies. The department head was a West Point Graduate. Later, when I was tied for outstanding cadet in the field of law, one of my law professors reminded the department head he had met my brother from West Point and that may have swayed the final vote my way!" Circa 1980.

"So can I count on you? Are you there for me, buddy? I need you as my wing man" Gregg pleaded.

"My brother is coming for the Army-Air Force Game on the 23rd. When is this weekend?" Tim asked.

"Not a problem. It is the weekend of the 17th. Really, I will cover everything: the room, the gas, even the food and beverage. You only need to keep her sister busy," Gregg pressed some more.

"What's this girl look like?" Tim questioned.

"It's Sarah's sister. Sarah is cute. How bad could her sister be? I have never seen her though," Gregg answered, "Just keep her occupied while Sarah and I are in the bedroom which I hope will be all weekend long."

"Okay, but you are going to owe me," Tim conceded.

"Awesome, I'll owe you a favor," Gregg smiled.

"Hey Gregg and Larry, have you met my brother, Dave? He's here from West Point for the game," Tim explained.

"That explains the stupid uniform," Larry quipped.

"Larry?" Dave started then turned to Tim, "Is he the hockey player you were telling me about that during first year challenged all of the seniors in the squadron to a fight?"

"That's him," Tim laughed.

"That was a pretty awesome story," Dave said.

"I only had to fight three of them. After I beat the first three, they came up with some lame reason why it couldn't continue," Larry said, "they got even though. Only Tim was rated lower in Military score that year. I had to spend the summer at Ft. Lewis."

"Nice meeting you, I will overlook the crack about my uniform," Dave said trying to act magnanimous.

"Ft. Lewis is way better than cleaning planes in Mississippi," Tim pointed out remembering his first summer at the academy.

"So you are a senior at West Point? Are you twins?" Gregg asked.

"No, I am a couple years older," Dave acknowledged.

"And I'm more athletic and better looking! He took a roundabout trip to West Point," Tim laughed.

Dave did not.

"Dave went to Annapolis, the University of Washington, joined the Army, went to Airborne Ranger School and then he went to West Point," Tim explained.

"What happened at Annapolis?" Gregg asked.

"I was not mature enough to accept or handle the grief as a plebe," Dave confessed.

"Yet you had no problem at West Point? Was the hazing different?" Larry asked.

"The hazing wasn't different, I was. After eighty six days training in the Mississippi swamps at Ranger School, having a couple of upper classmen yell at me didn't seem that big of a deal. Let's just say I was in a better frame of mind," Dave answered.

"That's cool, what were you two laughing about in Professor Boone's class earlier," Larry asked.

"That was pretty ridiculous," Tim said, "Dave, you want to explain?"

"Sure, I went to Tim's Economics class this afternoon. The Professor, Boone was it?, handed out an information sheet. It was riddled with typos and grammatical errors. I just so happened to have a red pen on me so I corrected it and gave it to Tim," Dave said.

"It was covered in red ink. On the top he wrote: Professors at West Point would never hand out such substandard material," Tim continued, "Dave, show it to him."

"I don't have it. I thought you had it," Dave said.

"That's okay," Larry said.

"You had better hope Boone didn't see it," Gregg laughed.

"Well, I am not going to worry about that now. Hey, Gregg, when are Sarah and her sister visiting again?" Tim asked.

"We broke up. You should have figured it out last weekend," Gregg said while clearly looking annoyed.

"What happened last weekend?" Dave asked.

"Sarah came out for the weekend. She brought her sister so I brought Tim to keep the sister busy. It turns out that her sister is cuter than Sarah. Then Sarah and I got in a fight on the drive to the resort and fought all weekend. Tim was getting it from her sister every couple hours. It was like being around a couple of rabbits. I paid for the whole shebang and didn't even get lucky. Meanwhile, Tim slept the whole drive back to the academy because he was so exhausted from having sex all weekend. To add insult to injury, your brother thinks I owe him a favor for him coming along," Gregg said to Dave.

Tim was laughing so hard all the others started as well. Even Gregg was laughing toward the end. "I am still worn out," Tim complained.

"Mr. Olwell, did you have a problem with Friday's class," Professor Boone asked on Monday. He looked really annoyed.

All the Cadets turned their attention to Tim as they were immediately trying to remember what had gone on last Friday.

"No sir," Tim replied cheerfully.

"See me after class Cadet," Professor Boone directed.

"Yes sir," Tim replied.

Tim found it really hard to concentrate during the lecture. He was concerned with how he was going to deal with the handout. He needed this class to be an A on his report card.

The bell rang and the other cadets filed out of the class. Tim remained at his seat. It was in the second row anyway so he figured it was close enough.

"Olwell, did you see this?" Professor Boone asked holding up the corrected handout.

"Yes sir," Tim answered.

"What do you have to say for yourself?" he asked.

Then it occurred to Tim that the Professor thought he corrected the paper as his and Dave's handwriting is similar. Tim saw an opportunity.

"I am glad I accepted the appointment to the Air Force Academy," Tim stated.

"I am sorry, I don't get the connection," Professor Boone said.

"My brother is studying at West Point. He was here in class on Friday. The West Point Cadets are so self absorbed that they feel it is necessary to show their superiority often at the expense of others. He did that. I am just glad I came here where we are more confident in our abilities that we don't have to show off," Tim spun.

"Your brother did this?" he asked.

"Yes, I don't care if one of your aides made a mistake on a handout," Tim offered knowing full well the handout was written by the professor. He just needed to offer the professor an out.

"Well, yes, aides do make mistakes. You may go Mr. Olwell," the professor said in a dismissive tone.

Tim quickly left because the conversation was going to make him late to his next class. He needed the entire period between classes to detour around the computer science lab to get to his aero science room. He was patting himself on the back as the bell rang when he was just inside the door. This professor pointed at his seat and started the lecture. Tim settled in and relaxed. He looked around and smiled as he recalled the victory party. Beating West Point at home had set off a huge weekend of frivolity. Dave had not enjoyed the post game as much as he had.

Dave in his West Point Uniform

PART III

TOUR ESCORT

By 1985, my mother was handling most of the Group Travel in Seattle. I was offered an opportunity to escort groups for her. After graduating with my second degree, I went to work with her. I travelled extensively for three years taking groups all over the world. I continued sporadically taking out groups until she retired in 1999.

Rice Paddy Kid with Passport

CHAPTER **22**

Hong Kong

Mom recalls: "It was unusual to assign an escort the week before a trip. I am trying to remember whether the Group annoyed me or the other escort cancelled. Either way, Robert was chosen. I just thought that he would be a great escort and it was time he did something other than dress up as a 'parlor maid'!" Circa 1985.

"Happy Birthday," Mom said waving me over to the table.

"Thanks," I said with a kiss.

"Did you find the restaurant okay?" she asked.

The restaurant was in downtown Seattle in the Federal Building. I had met my mother on numerous occasions in Seattle but never in this part of town.

"Yes, no problem. I had to park in a lot but other than that I found it," I explained.

The waiter came over and gave me a beverage and took our order. When lunch came, we started chatting.

"How would you like to go to Hong Kong for your birthday present?" she asked.

"Hong Kong? That would be sweet!" I said enthusiastically, "When did you have in mind?"

"Next week," she answered and let the timing sink in.

"Next week? I don't have a passport," I offered.

"That is just a detail. Do you want to go?" she asked directly.

"Yes, I do," I accepted.

"Great. That is why I picked this restaurant," she smiled.

After lunch, we went upstairs to the Department of Records and got a copy of my Birth Certificate. Then we crossed the street and got my passport pictures taken. After that we went back into the Federal

Building and applied for a rush on a passport. My Mom had it all planned.

Three days later, I received the passport. I went by her office to get the rest of the details.

"You are going to be the escort," Marleen informed me.

"What's that?" I asked.

"I said you are going to be the escort," she repeated.

"No, I heard you the first time. My question is what is an escort?" I clarified.

Marleen looked at me then shot a worried glance toward my mother.

"He will be fine," Mom assured her and motioned me to sit down.

I was presented with a binder which held all kinds of information pertinent to the trip. Copies of all the airline tickets, copies of the hotel contracts, a copy of the tour guide services, lists of the group names, copies of each of their passports and copies of all the payments made. My head started spinning.

"All you have to do is get them on the plane in Seattle, make sure in Tokyo everyone gets onto the plane to Hong Kong and get them through customs and baggage claim in Hong Kong. Then you will be met by Paul Chiu's tour guides and they will do everything else for the eight nights. You just need to take any issue that is brought to you to Paul Chiu's rep. Here is a check for $ 750. That is for miscellaneous tipping and group expenditures," Mom explained with Marleen at my side.

"Here is a list of purchases we want as well," Marleen said handing me a list with stores and items and the money necessary.

"I got this!" I said reasonably certain I could handle it.

A few minutes later, I pulled Marleen aside and asked whether she would need an accounting for the $750 expense money. She told me just to spend it and laughed. She went on to explain that it was twice what was necessary but because I wasn't an employee getting paid, Mom gave me extra.

In the few days before I departed, I spent a lot of time studying up on the escort binder. One of the things that really helped was looking at the copies of the passport pictures and placing faces with the names.

This allowed me to recognize the thirty members of the group more readily on the departure day at Sea Tac. Many of the group were surprised I recognized them by name. Part of it was my studying and part of it was seeking out the red All Around Travel bag tags. When everyone was checked in at the counter I went out to the terminal and chatted with the folks prior to boarding.

Once aboard, I relaxed and tried to get comfortable during the ten hour flight to Narita, the Tokyo Airport. There we disembarked the plane. As we walked into the terminal, everyone was looking to me for guidance. I just acted casual and looked for information. After a moment, I went up and asked the gate agent who told me where and when the connecting flight would be. I informed the group of this information and they thought I was well informed. I can handle this!

I did not enjoy the four hour flight from Narita to Hong Kong. I was just uncomfortable during the entire flight. It was probably because I had just gotten off a ten hour flight before it.

When we arrived, we collected all the luggage and started through customs. While in this line, I was trying to remember which way I was supposed to lead the group to the guides when exiting customs. Marleen had said, "go left" or did she say, "go right"? I could not remember. So I punted. I told everyone to just wait outside of customs until we all went through.

As I was the last through customs, I was surprised that no one from the group was there on the other side of the door. This could be a problem. I was in Hong Kong for twenty minutes and had already lost the group. I stood there for a moment and looked left then right. Which way to go?

"Robert!?" A guy in a blue blazer yelled at me.

I turned to him.

"Come on, we are waiting on you. I am Larry from Paul Chiu," he said and grabbed my suitcase. He led me to the waiting bus where everyone was already aboard. I just got on acting like that was the way things were supposed to happen.

When we arrived at the New World Hotel in Kowloon Peninsula a few minutes later, Larry gave me the room keys to hand out. I called the folks names and gave them their keys. Everyone was gone and I had my room key left. Larry invited me for a drink.

"I signed you up for all the optional sightseeing trips," he told me over a beer.

"What's that going to cost?" I asked alarmed that he was going to use all my money before I had even begun to spend it.

"What? No charge. Just tell the folks you are going and more will sign up. You want a Rolex?" he asked.

"Yes, besides there are a couple on Marlene's list," I said.

"Give me the list," he said taking it from me, I will get all this for you for $100."

"Okay, but what do I have to pay for all the stuff?" I asked thinking he was charging me to be my personnel shopper.

"No, you give me $100. I will give you everything on the list," he smiled, "I will make an appointment for the guy who sells the fake Rolexes to meet in your room after the Macau/China tour. Let the group know if anyone wants one to meet in your room. Got it? If you have any problems, see me. Before you buy anything, see me. I got you!" he smiled.

"Cool," I replied finishing my drink and saying good night as I was pretty tired. It was five a.m. my time. I was happy about taking care of Marlene's list, besides she had given me way more than a hundred dollars.

The next day we did a sightseeing tour of Hong Kong Island and Stanley Market. After our shopping, we went to Jumbo Restaurant, the floating tourist restaurant where we had dinner. During dinner, I was asked about the day trip to Macau and China on the hydrofoil.

"I am doing it! It sounds like a great time. Everyone I talked to said it was a great trip," I replied. I had only talked to Larry about it but hey, he was giving me a free trip and it was a hundred bucks a person.

Everyone signed up at my recommendation. We left the hotel and arrived at the pier early the next morning. We boarded the Boeing Hydrofoil for the two and a half hour ride to Macau. We cleared customs in Macau. After a brief tour of Macau, we cleared Chinese Customs. We were taken on an amazing adventure around the Chinese countryside. When we arrived at a resort for lunch, we were all excited and famished.

The first course was soup. Everyone just started eating away.

"This is pretty good. What is it?" I asked Larry.

"Pig stomach soup," he smiled.

All the spoons from our group hit the bottom of the bowls. Everyone glared at me. I decided I didn't want to know what we were eating after that. I also made a mental note never to ask what I was eating with a group again.

The next four courses came and everyone ate. Occasional, someone would say, "Don't ask."

On the trip back to Hong Kong, the China Sea was too rough to engage the foils. The trip took twice as long and was much rougher. We survived.

Since we were late, we barely made it back to my room in the hotel for the fake watch salesman. About five members of the group joined me. The sales guy opened up a brief case and displayed numerous versions of the Rolex line. It was quickly apparent that the gold watches looked pretty fake but the stainless watches looked really good.

I quickly picked out a two tone watch and Larry picked the watches from Marlene's list. As I paid the $40, others started picking and choosing their watches. By the time the salesman left, we were all wearing our new watches.

I went with the Bretlands and the Nixons shopping on Nathan Road the following day. The Bretlands had planned out their good cop bad cop shopping strategy. It did not include me. Soon they left me behind with the Nixons.

"You need to meet my son, Tim," Eudora said.

"I look forward to it," I replied politely.

"Tim is an optometrist but he is also fun to be around like you are," Bing stated.

We continued chatting through the crowded stores along Kowloon's main drive.

"I want three of those," Eudora told Bing. She was pointing to the Asian version of the Cabbage Patch Kids.

Bing and I negotiated at length to get the best price and Eudora got the dolls for her grandchildren.

The rest of the trip was a blur and soon I was in the Tokyo airport awaiting the flight to Seattle.

"Hey Eudora, " Mrs. Olsen said, " I got the Cabbage Patch Kid's passports stamped in Hong Kong when we went through customs."

Eudora looked at the stamp in the little passports and then she looked disappointed.

"Give me the dolls," I said.

Eudora complied and handed me the three dolls. I left the terminal and walked down to the Japanese Customs area. I asked a Customs Agent to stamp the dolls passports. He just laughed at the ridiculous request then stamped the dolls passports. When I returned to Eudora, she was ecstatic. She had gathered the other ladies to tell them what I was doing. They were all impressed with my success.

Then they all handed me their dolls. I went back to Customs and the agent again laughed but once again complied and stamped the passports. The ladies were thrilled with the little stamps. I was glad when our flight was called.

Upon arrival in Seattle, I thanked each member of the group and invited them to a reunion dinner a few weeks later to exchange the pictures.

I was relieved when I left the airport and headed home after a great experience.

In Hong Kong

R Donuts, Fort Lauderdale, Florida: We couldn't find it.

CHAPTER **23**

Prelude To A Cruise

Dave Bardy: "Topless donuts!? I prefer mine with a little icing."
Circa 1986.

"Will all non revenue passengers please leave the airplane and see the gate agent," the Flight Attendant announced over the intercom.

"Tom, ours are free tickets. Come on let's go see what is up," I told him.

We got up from our seats and grabbed our things. As we started to leave the plane, I told Dave Bardy, "We will be right back. You okay?"

"I got it handled," he said.

When Tom and I arrived at the desk at the gate there were a few people in front of us.

"May I help you," the Agent asked.

"They announced that we should get off the plane and see you," I said handing her Tom and my tickets.

She took the tickets and looked at them. She looked up and said, "Oh, this doesn't affect you. Please reboard the plane."

"The plane left lady!" Tom stated.

"I got this," I told Tom in a calming voice. Then I turned back to the gate agent, "Maam, we are with a group of one hundred folks on that plane that just left. The group is for KJR radio from Seattle and I am the escort. Although, there is another escort still with the group, we need to get to Fort Lauderdale as quickly as possible."

She hammered away at the keyboard to her terminal, "I can get you on a plane in forty five minutes. You will arrive about an hour later than your group."

"That will be fine. Thank you for taking care of this," I said.

"I have upgraded you to first class for the inconvenience and the misunderstanding," she said as she handed me back the tickets.

I thanked her and then Tom and I looked for a bar. I was unfamiliar with the Atlanta Airport but found a bar quickly enough.

"That is total BS," Tom said.

"Listen, Dave will have to deal with all the luggage and getting the group checked in at the hotel. If there is an issue, I can take care of it as an hour is not that big of a deal. Besides, we get to fly first class. I am glad you dressed for the occasion."

"What?" he asked.

"Like you didn't notice the bleach stain on your shirt and the ripped knee in your jeans?" I pointed out shaking my head.

"You're just jealous you can't pull off the look," he smiled.

"Yeah, that's it," I said and paid for our drinks, "I was going for hobo too this morning. Obviously, I didn't pull it off."

When they started boarding the plane for Fort Lauderdale, I decided I did not want to be associated with my brother in his current state of attire. I boarded rather quickly while Tom wasn't paying attention.

As Tom came into the first class section of the plane and started to sit next to me, I announced, "Hi, my name's Robert. It is nice to meet you," and extended my hand.

Tom took my hand and replied, "My name is Tom, your brother."

Well, that didn't work.

After an uneventful flight, we gathered our luggage and took a shuttle bus to the hotel. When we arrived everyone was already checked in and quite a few folks were by the pool.

"Where did you guys go?" I was asked.

"Airline issue. I see you all arrived okay."

"When we got off the plane, the other escort, Dave, held up a sign saying 'Lost Tour Group'. He directed us to the luggage and here."

"I knew he could handle it!" I said confidently.

Dave told me how everything went smoothly. He just ordered another drink on the plane after we got off.

Then we decided to hit Fort Lauderdale for the evening. We walked the boardwalk and entered The Candy Striper bar. All the wait staff and bartenders were women. They were wearing red striped bikinis and I liked it.

Dave, Matt, Tom and I enjoyed the evening. About midnight, I was talking to Dave and wasn't paying attention as I reached for my drink. It spilled in my crotch. I looked like I peed myself.

"It's time to go," I told him.

"It looks like you already did," he laughed.

"Good one, let's get a cab back to the hotel."

We went out onto the sidewalk and looked for a cab. Several people walked by me and laughed. I know, how rude!

We made it back to the hotel. We made plans for breakfast at 7:00am and crashed.

The next morning, I was ready for the new day.

"Where do you want to eat? We have to be back by ten to get the group to the ship," I asked.

"R Donuts," Dave said.

"You want to have donuts for breakfast?" I asked.

"R Donuts is a topless donut shop," Matt explained.

"Lead the way!" I said as I had heard enough to be convinced.

Well for the next two hours we wondered around Fort Lauderdale and never found the place. We finally ate at IHOP and made it back just in time to take the group to the pier.

As the busses arrived at the cruise ship, the busses stopped at the luggage area where the people offloaded the bags to the longshoremen to be sent aboard the Mardi Gras cruise ship . Then the bus took the people to the boarding area. The longshoremen were brow beating the people for tips.

I insisted that the bus offloaded the passengers first then Tom and I took the empty busses to the luggage area and saw that the luggage made it aboard.

"Where are all the peoples?" the longshoreman asked me when I got off the bus.

"It's just me," I said.

When the luggage was all transferred five minutes later, I tipped the guy fifty bucks. He was still trying to figure out where everyone had gone to. Tom was arguing with another longshoreman about the tipping when I walked up.

"I tipped that guy for the group. See him for your share," I told the longshoreman.

The longshoreman walked away to talk to the other guy.

"He told me he wanted a dollar a bag. I told him I wasn't giving him a hundred bucks for five minutes work," Tom said sternly.

"Let's get out of here," I said.

We rushed out of the luggage area and headed to the boarding area. When it looked like everyone from the group had boarded, Tom and I headed onboard, "Come on, I'll buy you a drink," I said.

Carnival's Mardi Gras

Dave Bardy acting casual behind me near the pillar.

CHAPTER **24**

Mardi Gras Cruise

Dave Bardy: "After graduating from college, Robert and I did several cruises together. After this cruise, the hula hoop contest was always a sure win for me. I still have the trophies as it's one of the highlights of my athletic career. Right up there with throwing a tennis ball into a toilet from about 75 yards to win free box seats for a minor league baseball game. Cruises were tough duty for a bunch of mid-20 year olds. Two of my friends met their future wives on these cruises. By the way, Matt went on to be the Chief Financial Officer for a regional lumber company. I think he can afford the pictures now. I guess nice guys do finish first sometimes". Circa 1986.

"I'll buy you a drink," I told my brother Tom as we boarded Carnival's Mardi Gras cruise in Fort Lauderdale.

I took a glass filled with strawberry daiquiri and handed it to him and took one for myself. I reached for and opened my wallet and realized I had no cash on me.

Tom shook his head and said, "I got it." He handed the guy a ten. Tom had pulled this stunt before on me but as the ship was boarding, he couldn't make me go get some cash.

I thanked him and continued onto the ship.

"Thank you," the waiter said.

"What? Give me my change! The drinks are $2.25 each," Tom demanded.

The waiter turned the tray around. On the other side was a sign saying the price was $4.75 with the souvenir glass. I had handed him a drink in a souvenir glass.

I caught up to Dave Bardy, the other escort and old college roommate, and his friend Matt Jeffries. Dave and I were babysitting a cruise group of a hundred folks. Once everyone was onboard, we didn't really have to work too hard until shore excursions started. After making sure everyone's luggage arrived to their staterooms, we would be done for the day. Carnival was an exceptional cruise line and I was pretty sure we would have the rest of the day off. Besides, once we sailed, I couldn't help any one left at the dock.

We were discussing what activities to do when Tom caught up to us. "Those drinks cost $9.50!" he told me.

"Thanks, I'll catch you later. Wait a minute didn't the sign say $2.25?" I recalled thinking Tom had been swindled.

"Yes, but not in the souvenir glass; with the glass they were $4.75."

"Sweet! I get to keep the glass!" I smiled.

"Let's go to the singles party," Matt suggested.

Tom and Dave agreed.

"It's for the needy not the greedy," I said pointing to my wedding ring.

"Come on," Dave insisted.

With that I headed into the bar area where the party was. Since I was in a large group and with friends of mine, I was feeling pretty safe. They were handing out free drinks so I grabbed two. I handed one to Tom and told him we were even.

"Nice!" he replied in disgust but took the drink I might add. Then I noticed he already had one in his other hand. I smiled as I turned to find Dave.

Just then, Dave and I were grabbed by the emcee. We were placed with a couple other guys on the band stage. Then we were each paired up with a woman. My pairing was spectacular. She was easily the finest looking woman in the bar. Bardy gave me a look acknowledging as much. Looked like greedy won out over needy this round.

Chairs were brought out on the stage and we were directed to sit down. I was handed three uninflated balloons. The game was the guy had to blow up a balloon. Tie it off and place it in their lap. Then the gal had to burst the balloon by sitting on it. I had an immediate understanding of how this game was going to go down. Winning would be easy. Instantly, I realized I wasn't going to win.

The key to win was to blow up the balloon as big as possible so it would burst more readily. Again, that is if you wanted to win. I was more interested in making the game last as long as possible rather than winning. Call me greedier.

"Go!" the emcee said. The room full of partiers with free drinks in hand roared their approval and the game was on.

All the guys started blowing up their balloons. After a couple of puffs I tied off my balloon when it was about the size of a softball. Dave tied his off when it was the size of a basketball. His partner landed on the balloon once and it burst. The other teams were having similar results. My partner with the incredible figure was hopping up and down on the balloon in my lap like no tomorrow and that balloon just would not burst. I placed my hands on her hips to help her keep her balance. She looked at me in surprise or was that an 'I'll kill you' look?

She was bouncing on my lap something delightful. I was delighted at least. The crowd seemed to appreciate the way her top was bouncing up and down. When everyone else was on their second balloon, she reached down and popped the underinflated balloon with her fingernails.

"She's cheating," Dave yelled pointing at my partner.

He had just tied off his second balloon and it too was the size of a softball. He smiled at me. It was a devious smile. I liked it.

By the time I tied off the second balloon, the other two guys were on their third. But now their's were small as well. These balloons were not popping but the girls were bouncing and their assets were too. The crowd was laughing hysterically and the gals were getting hopping mad. My partner had stopped bouncing and taken my hands off her hips. As she was about to get up, I was saved by the bell.

"Time!" the emcee called, "Folks, we have always had a winner before. These guys just don't seem to get this game. Let's have a big hand for our lady contestants though." The crowd had grown to over a hundred due to the continued free drinks and was loud with their approval. The male crowd members seemed overly enthusiastic about the game and display.

"My lap feels like a winner," I laughed.

"I won too!" Dave said.

The emcee finally gave the prizes to all the gals and told us to leave the stage. Awhile later, he caught up to Dave and me, "Really funny you guys. We are having another contest up on the lido deck at 9:00pm, want to participate?" he asked with pleading eyes. His job was to make sure he had volunteers and we were obliging.

"Absolutely. Got any free drink cards?" I asked because the open bar had just closed and we had been on stage the entire time.

"Sure," he said and handed me a couple. Then he gave Dave one.

Dave and I joined Tom and Matt. I handed Tom the free drink coupons, "Now are we even?"

"Four free drinks, hell yea!" Tom said. He hadn't quit drinking yet and always enjoyed a free drink.

"You know if you guys had blown the balloons up more you could have won," Matt said looking like we were idiots for not figuring it out.

"Really?" was all Dave could say to his friend then looked to me for support.

"Can I use your camera?" I asked Matt.

"Sure," he said and handed it over.

"Hey, check that babe out!" I said pointing behind Matt.

He turned around and I took a picture of my foot. When Matt turned back to me I gave him his camera back.

Dave pulled me aside a few minutes later, "What was that all about?"

"Every time Matt says something stupid, I am going to take a penalty picture with his camera," I laughed. I had not been around Matt much before but decided it was time to penalize his complete lack of situational awareness. He was a nice guy but missed a lot of our antics. Not understanding I had just received a free lap dance in front of a hundred people was just the latest example of his now famous cluelessness.

"Hi guys, want to join us for champagne?" a gal asked. She was hot and my mind immediately forgot about Matt, "We think you two are really funny."

I looked at Dave and he looked at me and we agreed. We sat down for some Moet Champagne with these two girls who explained they were from Boston. They ordered another bottle and we enjoyed the conversation. Every once in a while, someone from our group would stop by to comment on the stage act or ask about a shore excursion. I used that as an excuse to leave. I got up discreetly before the bill came. I was sure our free drink coupons did not cover bottles of good champagne.

That night at 9:00p.m., we arrived at the Lido deck. Our group from Seattle was well represented. Tom was already at the bar and told me that he was on his last free drink coupon. When the emcee saw us, he waved us over and then announced that the party was going to begin. He had us team up in twos. He grabbed Dave and me as the first team. Four or five other teams came up front with us. I wondered what we had gotten ourselves into when the emcee smiled at us with a sly grin.

"One of you need to compete in the Limbo, the other in the Hula Hoop competition," the emcee told each team, "Take a minute to pick who is doing which."

"I can't Limbo," I told Dave.

"Can you Hula Hoop?" he asked.

"I will figure out the Hula Hoop, but I know I can't Limbo," I insisted. I was about as limber as a two by four piece of lumber. I would have trouble doing the limbo under a suspended telephone wire.

"Hi guys, this is Stephanie and her boyfriend Steve," Matt said. Then he bought both of them a drink. He had stated he thought Stephanie was cute - but buying her boyfriend drinks?

"Hey Matt, let me use your camera for a minute," I said shaking my head.

He handed it to me and I quickly went into the adjacent bathroom and took three pictures of the urinal. I came out and casually handed the camera back. He took it without comment. Dave just shrugged his shoulders at me.

The emcee announced the Limbo and Dave went out to represent. The limbo bar started pretty high and everyone made it through. Round and round went until the bar was about three feet off the ground. Then a couple of the contestants dropped out. When it was just Dave and one other guy, the other guy cleared about thirty inches. Dave got an idea and asked the bar to be lowered to a foot, a foot!

"Everyone, Dave asked that the bar be lowered to a foot! Can I have your silence please?" the emcee announced and then told Dave to proceed. The emcee was building the crowd's interest as Dave stretched a bit. Dave was hamming it up and I wondered what he had in mind. Matt was following Stephanie and was in danger of missing whatever Dave pulled off so I shook him and made him turn around and watch.

Dave laid down on his back. He pulled his heels back to his sides about his waist. In that position, he kind of crab walked under the pole. I have no idea if it was a legal move but the crowd went wild when he cleared the height. The last contestant conceded and Dave had won the first challenge. He beamed at the crowd and walked over to our table.

He chest banged Tom as he went by the bar. I stood up and pretended to bow as he approached. He deserved it.

"Top that Olwell," Bardy challenged then laughed.

"I got this covered," I told him with false bravado. I was thinking hard about how I was going to hula hoop let alone win the contest!

While the others in our group came over to congratulate Dave, I came up with a game plan. I needed a game plan because I could not hula hoop; not even a little bit.

"Okay contestants, the Hula Hoop Challenge!" The emcee announced while handing me a hoop. "You can practice for a minute but when the music starts, start your hula hooping. If the hula hoop hits the floor, you are disqualified. Last man standing wins. If it is a tie, then the crowd will decide based on shear talent."

"Dave, come here," I said.

He leaned in and I told him my idea. He laughed and nodded. I maneuvered myself near a pillar by the corner of the stage. Dave went around behind the pillar. When the music started, Dave held the hula hoop from behind the pillar. I started moving like I was hula hooping and Dave was moving the hoop back and forth. Then he started raising the hoop to my neck. After that he moved it down below my knees, the whole time I was swinging my hips and dancing around.

The crowd on Dave's side of the stage saw what he was doing and was cheering for us. The crowd on my side had no idea what was going on other than I was this spectacular hula hooper. The emcee came over and realized what we were doing. He just laughed not knowing what to think of us. Since the crowd was enjoying the spectacle, the emcee played along. The response was the most interactive he had seen in his career. He wanted to play it up in case his boss was watching. This was too good.

There was one other guy standing when the music stopped. The emcee gave the decision to the crowd, many were laughing so hard they were nearly crying. I won hands down. I mean even the other guy's mother voted for me.

"Where did you guys come from?" The emcee asked while giving us our prizes.

"Seattle," I said.

"Portland," Dave said.

"I have never seen anything like that and I thought I had seen it all," he commented.

"Got any free drink coupons?" I asked.

"For you guys, no problem," he said and handed us each several. I left my hand out to get a couple more. The emcee complied with a shrug. He felt it was worth it to see the crowd have so much fun.

Tom came over, "That was good stuff you guys."

I handed him my stack of drink coupons and he thought I was great. Dave gave half his coupons to Matt. He told Matt not to use them on Stephanie's boyfriend.

"Why?" Matt asked.

Dave didn't say anything other than asking to borrow his camera. Dave took a couple of pictures of a bar stool when Matt wasn't paying attention. It wasn't even a cute bar stool. Meanwhile, the crowd started to disperse.

"Champagne?" the Boston girls asked while laughing and then handed us each a glass.

We were up late that night and the gals bought several more bottles of Moet. We were complete gentlemen and drank with them as long as they were buying.

The next day, we were sitting in the main ballroom after lunch having a glass of Champagne provided for us by the Boston chicks. The emcee announced there was a prize for the best looking guy dressed as a gal. The contest would start in fifteen minutes.

"Come on!" one of the Boston gals said.

We raced back to her cabin. Once there, she pulled out a wig and a French maid outfit. While I started dressing, these two gals started applying makeup. Dave just stood back and laughed at me. I was wondering who goes on a cruise with a French maid outfit? These girls knew how to pack for a cruise. I wondered what else these two girls from Boston had room to pack.

Fifteen minutes later, I was standing on the main ballroom stage in drag.

"You again? Nice outfit," The emcee face lit up as he saw me gracefully working my hips and laughed. He hoped that his boss was tracking how large his crowds were on this cruise and how great the excitement level was for the gimmicks. He beamed when he saw the ship's Captain standing in the doorway.

After a close competition, I won the free drink coupons. The emcee just gave me a stack this time. Tom was by the stage to collect them. He was having a great deal of fun at my expense. That was ok because I don't drink much and the free champagne was more than enough. The Captain came over to congratulate me but pulled back when I tried to hug him and give him a little peck on his check. He asked about how I found a French maid's outfit on such short notice. I told him to ask my wardrobe and makeup specialists from Boston. He didn't get the joke but the girls beamed with pride at our combined victory.

On the last night of the cruise, I commented to Dave how we had been drinking the Boston girls Champagne for the last few nights, "Maybe we should get a bottle?" I wanted to investigate why the girl would bring the French maid outfit.

"You're probably right," Dave said. He was still needy.

We went to the bar. "A bottle of Moet Champagne please," I ordered.

"Sir that is only sold in the main dining room. I can order one and have it for you in twenty minutes," the bartender informed me.

"How much is it?" I asked, now concerned.

"Thirty dollars a bottle, sir," he said.

"Forget that, give me two of the cheapest bottles of champagne you got here in the bar," I ordered.

Dave looked like he agreed. I paid with a twenty dollar bill that included a generous tip.

We arrived at the table where the Boston girls were carrying our champagne like it was Dom Perignon. The Boston girl I was hanging with thanked us. The one hanging with Dave was not impressed by our brand of champagne but she drank it anyway. Later that evening when the entertainment areas closed at 1 a.m., Dave and I led a group of about fifty folks into the main ballroom of the ship. We had accumulated an entourage by this time on board. Dave and I went up onto the stage. He sat down at the drums and started pounding out a beat with the foot petal. He used a pencil and started tapping the cymbals. Not to be outdone, I sat down at the piano and banged a couple of notes repeatedly. To both of our surprise, everyone else started dancing. We were an immediate hit!

About thirty minutes later, a huge security guard came through. He was easily six five and weighed three hundred pounds. He looked at us and we looked at him but we continued playing and the group continued dancing. He left the ballroom shaking his head and wondering where the emcee was.

A few minutes later, a short blonde gal from the purser's office came in and started yelling at us. We just danced the meringue out of the ballroom. The crowd broke up as the security guard was waiting about ten feet outside the door. He looked more menacing since he had combed his hair up into a fro that made him look 4 inches taller and meaner.

When checking out later that morning, the emcee walked up to Dave and me, "Was that you in the ballroom at 1am? Everyone in the Purser's office is talking about it."

We both just laughed a nodded. Even a small nod hurt, though.

"I knew it was you guys, thanks for the fun and have a safe trip home," he said.

The Boston gals came over to say goodbye. Mine was very pleasant.

"I've got a hangover from that cheap champagne you bought," said the other.

"Sorry, we tried to buy the Moet but the bar was out," I told her truthfully.

She just gave Dave a hug and stormed off. I waved to my new friend as they left. She smiled and waved back.

I left the group in Fort Lauderdale because I had to fly to Europe to meet another group flying there from Seattle.

About a month after the trip, we had a group dinner to get together and exchange photos. It was a ploy to get the travelers to start thinking about their next trip with our travel agency. I was pretty sure most of the group would travel with me again as their escort. As a rule, Tom didn't attend these functions as we only supplied free soda and iced tea. Dave was there with me because he was an escort and it was the last official function of that duty.

"Hey Dave, what did Matt say about the photos?" I asked.

"He didn't say anything. I don't think he has looked at them. He just went in and asked for three copies. He spent a ton of money on those photos though," Dave replied.

Matt walked up to a cute gal from the trip, "Want to see my photos?"

"Sure," she said and he sat down next to her. He was still needy.

He opened the envelope and took out the pictures. Toilet, toilet, toilet, Foot, Foot, Foot, Closet, Closet, Closet, Bed, Bed, Bed, Urinal, Urinal, Urinal.

"How'd those get in here?" he said out loud seeing they were not having the effect he had hoped on this lovely young lady.

"Yea, those are real nice," the gal said as she slowly moved away from him. She was asking herself what kind of guy takes pictures of urinals on a cruise ship?

She got up shaking her head and left him sifting through his pictures. By the time he was done, about eighty per cent of his photos were trash pictures. He just sat there mystified as to where they had come from. It was clear he did not know so Dave and I decided not to fess up. Stupidity deserves company. Matt had lots of pictures to keep him company. I hope by the next trip he buys a digital camera otherwise it may be even more expensive for him. I wonder how you teach an adult man situation awareness. It may be hopeless.

Note: The trip was such a success that Dave was asked to solo escort after that for KJR's trips hosted by Stacie Hansen. I was doing Gary Lockwood's trips. So over the next few years Dave and I only escorted together twice more. Tom started escorting trips as well.

Oh yes I did!

CHAPTER **25**

Tim Nixon: Highlights

Circa 1986.

Bing and Eudora Nixon were on the first trip I ever escorted to Hong Kong. The trip was a great success. The following year, they signed up for the trip to Portugal I was escorting. They also convinced their son, Tim, to come along. Rather than require him to pay the single supplement for travelling alone, I suggested that he room with me as I usually had a room to myself. This would save him about four hundred dollars. He accepted.

I was pretty tired when I arrived back at the airport in Copenhagen. I flew in the previous day from Ft. Lauderdale where I had been on a Carnival Cruise to the Bahamas with a different group. The other escort, Dave Bardy, was taking that group to Disney World then home to Seattle. I was at the airport to meet the group flying in from Seattle. Then I was taking them to Portugal. I would catch up on my sleep when the group was bunked down in Portugal.

I looked up at the arrival board to see the flight had landed. I went over and waited outside of the Customs area. Customs at this airport was usually quick and efficient. About twenty minutes later, members of the group started coming out. The door would slide open and the people would push their luggage carts through and the door would quickly close behind them. I could get a glance in but the hallway did not reveal much. I had to wait until they actually came through the doors to communicate with them.

Waving to the members of the group, I greeted them and pulled them aside until the whole group was assembled. Finally, I saw Tim Nixon and waved him over.

"Hey Tim, I think we are just missing the Hills. Did you see them?" I asked.

"Robert! Good to see you. The Hills? Yea, they're coming," he said and started laughing. I didn't see the humor in my question.

"What?"

"You'll see," he said continuing to laugh.

The customs door slid open and Mrs. Hill came out. She was carrying her handbag. She was closely followed by the luggage cart Mr. Hill was pushing. The cart was overloaded with more luggage than the trip length should dictate. He took too long maneuvering the cart through the door and the doors shut, hitting the sides of the luggage cart. The luggage started cascading off the front of the cart. Mr. Hill leaned down and tried to stabilize the luggage from inside the doorway. It was like the whole thing was in slow motion. Mr. Hill was six feet eleven inches tall. He was bending over the cart and grabbing at a piece of luggage on the other side of the door. I did not know when the exact moment was that I realized he had passed the tipping point and was going to fall over the front of the cart but he did. So their luggage is all over the place, he is on top of the luggage sprawled out like only someone who is nearly seven feet tall could be. It was too bad for such a nice old guy to end up that way.

Then his wife starts screaming at him, "Get up! You're embarrassing us!" She had previously offered no help or guidance as he was trying desperately to navigate the hallway and doors.

I grabbed Tim and we quickly rushed to Mr. Hill's aid. We each grabbed an arm and lifted him to his feet. We forced the door and pulled the cart completely through the door. We then started reassembling his luggage on the cart. I could still not believe how much luggage there was.

"I can't take you anywhere!" Mrs. Hill continued, "Hurry up right this instant!" She shouted as if that would make matters better or her supposed embarrassment go away. Mr. Hill now did look embarrassed and older.

"It's okay lady, we got this," I told her hoping she would just get out of the way so I could reassemble the collection of luggage onto the overloaded cart.

"Just get out of the way," Tim said gently moving her to one side with his arm. She huffed at being gently moved aside but stopped berating everyone and everything.

I knew we were going to get along. Once we had the group's luggage onboard the bus, I boarded the bus. After verifying the head count, I nodded to the driver to start. I went and sat down by Tim.

Robert L. Olwell

"That was fun," I said sarcastically. I couldn't figure out what had transpired to cause such a ruckus.

"The Hills drank a whole fifth of whiskey on the plane. They carried it on and kept pouring themselves drinks until it was empty. Then they bought some drinks from the flight attendant," he laughed.

"Wow, that explains it," I laughed.

"Are your trips always this fun?" he asked.

"Wait and see for yourself," I smiled. In the short time I had been leading trips, I learned that each group was different and no trip was easy.

Later on the same trip, I was in the bar of the Hotel in Cascais just outside of Lisbon. There was another group of rowdy men staying at the hotel from England. They were on a golf adventure. I was holding my own with them when Tim came into the bar. Tim was wearing a tank top and running shorts.

"Hey," I said, "Can I get you something?"

"How's it going? I'll take a draft beer," he said looking tired and sweaty.

I ordered a beer and introduced him to Trevor, one of the Brits.

"You were running?" Trevor asked.

"Yes, I just got back from running a 5k," Tim said then accepted the beer from the bartender.

"Well I ran a 10K this morning," Trevor said loudly enough for his friends in the bar to hear.

The other Brits howled in approval.

"Yes but before I went running I played tennis for an hour," Tim replied casually.

"That's nice, but I played tennis for two hours this morning," Trevor said smugly.

A small cheer went up amongst his friends. It was definitely on.

"Well before I played tennis, I played eighteen holes of golf," Tim responded with a smile and a hit from his beer.

Trevor's friends showed some love by yelling a bit at that.

"I played thirty six holes of golf and then went and rode bucking broncos on the beach with the wind in my face," Trevor said triumphantly.

The bar crowd went nuts with that. Tim waited until it calmed down a bit then said, "While you were playing your thirty-six holes of golf and riding your bucking broncos with the wind in your face, I was

133

making love to your wife," he paused long enough to put his open hand in front of Trevor's face, "five times!"

That did it! Everyone burst into laughter and cheering, even Trevor who offered to buy Tim a drink. I added my request to the same order.

When it quieted down, Tim asked, "What was that all about?"

"I have no idea but you're the man!" I said.

"That was pretty good, huh?" he smiled.

"Not that, I meant you're the man because I only slept with his wife three times," I laughed.

"Really? Let me buy you a beer then."

The following year, Tim joined me on a trip to Spain. We were staying at a Hotel in Torremolinas that over looked the Mediterranean Sea. We had a room adjacent to the pool and pool bar. The temperature was hovering around seventy-five but the water in the pool was cold. Not surprisingly, there were lots of folks sitting around the pool but no one swimming. I reflected at what a pleasant way to end the day, smiling as I surveyed the pool area.

We had just returned from a sightseeing tour. We were invited to the pool bar for a drink. When we joined the group in the bar, there was a serious conversation going on. Half the folks thought it was inappropriate for the American women at the pool to be sunbathing topless. The other half thought "when in Rome, do as the Romans do".

"What do you think, Robert?" Tim asked sucking me into this conversation.

The whole group looked at me. "I think this conversation needs a beer," I replied wanting to avoid being the arbiter of a silly problem.

This was mixed with laughs and boos. People were booing me, really. Finally, I got a beer and was hiding behind a long, cool draw on the mug.

"Quit stalling," Tim laughed as he took my mug from my hand. I wiped my mouth and thought about my response.

"I think both sides are right. She should definitely not be sunbathing topless," I said laughing and pointing in the direction of a rather large woman.

Everyone laughed but it was short lived. It seems this was a more serious argument than I realized. I paused to think about another way out when another woman asked me my opinion.

"No, really what do you think?" A lady asked.

"It is unfair to use American ethics and mores to evaluate behavior in a different country. If sunbathing topless is okay here then it is okay here. Plain and simple," I answered. "If you are comfortable enough then join in. If not, enjoy the view. If that is uncomfortable, then avoid the view."

"What he said," Tim nodded and I hoped that solved our debate on topless women in Spain.

It was soon obvious that this discussion wasn't going to have a resolution. Although the beer was free, I decided it was time to move on. I really hoped some would be too uncomfortable to join in.

"Tim, we have to go to that meeting now," I said and got up.

"Right, we had better hurry," Tim said and thanked everyone for the drinks.

As we left the pool bar and headed around the pool to our room, Tim asked, "What meeting?"

Just then Tim stepped across the corner of the pool, I stiff armed him and he went flying into the cold water. He surfaced in the middle of the pool with a smile and swam over to the edge and got out.

"Great! The room key fell out of my pocket. We both looked and could see it on the bottom of the deep end. Then we noticed his money floating in the pool as well.

Everyone around the pool was laughing and looking at us. I felt bad that the key was at the bottom of the pool.

"I will get the key," I said and removed my shirt and handed it to Tim.

I dove in and swam to the bottom and collected the key. I surfaced and retrieved his money. He would need it to buy my next drink. Everyone was laughing when I climbed out of the pool. I looked around to see my shirt floating in the middle of the pool. Apparently, after I dove in he looked at my shirt in his wet hand and just threw it in the pool.

"So that's how it's going to be?" I asked.

"You really thought I was worried about keeping your dirty stinking shirt dry?" Tim laughed. "I am comfortable with you being topless!" he exclaimed and left me laughing at him and my shirt. One of the pool hands used a lifeguard pole to reach my shirt. I thanked him and used the time to review the women around the pool. I came to the conclusion that women should be able to sunbathe topless and I didn't have to look at the ones that showed poor judgment by wrongly joining in. I was at peace with the Spanish mores.

Tim Nixon and me.

Note: Tim is an Optometrist with his own practice. He joined six of my trips after Portugal. He was great fun to be around. This is a picture from the Pacific Princess on a Caribbean Cruise.

CHAPTER **26**

Unrest In Spain

Mom remembers: "Not every group worked well with every escort. Robert, Tom, Cheryl and Dave Bardy created loyalty among their groups. Al and Sadie Baines ended up as some of Robert's favorite passengers. They always came in laughing and then told me stories of his antics. They usually asked if "Capt. Bidet" was in. Oh, well, I guess that's another of Robert's tour escort stories." Circa 1987.

"Do you believe they are charging us twenty five cents for butter? They said all meals were included. I think we should all complain," Mr. Rhodes said very loudly in the hotel restaurant.

I looked up from my lunch and sighed. The meal was hot, tasty and had been served immediately when we arrived. I noticed a few others of the group were now discussing the butter charge. I got up and walked over to Mr. Rhodes' table.

"Hi Mr. Rhodes, is there a problem I can help with?" I asked. I was using 'my everyone needs to hear this' voice.

"I just got charged twenty five cents for butter. This trip said all meals were included. What do you have to say about that?" he glared at me.

Really? All this fuss about a quarter? What a jerk. I knew this needed to be addressed.

I smiled. "Let me explain Mr. Rhodes."

"If you think," he started.

"No, let me finish," I said holding my hand up to his face, "you paid $699 for this ten day trip to Spain. SAS Airlines had to make money. The transfer company in Copenhagen had to make money. The hotel in Copenhagen had to make money. Sterling Airways had to make money. The transfer company here in Spain had to make money. The sightseeing company that provided the three tours here had to make money. This hotel had to make money. This restaurant where you have been offered twenty one meals had to make money. KJR radio that advertised the trip had to make money and even All Around Travel had to make money. So you see there wasn't enough money left to pay for your butter." I just smiled and flipped him a quarter and walked away.

I could see by the expressions on the other tour members nearby that I had achieved the goal of pointing out the value they had received on this trip even if it was lost on Rhodes.

I was talking to the Tour Operator outside the restaurant when Tom Thompson approached me.

"Will you join us for a drink?" he offered.

I looked and he was with his wife and several other couples.

"Absolutely, give me a minute and then I will meet you in the pool bar," I said picking the pool bar because I could scan for beautiful scantily clad Spanish women while pretending to listen if the meeting didn't go well.

A few minutes later, I arrived to the group of about eight tour members. I said hello to all and was seated so I had an unobstructed view of the tanning area.

"You're not much of a Tour Escort," Al Baines said with his hands folded across his chest.

Ouch! This is going to be interesting. "First, someone offered to buy me a drink," I said and waived to the bartender, "I'll have a liter of draft beer." No sense ordering a small one for this. I could always sit here and watch the women with the large beer they were paying for.

"We were talking and we have been on numerous trips and you don't measure up to any of the escorts we have had in the past. Hell, compared to Juan Carlos from the other group in the hotel, you suck", Norm Olsen said.

With that I just smiled, I waited for my beer before I said anything. Juan Carlos was the Escort for another group that flew in from Copenhagen with us. He was always very busy. I was busy watching a micro bikini get settled into a lounge chair and waiting for my beer.

"Thanks for the beer," I said and raised my glass to the group and took a sip, "Now let's discuss this, shall we? What do you like about Juan Carlos?"

"The first day at the airport here, his group just got on the bus and he took care of all the luggage. Then he got on the bus and took roll call to see if everyone was there," Tom started.

"When they arrived at this hotel, they checked in. Then Juan Carlos spent all evening checking in with his group to ensure their luggage arrived. He even went back to the airport to retrieve luggage that was missing. He went way above and beyond," Al Baines said.

The whole group of folks in the bar was nodding.

I smiled and took another sip of beer. This seemed to annoy several of the folks. The micro bikini rolled over and adjusted her thong strap.

"See! Even your attitude right now suggests you think this is funny," Norm accused.

I smiled again then set my beer down, "Let's talk about this. Upon arrival into the Malaga airport, I asked that you identify your bags to the porter. Then I insisted that you do not get on the bus until you saw your bags placed in the cargo compartment on the bus."

"But Juan Carlos took care of all that for his group," Sadie Baines said.

"I will get back to that Sadie. Then when all the bags were on the bus, I boarded the bus and we left for this hotel," I continued.

"Juan Carlos took a roll call before he left the airport, he was making sure everyone was with his group," Betty Olson pointed out.

"I will get back to that Betty. Then when we arrived here at the hotel, I asked that you wait to see your luggage was taken off the bus before you entered the hotel," I said.

"Yes, but after a long day we just wanted to check in like Juan Carlos' group," Al Baines offered.

"I get that Al. You also said you were impressed that Juan Carlos tracked down his groups missing luggage that night."

"He was amazing. You did not even check in with us, you just stood around the lobby," Sadie Baines commented.

"Okay, I got it. Now let me explain. You all may first wish to have a drink," I laughed then took another hit of my beer. Another micro bikini appeared and I adjusted my sun glasses.

So far this had clearly not gone down like they had expected it would. They were having their drink and looking at each. I was neither upset nor defensive. I wasn't even really displaying much concern. They could not tell if this reinforced their belief I sucked or if I knew something they didn't know. Obviously, I did not know my part in this intervention.

"First the luggage at the airport: by pointing out your luggage to the porter and your watching it get loaded on the bus prior to your boarding, I knew all the luggage was on the bus. Juan Carlos counted the bags as they went on his bus. When he had the right number, he got on the bus. He did not know if he had the right luggage only the right number of pieces," I said and waited for that to sink in.

"So your method is to make sure we account for our own luggage?" Tom Thompson asked.

"I am not the one inconvenienced if your luggage gets lost and I do not know what everyone's luggage looks like with the exception of our bag tags. You are probably not aware of this but I told Juan Carlos that there were two pieces of luggage still on the airport baggage carousel that belonged to his group."

"You did?" Tom Thompson asked skeptically.

"Yes I did. You can ask him. Anyway, he blew me off because he thought he had the right number of pieces. He did not account for carry ons being placed with the other luggage to be loaded onto the bus. I didn't have to worry about additional carry on bags being placed in the cargo space as you watched and ensured your luggage was loaded."

"I see but he took roll to make sure everyone was on the bus when they departed. You just got on the bus and we left," Sadie Baines pointed out.

"How many people are in our group? Anyone?" I asked. Another bikini clad hottie joined the small cluster in the tanning area. I had to get through this meeting so I can start another one with them.

"I don't know forty-something?" Norm guessed.

"Good guess Norm. There are forty-eight. Our's is a fifty-two passenger bus. It only takes me a few seconds to count four empty seats while at the same time scanning for anyone who shouldn't be on the bus. That is much faster than calling your names. We actually left for the hotel faster than taking roll." I stood and reached for a napkin. I pretended to scan the small group but was really standing briefly to get a better angle on the newest Spanish goddess getting ready to tan by the pool. She had on a pink suit.

"Oh," was all Al had to say.

"When we arrived here, you verified your luggage got off the bus before checking in. I announced I would be in the lobby for the following two hours to deal with any concerns. As Al stated, everyone was tired from a long day of travel. You coming to me with an issue versus me banging on your door asking if everything is okay achieved the same goal. I was available to everyone by being in one place. Also, Juan Carlos' group had a bag that was hidden behind the spare tire in the cargo hold of their bus. The bus left here that night and went to Portugal. It took two days to get the suitcase back."

"Two days? That would have been awful," Betty said. The pink suit was applying lotion now.

"Mrs. Johnson came down the first night saying she was missing a suitcase. She found me right where I said I would be in case of any issues. She confirmed it had come off the bus. Therefore, I knew it was in the hotel someplace. A few minutes later, you called Al, to say you were delivered an extra suitcase. Since I was in a central place, the call was put right through to me. Mrs. Johnson got her bag in no time and I did not have to run to the airport because I knew it was at the hotel."

The demeanor of the group was changing as they started to understand the method to my madness. I was showing no emotion because I didn't want anyone know how much I was enjoying my vantage point of the pool.

"I have escorted nearly fifty groups out of Seattle. I have learned a lot of ways to ensure everything is being handled without having to be demonstrative in my approach. The success of a group escort is not handling lots and lots of problems but preventing as many as possible. Look, I'm not perfect and neither is anyone else working to pull off this trip. But, we are all trying to ensure as trouble free and enjoyable a trip as possible." I was finishing this beer faster that I wanted.

"What about that stunt you pulled at lunch with Bill Rhodes?"

"He was making a scene and creating unrest. I had to put a stop to it."

"He probably will never travel with you again," Norm laughed.

"I would prefer it if he wouldn't. Listen, you all are on vacation. You are here for a great time. No one wants to hear complaining over stupid stuff all the time. He may not travel with me again but how about you guys?"

"I will," Al Baines said.

"Okay, me too," Norm Olson said.

"Do you need another beer?" Tom asked.

"Sure, listen there is a cool bar in town that serves excellent fish and chips. I am going there for dinner tonight. Anyone want to come along?" I asked getting ready to slowly sip another free beer and gaze over the Spanish pool scenery.

They all came to dinner along with many of the others from Seattle. Al Baines bought my dinner. I had several free beers. I told stories of past trip complainers and we laughed into the evening since dinner in Spain was usually a late social event. We had a great meal, the fish and chips were excellent, and the service was fabulous. Since it was a local establishment, the price was very reasonable. The evening was a great success. As we walked back to the hotel, I wondered if the pool area was lit at night.

After that, every time Juan Carlos took roll on his bus someone commented to me about it. One lady even called out "4 empty seats" as I boarded the bus for the last airport ride. When we returned to Seattle, Mr. Rhodes complained to my boss about the quarter. He didn't know my boss was my mother. She expressed concern to Mr. Rhodes but thanked me for handling the situation. She had received numerous compliments about the way I had handled the "quarter incident" as it was later called. She even used it as a story during future sales presentations to explain that sometimes free wasn't all inclusive but to not lose sight of the value and enjoyment of a fabulous trip over such a small item. The Olsons, Thompsons, and Baines travelled with me extensively. Al and Sadie even attended my wedding. Since it had an open bar, I offered to buy them a drink to return the favor.

Portuguese Coin Ring: Not the actual ring from the story!

CHAPTER **27**

Coin Ring

Circa 1988.

"That's the Eiffel Tower?" Dan asked scratching his head.

"It looks like an elevator," Gary suggested.

"It is and it is," I said.

"What's that?" Teddie asked joining the conversation.

"Okay, gather round everyone," I told the group as I did not want to have to go through this again. When the Crippens and Lockwoods came closer, I attempted to explain, "Gustav Eiffel built this tower. It acts as an elevator from this street to the top of the hill above. It is a little over three stories high and costs about twenty cents to ride. So here in Lisbon, they refer to it as their Eiffel Tower."

"Because it's named after Eiffel you made us walk four blocks out of the way to see it?" Teddie asked in one of those tones.

I was about to comment on how she could use the exercise when Gary helped me out.

"Dan get control of your wife will you," Gary said and laughed.

"Teddie let it go, now we can tell everyone we were on the Eiffel Tower," Dan laughed.

Teddie just gave me another scowl and walked away with Lisa, Gary's wife.

Dan and Gary went over to an adjacent jewelry shop and started window shopping. Dan pulled out his calculator and pointed to the Rolex in the window, "They only want $345 for that Rolex. I am going in to get a better look at it."

Dan went in the shop and Gary waved me over, "This should be good."

"What's that?" I asked.

"Dan thinks that Rolex is $345," Gary said pointing at the watch in the window.

"I don't have a calculator on me but I think it is closer to $3500," I pointed out.

"I know that's what I thought," Gary smiled.

We both watched as the clerk came over and gently removed the watch from the window. He took it back to the counter where Dan was standing. The clerk placed a piece of black velvet on the glass case and set the watch carefully down so Dan could inspect it. Dan reached out for the watch. He opened the clasp and went to place it on his wrist. He lost grip and dropped it. The clerk yelled. Dan lifted his leg in time to trap the watch against the case.

The clerk snatched the watch out of Dan's hand. We couldn't hear anything other than the one yell but it looked like the clerk was not happy at all. Dan looked like he wanted the watch and handed the clerk $350. The clerk looked at the money then looked at Dan. He started shaking his head violently and yelling. Gary and I couldn't make out what he was saying but clearly he was annoyed. Dan just stood there not knowing what was going on. The clerk slid his big calculator in front of Dan and pressed the buttons.

Dan looked at the calculator and placed one hand on the side of his face and reached out to get his money back with the other. The clerk gave him the money and pointed at the door.

"Act casual," Gary told me.

When Dan came out, Gary asked, "Can I see your watch? I think I will get one too."

"That watch was $3476 and I nearly dropped it on the floor! The clerk sure was pissed at me. He thought I was low ball negotiating with him and I thought I was paying full price. I think he was swearing at me in Portuguese at the end," Dan said with a nervous laugh. "Please don't tell Teddie," he added very seriously.

We promised not to tell. When we caught up with their wives a few shops down, I suggested we walk over to the river to see the monument to the Navigators. I explained there was a map carved in the stone and the dates marked when the first European reached that point.

"That sounds cool," Lisa said.

The others agreed. I directed the group toward the riverfront. Every time we passed a woman in a doorfront on the way, Dan would tell me she was a prostitute.

"Dan that lady has got to be ninety, really?" I said skeptically.

"You could probably get a good deal on her," he suggested.

"No thanks!"

"What about her then? She's probably only sixty. That's the way prostitutes are in Europe," he told me.

"You're the one who would know," I just laughed not sure if he was serious or not.

The group just spread out when we reached the monument. I was answering the many questions with my favorite non answer, "Well maybe, or then again maybe not." I was always amazed how readily people accepted that for an answer. It was difficult keeping a straight face when saying it.

Gary came over and showed me a ring he purchased. It was a gold coin ring although I am sure there was no gold in it. The face of the ring was a small coin. It looked pretty cool.

Dan came over and took the ring right out of Gary's hand, "That's really nice. Where did you get it?"

"I bought it from that guy," Gary said pointing to a street vendor, "I got it for ten bucks."

Dan looked excited. He gave the ring back to Gary and raced over to the vendor.

About fifteen minutes, Dan came back over with a ring just like Gary had purchased.

"What did you buy now?" Teddie asked him with attitude.

"I got this amazing ring," he said showing her the ring.

She took the ring and inspected it. Then she held it up to him and asked, "What did you pay for this?"

"Only twenty bucks," Dan replied happily.

"Twenty? I got mine for only ten from the same guy," Gary interrupted. I think he knew that was going to blow Teddie's gasket.

"What? You paid twice as much for the same ring from the same vendor five minutes after Gary? You have got to be kidding me," Teddie tore into him.

"I know! He was a really good negotiator," Dan laughed nervously.

"Hand over all your cash," Teddie insisted, "Now show me the guy you bought the ring from."

Dan turned and pointed him out.

"Come with me!" she said to Dan and off they went.

Gary and I spent the next ten minutes watching Teddie alternate yelling between the vendor and her husband. Reluctantly, the vendor handed a few dollars back to Teddie. She stormed away with Dan following at her heals.

I went over and talked to the vendor for a few minutes.

When I returned, Gary asked, "Did you buy a ring?"

"No, I gave the guy another ten bucks. It was too funny to watch that for free," I laughed.

"What did the vendor say to that?"

"He started laughing. When I started to walk away, he gave me these," I said holding out my hand displaying the two coin rings.

Gary was still laughing when we came up to Teddie and Lisa.

"He gave me five dollars back," Teddie said triumphantly.

Gary just laughed harder.

Both women looked at him but neither asked.

Note: I escorted six different trips with Gary Lockwood. He was the morning drive DJ for KJR radio in Seattle for many years. Dan and Teddie went on all of his trips. They were good friends and golf buddies with the Lockwoods. We never let Dan negotiate anything after this, even a cab fare!

Dan's son admired the ring back in Seattle so Dan gifted it to him. His son thought it was a wonderful gift until he took the ring to a jeweler to have it sized. The jeweler said there wasn't enough metal in the ring to size it.

Lisbon's Eiffel Tower.

Robert L. Olwell

PART IV

TRAVEL

I love to travel. Scott and Mike are included in several of the following stories. Mike was in the same dorm with me at Washington State University. Scott and I met as managers for McDonald's in 1993. A few years after that, Mike was Scott's Assistant Manager at McDonald's and we became reacquainted.   When I left McDonald's and joined Costco, Scott and Mike followed. I truly enjoy the experiences we share when traveling together.

Cheryl and I usually take a trip of some kind every year. Our cruises with the family have been very eventful as you will see.

Reno Hilton.

Reno Hilton's Pool.

CHAPTER **28**

Reno

Scott: "This was a classic Robert vacation, $139 out the door. On day one, we wandered for hours among the walking dead in Reno, no one under eighty five years old goes to Reno anymore. The biggest show was a qualifying event for the U.S. bowling tour in a bowling alley that puts Madison Square Garden to shame. To Robert's consternation, Cheryl bought a strawberry margarita in a glass that was nearly as tall as she was. This led to Cheryl soon becoming one of the walking dead and causing a bit of friction. That was how Cheryl and I ended up sharing a table at the comedy show. We did enjoy Robert and Chad getting roasted, Robert didn't look amused as the comedian continually referenced the abuse the hotel bed must be taking as both Chad and Robert were not small boys."

Cheryl adds: "Robert bought me the enormous drink, and I am sure that it was intended to console me for the 'pool'. I ended up sitting next to Scott because the other two refused to be stuck at a table with him. All the stupid crap he says doesn't bother me like it does everyone else who knows him. It's true I don't like to gamble, so the only reason for me to go to Reno was to enjoy the sun by the pool. That and the perpetual comedy tour starring Robert and his friends." Circa 1999.

"I don't want to go to Reno with your friends. I don't even like to gamble," my wife protested.

"Cheryl, it is only $139 for three nights including airfare. We'd be staying at the Hilton. Just come along, you can sunbathe by the pool for three days," I explained.

She finally agreed and the four of us, including Scott and Chad, booked the trip.

After arriving at the Reno Hilton, we checked in and got our room keys. I handed Cheryl our key. She smiled then she walked straight over to the concierge desk.

"Where is the pool?" she inquired.

"It is on the eleventh floor but it is closed this time of year," the concierge answered.

"What?" she said and turned toward me.

"I said, 'sunbathe,' " replying to her while slowly moving behind Chad.

I had to listen to it all the way to the room. After checking out the rooms, we went and checked out the casino.

To make it up to Cheryl, I purchased four seats to the Hilton's cabaret show called "Skin Tight". As I had bought the tickets fairly early in the day, they were pretty good seats as the table touched the stage.

When we arrived before the show, I handed out the tickets keeping the stage side seat for myself. With the other three moved away perpendicular to the stage, I sat down.

"That's BS, man," Scott said to me shaking his head.

"What?" I asked.

"Why do you get the stage seat?" he asked and Chad now was agreeing with him.

"Really?"

"You brought your woman," he complained.

"I made the arrangements for the show but if it's going to be a big deal switch with me," I replied expecting that to be the end of it. It wasn't.

Scott got up and motioned for me to move. I just shook my head and sat in the fourth seat from the stage.

I was ordering a drink when a couple of guys sat down across from us. They were clearly not here to see women in skimpy clothing.

I said, "Hello."

They responded in kind and the lights started to dim.

The curtains started to open and a singer came out. Then they opened the curtains the rest of the way and exposed thirty or so dancers only wearing thongs.

"I hope they don't catch a cold," I laughed.

"I'll warm them up," Scott said and Chad gave him a high five.

I just hugged my wife and tried not to stare too much.

Within thirty seconds, a dancer came over to the edge of the stage next to Scott. A moment later a glistening thonged butt was being gyrated in his face. I swear sweat was transferring from the dancer to Scott's face. Unfortunately for Scott, it was the only guy dancer on the stage. Scott looked like he wanted to change seats back but I wasn't having any of it. Cheryl and Chad were laughing out loud. Then the guys across from me started complaining.

"How come he gets that seat? We paid the same amount as he did. It's just not fair," they said to each other.

"Yeah, but if you had that seat the dancer would have been a woman," I consoled them.

"Ewe," they replied together.

Chad laughed again loud and slapped Scott on the back. Scott scowled and wiped his face and took a rather large gulp of his drink.

After the show as we were leaving, Cheryl turned to Scott and asked, "Did you get his number?" referring to the dancer.

"Funny," Scott replied without a smile.

"Hey I think you have a little ass glitter still on your face," Chad said handing Scott a napkin.

Scott started to reach for the napkin then realized he was being had.

"I knew it was a good idea to bring you along," I said to Chad.

The next day we were having a late breakfast and discussing what to do. We decided to go over to the go kart track in Sparks. On the taxi drive over, the driver kept trying to talk us in to going to the Moonlight Bunny Ranch. It was odd as my wife was sitting next to me in the cab. I don't know what Scott and Chad were thinking but I was glad when we got to the Fun center.

"Let's get the hour pass for the go karts," Chad suggested.

It was agreed and we went over to the track. I was impressed these were not the go karts of my childhood. These were fast karts with little fiberglass NASCAR bodies. What was really cool was the fact that the four of us had the place to ourselves.

The attendant adjusted our seatbelts then gave us his well practiced speech, "There will be no touching between cars. If there is a yellow flag you are to slow down. You must follow any verbal commands. Failure to adhere to the rules will lead to immediate revocation of your passes and you will be asked to leave the premises."

Scott rolled his eyes at me, "We've been driving longer than he's been alive."

151

Cheryl punched the gas and we followed her onto the track for the six lap race. Scott was very intent on winning as he is super competitive. As previously discussed, Chad and I went about harassing him.

The first couple of times we bumped Scott we were worried about getting red flagged. The attendant didn't seem to care so we continued. Cheryl won the first race.

As there were still no others waiting for the karts, we just restarted another race. This time Chad and I kept trying to hit Scott's back wheel to spin him. Chad finally got him on the last lap and Cheryl won the second race.

Scott exchanged a few choice words with us as we started the third race. This time I worked to position myself just ahead and to the left of Scott. As we raced to the next right hand turn, I cut the corner super close and drove Scott into the tires. He yelled after me as Chad who was trailing us t-boned him like we were in bumper cars.

This required the attendant to come and pull Chad's and Scott's Karts back onto the track. While they were restarted, Cheryl crossed the finish line to win the third race.

Before we were started for the fourth race, the attendant warned us again. He was "Serious" this time. We agreed amongst ourselves to race fair and off we went.

Chad and I were in front of Scott and we just focused on not letting him pass us. Cheryl won again and Scott finished last.

Scott decided to work his revenge by convincing us to play Putt Putt golf with the loser buying the winner's dinner. As he was the best golfer, he easily won.

When the cab dropped us off in the parking lot at the Hilton, we were next to some contraption ride. Chad convinced me to go on it with him. It looked like a ginormous swing. We were put in a harness then cabled. We were raised to about twenty feet off the ground then a second cable started pulling us backward and up. When we were about eighty feet off the ground, we were told to release the second cable. I wouldn't. Chad just pulled the release and we dropped then swung like a pendulum back and forth. Chad was having a blast and I wanted off.

When the ride was over, the attendant offered to let us go again for free to attract others.

"No! Get me off this thing," I demanded.

Scott and Chad were giving me a hard time while walking through the Hotel's arcade.

I stopped in front of the virtual roller coaster. Chad wanted to do it and Scott agreed to go on it with him. They got in and closed the door. From Cheryl and my vantage point it went something like this.

The seats dropped face down, rotated completely around three times. We could hear their yelling at this point. Then the seats started doing vertical 360s while rotating horizontally five times. I think Scott was crying by now.

Cheryl and I were shocked and started laughing at the spectacle.

Scott was embarrassed upon exit. He got even with us by ordering Steak and Lobster for dinner. He got the most out of his Putt Putt victory. I was annoyed at his dinner's expense but I got over it. While eating, we decided to see a comedy show.

The tables at the comedy club at the Silver Legacy were small set up in twos. I sat down with Chad with Cheryl and Scott sitting at the next table. We ordered drinks and started chatting until the comedians started.

"Honey pack your bags, I won the lottery," the comedian started " 'Where are we going?' my wife asked. Nowhere, get the hell out b*tch."

Well the crowd responded with a good laugh.

"I'd never do that to YOU honey," I said sarcastically and loud enough for Cheryl to hear at the next table.

It was loud enough where everyone heard and that got a bigger laugh than the original joke.

When the laughing died down, the comedian asked, "Who said that?"

Chad pointed to me.

So the comedian sees me sitting with Chad and comes to the conclusion I was referring to Chad not my wife sitting at the next table on the other side of Scott. Then the gay jokes started. He roasted Chad and me. It was pretty funny.

"Where are you from?" he asked us.

"Seattle," Chad answered.

"What's that thing up there that comes out about twice a year, the Sun?" he joked.

"What's that thing in Reno that comes out about twice a year, a funny comedian?" Chad responded.

Everyone had a good time. The comedian actually sent us a beverage during the next performance.

After the show, Scott was all over Chad and me, "He burned you bad with those gay jokes."

"Yeah, but I'm sleeping with her tonight and you're sleeping with Chad," I laughed referring to Cheryl.

Scott laughed and Chad told him, "No spooning tonight."

Lili Marleen

Canary Islands

CHAPTER **29**

Lili Marleen

Scott: "As we began this trip, Robert took great joy in reminding me that I had never been on any kind of an ocean sailing vessel. He reminded me repeatedly about the fact that I would probably be sick to begin with and how he looked forward to that. Robert also took great amusement in explaining the toilet in the room was operated by vacuum and it was not advisable to fully sit on the seat and flush as he knew of cases where people's bowels were sucked from their body. I spent seven days making a concerted effort to create an air gap to protect my colon only to find out later he was full of crap.

Now Robert wasn't just seasick, he recreated the famous scene of Linda Blair's head spinning and cascading vomit throughout our cabin. The ship was rocking as I walked down the hall to our cabin. There seemed to be a green fog of sickness. I knew I only had a few minutes to check up on Robert before I would be sick. As I entered the room it hit me like a sledge hammer.

"Holy crap, how can you stand this?" I asked as I observed Robert sitting in his bunk reading his Star trek book.

He said, "I've gotten use to it."

I kept telling him he needed to get on deck as I knew my time was running out, finally he gave me the Robert look and said "I'm not moving, do whatever you want."

On my next visit down below I finally got him out of the bunk. I said, "You are going to clean this up before you leave right?"

"That's why we have a cabin girl!"

"You are not making her clean this, get it done!" I said and left. (Let's face it, she was really hot).

By the second day the ship's doc hadn't seen Robert and asked how he was.

I replied, "Not good."

155

He said, "Come with me. I have something for him."

As he came out of his cabin, he handed me a package and said, "Give this to him and he will be fine."

As I walked away I began uncontrollably laughing. This was a seasick pill, and not an oral one, it loosely resembled a Cousteau deep sea exploratory submersible and looked as though it would take a professional to insert it. As I gave it to Robert he looked at it and said, "What do you want me to do with this?" and then the light came on "oh no, no way in hell!!"

I said, "Suit yourself, I'll be on deck enjoying the weather."

About 20 minutes later Robert wandered up on deck, lower lip pouting and walking as if he had just had a prostate exam from a big handed doctor.

Finally, our trip to the Carnival: All I can say is after 2 liters of beer Robert was lit up like a Christmas tree and said, "Let's head back."

I replied, "I am having another."

"I'm going back to the boat."

As he left I watched him march away, uphill. Falling back on my geography, it was not hard to come to the conclusion I would soon see Robert again, hopefully soon as I did not want to go looking for him. I could see the boat from where I sat. Soon Robert came trudging back down the street, downhill and to the boat."

Cheryl's insight: "I can vouch for witnessing Robert in rare form aboard a ship. I took my first cruise with Robert shortly after we were married. We experienced gale force winds one evening. I knew I was going to be sick. I grew up fishing and boating with my Dad, I started every outing by feeding the fish. Robert, on the other hand made quite a show about how he "never gets sick on cruise ships." That night was captain's dinner. I will never forget how dashing Robert looked all dressed up for our steak and lobster that night as we took a stroll on deck before the night's festivities. I will also never be able to erase from my memory how dashing my husband looked spewing what seemed like a week's worth of food and drink the entire length and width of the grand staircase. But he never gets sick on a cruise ship." Circa 1998.

In February of 1998, Mom's travel agency was doing a lot of river boat trips in Europe. A representative of Dielhmann Cruises called me. I had met Ron aboard the riverboat Mozart on the Danube a few months before.

"But only German's are Sailing the Canary Islands. We haven't been able to get the American market interested. Do you and your wife want to come over and check out the ship? I will comp the cruise but you have to cover the airfare," he explained.

"Absolutely!" I told him, "and thanks!"

Cheryl was unable to make it. I asked my friend Scott to join me. He obliged and made a rush order on a passport.

Scott and I finally arrived. As we walked down the pier toward the Lili Marleen, the fatigue from flying from Seattle to Grand Canary Island via London and Madrid left us. The sailing vessel was two hundred and fifty feet long and held fifty passengers. I climbed the gangway as Scott took pictures from the dock.

The purser walked up to me with a clipboard.

"Hi, I am Robert Olwell," I introduced myself.

"You are Mr. and Mrs. Olwell?" she asked quizzically looking at me then Scott. She was very concerned about two guys traveling as man and wife.

I paused for a moment trying to understand her angst, "No, that's Scott Beedell. There was a name change as my wife could not make it. You should have received notification last week."

She looked relieved. Then she worked hard at accommodating us as our original cabin only had one bed. When the arrangements were finalized, we were shown to our cabin. It was small but well appointed. Two twin beds, bathroom, small dresser and a port hole were more than adequate. We put away our belongings and headed up on deck to explore the boat.

"They looked pretty concerned that you were my wife," I laughed.

"What?" Scott laughed.

"Yeah, they had not received the name change from Cheryl's to yours. The Purser was all upset when she saw you. Normally women get upset when they see you but this was different," I told him.

"They are only upset when they see me next to you!" he chided.

"What are you trying to say?" I feigned being hurt.

"I think you can figure it out. Let's get a beer."

We stayed in port that night. We explored the city but made it an early night.

After breakfast, we set sail. The ship sailed smoothly out of port. I enjoyed a beverage with Scott on the sun deck as we sailed across the front of Grand Canary. When we left the protected side of the island, the Atlantic Ocean hit us with its full force. The Lili Marleen really started swaying.

I looked at Scott.

"You better hold on," he laughed and smiled.

As the Lili Marleen rocked back and forth and up and down, passenger after passenger left the deck. I tried holding on as long as possible.

"I am going down to the room," I finally said.

"You are looking pretty green," he laughed, "but you are probably better off up here on deck."

"I got to go," I answered as I rushed toward the stairs.

I made it to the room and sat down on the bed. I was trying to hold it together. Every time the Lili listed to my side of the ship, our port hole went under water. When it became apparent I was going to be sick, I stood up and stepped toward the bathroom. That was as far as I got, I blew through the door into the bathroom. I continued to redecorate for a few minutes before making it back to the bed.

Scott came down a while later. He opened the door and was hit by the smell of my seasickness.

"Oh God?! Are you okay?"

"I will probably survive," I said bravely.

"Dude, I have to go up on deck. This is going to make me sick," he said and closed the door.

He came back later, "Here," he said handing me a pill the size of a golf ball.

"What is this?"

"I told the ship's doctor you were sick. He said you should take it," Scott informed me.

"Okay, now I know where you got it. What is it?"

"A pill to help with your seasickness," he explained.

"It's the size of a golf ball!" I protested.

"More like a ping pong ball," he laughed.

"I can't swallow that!" I protested, "and even if I could, I don't think I could keep it down."

"You don't swallow it," he laughed.

"What do you mean? How do you? Oh!" I said finally understanding.

"Well, I will just leave you to it then," Scott said and departed.

There was no way I was going to use that pill. Then I got sick again. I was sure I wasn't going to take that medicine. Then I got sick again. Okay, I 'took' the damn pill! Are you happy? I dropped my pants and inserted the ping pong ball sized horse pill in my butt! I had Scott's tooth brush handy in case it wouldn't go in. Fortunately for Scott, it did.

About an hour later I started feeling better. Oh, feeling better regarding my nausea not about taking the medicine.

I did a half hearted attempt at cleaning up the bathroom. I went up on deck to find Scott at the boat's rail. He was swinging down and touching the ocean with his hand. He was king of the ocean.

"You look better," he said noticing me.

"Feeling better," I answered.

"You seem to be walking funny," Scott said but he couldn't keep a straight face.

"I better work on that or the Purser will think we are gay again," I told him, "Are you the only one up on deck besides the crew?"

"Yep, it has been that way since about the time you went down to the cabin."

"Okay, this medicine is making me drowsy so I am going to head back down to the room. Thanks for getting me the meds," I offered and headed back down below deck.

I awoke early the next day. I got up and dressed without waking Scott. I had my appetite back so I headed to the dining room.

During the meal, I was presented with a print out of our room charges for the previous day. I was asked to sign off that the charges were correct. I had no idea what drinks Scott had ordered the previous evening but the bill seemed reasonable. So I signed it.

Just before noon, Scott found me on deck, "You need to clean that bathroom better!"

"That's what the room steward is for," I explained.

Our room steward was this beautiful twenty year old German girl. Scott kept calling her Heidi although that was not her name. There was no way Scott was going to make her clean our bathroom even if it was her job and he said as much.

"Alright, I will tidy it up, Romeo," I laughed.

We enjoyed sailing to our next port.

I convinced Scott to sign up for a sightseeing tour. We boarded the bus and headed across the island. When we got near the top of the volcanic island, we off loaded and were offered a camel ride.

"No thanks, " I replied as I had ridden a camel before.

"Well, I'm not doing it if you're not," Scott declared.

"What do I care what you do?"

"Come on," he pleaded.

"Okay," I conceded.

I wish I hadn't. The camels had a saddle over their backs where one person sat on either side. I was placed in the metal seat. Scott was placed on the other side of the same camel. Then the guy looks at both of us and starts adding sand bags to Scott's side to balance my weight. Scott started laughing at me and the camel gave me a dirty look.

Once enough sand was added to thoroughly humiliate me and feed Scott's amusement, the camel was directed to stand. Then we were walked up a hill and down a hill for a three minute ride. The whole time the camel kept looking at me and spitting. I was going to be chastised for years about my weight for this three minute ride. Then the Camel owner wanted me to tip him. Right! He then took the camel we rode out of service like I broke it or something. Scott tipped him generously enough for both of us.

The tour took us to a National Park at the top of the volcano. There was a barbeque there. It consisted of a metal grill over a hole in the ground ten feet deep. The heat from the volcano cooked the food. We dropped a piece of paper in the hole and it caught fire before hitting the bottom. It was pretty cool.

Then the guide explained it was a Park and no rocks could legally be removed from it.

"However, if you can hold onto the rock I give you then you can keep it," he said.

He took a shovel and dug down about a foot and picked up some gravel. He walked around the group and shook a rock off the shovel to the group's hands. When he got to me, I refused.

Scott put his hand out to receive the rock. It dropped into his hand and he yelped and tossed it to his other hand. He did this many times. He was determined to keep his volcanic rock. He was the only one who held the rock. Everyone but me was rubbing their burned hands.

"Check it out," Scott displayed with pride.

"Nice rock," I said sarcastically.

"You're just jealous," he said.

"That's it! You got me. I am so jealous you have a pebble and a burned hand and I don't," I laughed.

When the tour ended by the boat, we went into a local bar to have a beer. The timing of our trip was pretty cool as Carnival was going on. Each night there were parades and partying. We hung out at the bar for a couple of hours. I had a few too many beers and decided I needed to head back to the Lili Marleen.

I told Scott as much and headed up the road toward the ship. I could see the Lili but I could not figure out how to get into the Marina. After about a half hour I came walking back to the bar, Scott was laughing at me because he knew the way. He knew the way but didn't tell me when I was going the wrong way.

He pointed the way. I safely arrived back to the sailboat.

On several occasions, the Captain held discussions about sailing. It was during one of these discussions, I determined German was not a concise language. I know because the Captain would go on and on and on in German for fifteen minutes then in English translate, "The wind would then change direction." Then he would proceed in German. I decided I would not attend another meeting.

I had the opportunity to climb the rigging to the crow's nest. I was not about to pass up that opportunity. I watched as a couple of the passengers went before me. I noticed where the need to transfer from one set of ropes to another set of ropes was causing a lot of problems. I studied the rigging and made a plan.

When it was my turn, I grabbed the ropes and left the deck and swung to the outside of the rope ladder. I climbed away and smoothly transitioned the ropes and rapidly climbed into the crow's nest.

"Excellent work sailor!" the crewman said to me.

As I smiled to thank him, I realized that the motion of the deck was amplified forty feet above the deck.

"Thanks, can I get down now?" I responded.

He laughed until he realized I was serious then he laughed hard. He allowed me to return to the safety of the deck.

"Why didn't you stay up there longer?" Scott asked.

"Just giving everyone a chance," I said.

"Really?" Scott asked looking right through me.

"Dude, if you think the ship rocks down here, wait until you are up there! It is swinging like crazy. I was not about to risk needing another of those horse pills if you know what I mean!"

He just laughed and took his turn on the mast. He stayed up longer than I did but did not manage the climb as easily.

On the last night, there was a sing along on deck. There were about thirty sixty year old Germans, Scott and me. I was laughing as the songs always came back to the children's songs of their youths. Their youths in Nazi Germany! I mean really! They were singing about war and disease and pestilence while standing at attention. Before my eyes, in two songs they all reverted to Hitler youth. The Doctor translated the songs and they were horrific. For once in my life I decided to keep my thoughts to myself.

Scott and I had been drinking with these guys for a week and they were really cool. I guess growing up in Nazi Germany as a kid left an impression.

"I won't be teaching any of those songs to my kids," Scott laughed as we returned to our cabin.

"That was too funny! I wonder if they realized that they went right back to the 1940's when they started singing?"

"I'm not asking them! I am glad we are off to Madrid tomorrow though!"

Royal Palace, Madrid, Spain

CHAPTER **30**

Madrid

Scott: "I had recently been divorced prior to this trip and Robert invited me as Cheryl could not go. This was my first trip out of the country other than Canada, which really doesn't count as foreign travel, just a travel back in time. Now Robert is a seasoned international traveler, just ask and he will tell you. Though he likes to tell the story of my utter fear in the Taxi, (which is not far from the truth), I was not the only one frantically trying to lock my seatbelt into place, and from the soiled spot on Robert's seat I could tell he too was affected by the formula 1 wanna be driver. Robert neglected to mention our first encounter with the law: on the way to the museum we ran into small groups of stoic soldiers armed with AK's. I enthusiastically asked him to take my picture standing next to one such soldier. Robert went a bit pale and said "not a good idea, stay away from the soldier."' Circa 1998.

The flight from Grand Canary to Madrid was fairly uneventful. We caught a cab into the city and checked into our hotel. The hotel was situated right on the edge of the shopping district and a few blocks from the capitol buildings.

"Let's go explore," I suggested.

"Cool," Scott said.

We left our room and took the stairs down to the lobby. On the way out we were stopped by the front desk employee. We were informed that we could not take the key out of the hotel. Scott handed over the key and we headed out.

We walked over to the Royal Palaces and were impressed by the majesty of the buildings. We were heading back towards our hotel when we came upon an English pub.

"Want a beer?" Scott asked.

"Why not," I replied.

The bartender came over as we sat at the bar. I ordered a beer from tap and so did Scott. The Bartender returned with our beers in liter sized glasses.

"Really?" I asked.

Scott just laughed knowing that I was a lightweight. We chatted about the Canary Islands until I had finally nursed that beer down to the bottom of the glass. I was really proud of myself.

"Happy hour," the bartender said and placed a half liter glass of beer in front of each of us.

"Thanks," Scott said and reached out for his glass.

"I'm not drinking that," I told Scott to his amusement.

He drank it. We paid the bill and headed back in the hotel's direction.

"I need to eat something," I said,

"Wow, I am really feeling that beer. I need to eat too!" he replied and we started to look for a restaurant.

The only problem was that most of the restaurants in Madrid are closed between two and seven. It was only five! So restaurant after restaurant we came to was closed. Scott was getting really annoyed when I saw a sign for the Picasso Museum. We went in.

Picasso is pretty out there as an impressionist. I don't know if the beer was getting to me but his paintings started to make sense. There was a nice display of sketching and paintings. We should have stayed longer but we had not eaten since breakfast and the beer was hitting us hard.

After finding a restaurant and enjoying our meal, I decided I wanted to pick up some souvenirs. We entered a store near the hotel. Here I found a sword that I liked. After buying it, I did not want to have to carry it around with me. I returned to the hotel. There was no one at the front desk so I rang the bell. When the attendant came out, I got the key. I dropped the sword off in the room and went back to the front desk. Again it was vacant so I rang the bell, when the attendant returned again I gave him the key.

I left the hotel where Scott was waiting.

"You know what? I want a sword too," he said.

"Well let's go get you one," I said.

We went back to the store where Scott purchased a sword and a few pocket knives. Upon departing the store, he decided he did not want to carry the stuff either. The hotel was close by so we returned. He rang the bell for the front desk attendant. He came out and looked annoyed that it was us again. He gave Scott the key. Scott went and dropped off his things in the room. Once again the attendant had left the desk. Scott rang the bell. The attendant returned and collected the key.

That started a cycle where I would buy something like a stein or Lladro and return it to the hotel. Then Scott would decide he wanted one and go back to the same store and buy it. Then he would return it to the hotel. Each time we would bother the front desk attendant to get the key and again to return the key. I did not feel bad about it as they would not let us leave the hotel with the key. The fact that Scott would not make up his mind was doubling our trips but by now I thought it was rather amusing, even if the attendant did not.

When we finally finished our shopping we called it a night. The next morning we caught a cab to the airport for our flight home. Once we were in the cab, the driver raced through Madrid. It was raining and the roads were wet. When I mean raced, I mean the driver did not go under seventy miles an hour through the city. If that meant going into oncoming traffic or driving on the curb, it did not seem to bother the driver. Scott was freaking out.

"We are going to die in Madrid," he told me as he was turning white.

"Technically, we just left the city limits so I think we won't be dying in Madrid," I said acting casual. I was freaking out on the inside.

We arrived at the airport twenty minutes after leaving the hotel. This was the fourth trip to or from the hotel to the airport. The other three trips took a minimum of an hour.

"Get me out of this cab! I will pay the driver," Scott said.

"Right on," I said exiting the taxi.

"How much?" Scott asked.

"185 pesos," the driver said which was about $25.

Scott proceeded to count out exactly 185 pesos even though we had larger bills. He made sure the driver got the exact amount and not one peso more. This was odd because Scott usually tipped quite well.

I said as much.

"I'm not giving that guy a tip for nearly killing us. He drove on the sidewalk! Are you kidding me?"

We grabbed our suitcases and swords and went to the ticket counter. As we were checking our luggage, the supervisor noticed our swords.

"Excuse me senor? Are you planning on taking a sword aboard the flight?" he asked.

It dawned on me at that moment how ridiculous it was for us to think we could bring our swords and all of Scott's knives onto the plane with us. So I looked at the supervisor and said, "Of course, why wouldn't we?"

The airport police were very quietly surrounding us. Scott pointed it out to me.

"Can we check our weapons?" I asked before the police tazzed us.

The British Airways attendant looked relieved and made arrangements for some boxes and bubble wrap for us. We wrapped the knives and swords and checked them under the close scrutiny of the police.

When we boarded the flight to London to connect to Seattle, Scott said, "I bet we never see those swords and knives again!"

"We either could check the swords or check out a Spanish Jail. I think the choice was obvious," I said, "Want a drink?"

"It's nine am! Hell yes!," Scott then sighed and said, "I need a drink."

When we arrived in Seattle, we collected our bags. The swords were not to be found. Scott was convinced they were gone forever. I asked a Customs employee.

"The swords are yours? Please come with me," he told us.

We were taken into a small room where we were lectured by federal agents about carrying weapons onto a plane and into the U.S.. Finally, they released us. We were escorted out to the airport parking lot and only when we got to my car did the Officer give us the swords.

Note: Scott had to remind me of the Police escort out of the airport as I had forgotten. It seems Scott remembers our interactions with law enforcement much better than I do. Probably because I don't think of it as such a big deal like he does.

CHAPTER **31**

Laugh Of The Hyena

Scott: "Now if you know Robert, you will know that Cris Angel, the magician, recently approached him on a feat that Robert regularly performs that hasn't been duplicated. Robert can actually pinch 1 penny into 2, I kid you not, and therefore feels it is his mission to never take those two pennies for granted. This leads to endless whining about the cost of EVERYTHING. Robert can't fly anywhere because apparently San Antonio is the hub to nowhere, requiring you to buy tickets to the east coast to get to the west coast (so he says). We couldn't go to Vegas because apparently to get there from San Antonio you must transfer planes in Moscow. Because of this, most of our vacation discussions would pale the negotiation process for Middle Eastern peace." Circa 2010.

"What do you want to do for my birthday?" Scott asked.
"Nothing," I replied. I always looked forward to Scott's calls.
"No really, what sounds good?" he tried again.
"Really, nothing. I'll send you a card," I offered.
"Dude, I'm going to be fifty. We need to celebrate."

That's what started a two month dialogue into what, when, where and how much for his birthday trip. Now discussing travel plans with Scott is difficult. He hasn't been anywhere or done anything but he thinks he is an expert on everywhere. Then he pretends to consider all the options but always comes back to what he wants to do. I knew this but for some reason I allowed it to drag on. I mean way past the point when I should have just said, "Fine, do what you want." Ultimately, that is where it ended.

When the decision was finally agreed to or at least communicated, I had new found respect for Scott's ex-wife but enough about that. Plans were made for San Diego for a three night stay.

While changing planes in Houston, I texted Scott to get an update as to his and Mike's status. He replied that their flight out of Seattle was delayed due to a problem in San Francisco where they were to connect flights.

"When can we expect to depart?" Scott asked the agent politely.

"There is a flight I can get you on that leaves at 5:30 this afternoon," the desk agent replied in an upbeat manner.

"WHAT?" Scott exclaimed, "That is nine hours from now."

"That is the best we can do right now," she said and returned the tickets and boarding passes. She then dismissed him turning her attention to the stressed out mob before her.

Walking back to Mike, he was pretty fired up. As they left the crowd of folks at the counter, he explained the situation.

Mike saw an agent a couple of gates down where there was no one in line and suggested they go talk to her.

"Hi, my friend and I were scheduled to fly to San Diego this morning and due to something going on in San Francisco we will not be leaving until 5:30. It is my birthday and I do not want to spend it in an airport. Besides my best friend is flying in expecting us to pick him up," he explained.

She looked bored so she held her hand out for his tickets and started typing furiously on her keyboard. She looked up, "How old are you?"

"Fifty," Scott answered.

"Did you say fifty?"

"Yes," Scott replied.

"Aren't you a little old to be whining about your birthday?" she asked without looking up from her computer.

Scott glared at Mike who stifled a laugh.

With one final exaggerated keystroke, she looked up and smiled, "There you go. But if you're picking up your best friend, who is this?"

Scott looked at her then at Mike, "My other best friend."

"Nice save, have a pleasant trip and thank you for flying Alaska."

As they walked away, Scott started to complain about her dogging him about the birthday. Mike stopped him. She had gotten them on a 1:00 p.m. direct flight and upgraded them to first class. That shut him up. You may want to note the date and time.

I arrived in San Diego. The plan was for Scott to pick me up with the rental car. As he was still in Seattle, he texted the info and off I went to the rental agency.

While am standing in line at Budget, I flashed back to the rental car fiasco when my car broke down during a family ski vacation. I could not rent from an agency because I didn't carry a credit card. I still didn't.

"How may I help you?"' the rep asked.

I gave her the reservation and then the hassle began. They allowed for a debit card with an outrageous deposit and a copy of your return flight ticket. I reluctantly agreed to the deposit but my ticket was all done on the computer. So I had to take out my computer, connect to their wifi, enter their secret password, look up my reservation and show it to her. Meanwhile she checked with the manager who acted like he was looking to see if my photo was in their log of people who steal Ford Focuses and known criminals. I was aggravated by the accusatory looks and tone so I held up my cell phone.

"I can get my mommy on the phone if it will speed things up," I was a little bit sarcastic. They weren't amused.

The manager came over to say something when a customer came in and started yelling about the exit security. He pulled in the wrong way and punctured all four tires. During the scene that followed, the gal just gave me the keys and sent me on my way.

I got in the rental car and headed to the Paradise Point Resort with map and lame directions. After driving by it a couple of times, I pulled in and went up to check in.

"The reservation is in Scott's name. You cannot check in without him." I was informed.

"He will not be here for several hours," I explained.

"You're welcome to have a seat in the lobby."

I took a seat in the lobby just as my phone rang.

"Hi Dad, can I spend the weekend with my boyfriend?" Claire, my eighteen year old daughter, asked.

Wow that is a loaded question. I was sure I needed to tiptoe through this minefield.

"Why are you asking me?" I dodged.

"Grandma doesn't think it is a good idea."

"Ya think!" I replied.

She went on to tell me all kinds of stuff. When she announced that she wasn't sexually active, I was over the conversation.

"Call your mother. Either your grandmother or your mother needs to give you permission. I am not making this decision," I said and pretended to lose signal.

I was thinking about Claire's call when I went back to the fact Scott had arranged this weekend. Having been on trips like this before, I decided to investigate this a little.

"Excuse me; did my friend book the Honeymoon suite for polygamists?" I asked.

She laughed but looked confused.

"There are three guys staying in the room. Is there more than one bed?" I clarified.

"It is a King room."

After talking with her, we changed the room to two queen beds and a roll a way.

I decided to find lunch. I headed toward the airport. When I passed it, I started looking for somewhere to eat. My phone rang.

"Did you talk to your daughter?" my wife asked.

"Hello to you too and yes, I told her to talk to you," I explained.

She started giving me the rundown when I saw a Subway. I changed lanes rather abruptly toward it and in doing so cut off a Cab. I am listening to my wife, trying to figure how to get into Subway and doing my best to lose the irate Cabbie who is honking and raising his fist at me.

Three u-turns later, I lost the Cab. Cheryl was still laughing when I arrived at the Subway parking lot without the cabbie. Apparently, she was hearing the whole honking and screeching of my tires during the U-turn stuff.

I was saying goodbye to her as I entered the Subway. My phone rang again and it was Scott announcing his arrival. Explaining where I was, I asked if they wanted anything to eat.

"No, we ate on the flight down. The meal was first class. Hurry up and come get us," he demanded and hung up.

"Yes, I would like that toasted. Take your time," I told the Sandwich Artist. You can't rush an artist.

A few minutes later, I picked up the guys and we headed back to the hotel. I informed Scott and Mike about changing room so that there were at least two beds. Scott promised to work his magic when we got to the hotel.

Scott returned with the keys to the room after a brief exchange with the hotel receptionist. When we arrived at the room, Scott commented on how nice it was and placed his luggage on the one King Size bed in the bedroom. Mike and I were facing a rollaway and a fold out couch.

I was annoyed. So we discussed it a bit and headed to the bar.

While enjoying the view of the water and having a beer, a group of folks came to the bar and they were all wearing name tags which said their name and "Heart of the Samurai".

I commented as much, asking what it meant and one in their group replied, "If I told you I would have to kill you," and started to laugh.

I made a mental note that it was game on!

After our drink, Scott was annoyed that Mike and I were annoyed about the room situation. He also learned that there was a wedding reception taking place across the way from us.

"That is totally unacceptable," Scott said.

"Ever seen the movie Wedding Crashers? This could be fun," I offered.

"Nope, I'm going to take care of this."

About a half an hour later, we arrived at our new room. The fourth room now if anyone is counting. It was identical to the last room except farther away from everything. Mike and I were still facing three nights on a rollaway or couch.

"Yeah, this is way better!" I pointed out.

I opened my computer to find out that 'Heart of the Samurai' was a Leadership class and these people paid five thousand dollars to attend.

With the new found knowledge, we went to the lobby and asked for some name tags. After dinner, we went back to the bar. I ordered our beers and waited for the fun to begin. As you may imagine, if you paid five thousand dollars for a seminar, you probably would not appreciate three guys making fun of it. We were asked by the bartender to leave. It seems our name tags hit a few nerves. We were wearing the following:

"Laugh of the Hyena" – me.

"Teeth of the Pirhana" – Mike.

"Prize of the Cougar"- Scott.

We were still laughing when we got back to the room and I folded out my bed.

Scott and Mike.

CHAPTER **32**

Mella Bella

Scott: "Yes, our trip to San Diego. I would start by saying the Olympics were over before they began, the only real competitive event was croquet as Robert became winded watching us. The real fun was at the resort bar, if you know Robert he will find any way to get a deal or save a dime, which leads into the bar story. Retired gang banger? No! I would say active and extremely drunk. When Robert realized these guys were buying it was game on and I was looking for a place to duck and cover if it went sideways. Even the Bartender was looking at Robert with the "Dude... what are you thinking?" look. Luckily we all survived and Robert got out of paying his debt!" Circa 2010.

The second morning of Scott's birthday trip began with Scott's San Diego Olympics. It was his birthday so we amused him. The events consisted of Ping Pong, Croquet, and Horse. Scott, Mike and I embarrassed ourselves to such a degree that when asked I had to tell people I represented Bolivia. The USA deserved better. It wasn't all bad, I won the Bronze Medal in all three events. I am kind of glad I didn't win as I did not know Bolivia's national anthem. Scott probably would have expected me to sing it.

We then decided to hook up with Mike's daughter and his sister's family for a late breakfast. We arrived at the restaurant and met his family. Mike inquired and was told the wait was about an hour for our tables. The hostess pointed to the bar area and said she would call us. The previous day when walking the beach, I had found a plastic set of pilot wings. They were the kind little kids were given at the Navy Museum of Flight. While Mike and his family went into the bar, I pinned the wings on my shirt. I went back up to the hostess.

"Now how long is it going to be?" I asked pointing to my wings.

She gave me a weird look and a nervous laugh.

I just gave her a nod like I knew something and headed into the bar. Three minutes later, they had two tables next to each other for our group. Mike and his sister were happily surprised. I just pointed to the wings.

Our two tables had different waitresses. We ordered pretty close to the same time. A few minutes later, quicker than it should have been, my table was served our brunch. We were eating and carrying on for about forty minutes before we realized the other table had yet to be served.

"Here," I said, "put these on your table." I unpinned my wings and handed them to Paul, Mike's brother in law.

He placed the wings on his table and thirty seconds later the waitress arrived with his food and apologized for the wait. Now reading this you may think that this was all a coincidence and had nothing to do with the power of my plastic wings. But are you really sure?

After visiting Coronado Island and spending a few hours with Mike's family, we headed back to San Diego State University to drop Mike's daughter, Kylie, off at her sorority. As we pulled into the sorority parking lot, we dodged the beer bottles and telltale sixteen ounce red plastic cups strewn across the grounds.

Mike pretended to ignore them. I figured I may as well let it go, not commenting was hard for me. But it wasn't my daughter!

We went in the sorority and met the house mother. Then Kylie introduced us to her "little sister". We made small talk for a while then Mike said it was time to go and spread his arms to his daughter for a hug.

So I spread my arms to Kylie's little sister. She looked horrified but must have really valued Kylie so she gave me a hug. Mike started laughing and Kylie looked apologetic. I feigned annoyance. We made our exit after that.

We headed to Old Town and had dinner. Scott and Mike wanted to hang out there but I said I would buy the drinks back at the resort. They figured that was a good deal so off we went.

We sat down at the bar. I ordered a round and gave the bartender my debit card to run a tab. Across from us two guys in their late thirties wearing Laker's jerseys and Ball caps off center sat down. With the tattoos and garb, I would venture to say they were retired gang bangers. I hoped I was accurate about the retired part.

They ordered a couple of shots each and pounded them. They ordered another round. One started talking to the folks at the bar. He was kind of loud but no one really acknowledged them.

"How's it going?" I asked the guy. I felt it was rather rude everyone was ignoring him.

"Good man," he started, "I like you. You talked to me. I'm going to buy you a drink. I'm going to buy your friends a drink also." Then he threw the bartender some money.

The bartender was annoyed with the guy. He came over to me and said as he had not charged the first round yet he would just count that as the drinks my new friend was buying. He handed back my debit card. Score!

We talked across the bar for a while. Mike talked a bit but Scott looked like he wanted to be somewhere else. Then the guy decided to buy us another round. We were milking our drinks and these two guys across the bar were throwing down two shots at a time faster than the bartender could refill them. The guy was getting louder and was swearing at the bartender to hurry up. The bartender just stopped coming to our end of the bar after that.

"Do you speak Spanish?" he asked me.

"Nope," I replied.

"Do you want me to teach you Spanish?" he continued.

"Why not?" I agreed, heck he had already bought us three rounds.

"Say Mella Bella," he said.

I really didn't catch what he said, "Bella Bella?"

"No, say Mella Bella," he tried again.

Again, the bar was noisy and he was hammered so I tried again, "Mella mella?"

"No, it's MELLA BELLA!" he exclaimed.

"Mella Bella?" I offered.

"That's it. It means you wax my balls!" he said and they started laughing.

"Yeah, I don't want to learn anymore Spanish. But hey let me buy you a drink," I suggested and called for the bartender.

"You wax his balls," Mike laughed in my ear.

The bartender came over and told me the guy was cut off and I could not buy him a drink. Works for me! At least I tried.

We waited until the cab came to take our friends away. Then we went back to the room where again, I folded out my bed for the night.

"Night Mella Bella," Mike laughed again.

"I didn't have to pay for any of our drinks tonight. Who's laughing now?"

"You didn't stick that guy with the tab did you?" Mike asked in amazement.

"Yep and with the money I saved I might get bikini waxed! Goodnight Teeth of Piranha."

Belize Cave Tubing

CHAPTER **33**

Cave Tubing

Tim: "We had a great time cruising as a family. This story is all true and adds to the stories we can tell when we were all part of it together. I loved Belize and the island off of Honduras." Circa 2010.

Cheryl: "What can I say, besides this is my daughter Alex. She is from an alternate universe. So when a river guide in a third world country that has no governing body to look out for its own citizens safety let alone the safety of tourists tells you to hold on to the rope with BOTH hands or you risk being dragged down river and out to sea by the currents brought on by the torrential rains of the previous day, you might want to do as you're told. This was truly a day to remember. It was great fun and we did it again the next year. This time without Alex acquiring more scars."

I gathered the family up on the pier as they got off the tender from the cruise ship. When everyone was accounted for, I looked at the directions I had printed off the internet and confidently pointed the way. We exited the cruise terminal onto the street.

"Hey, this bus says 'Cave Tubing,' " my brother, Tim, said pointing towards a brand new European Air Conditioned motor coach.

"That's not ours. That is the Carnival Cruise shore excursion. We go this way," I directed.

I was confident because there was a local guy standing across the street with a piece of cardboard with 'Island Marketing' written in crayon. I motioned to him and he led us past the Carnival busses where others were boarding. About a block later we found the excursion office; we sat down and waited for our tour to be called.

"Crayon?" Cheryl scowled at me.

"Look they sell soda," I said changing the subject and walking away from her.

I handed everyone a beverage and sat down. We did not have to wait too long but it was long enough for my two daughters to start screaming at each other. When directed, we grabbed our things and headed back out toward the bus area. The European Air Conditioned busses were gone and our bus waited. I had always wondered what happened to the Partridge Family bus. I was pretty sure I was looking at it.

"Who booked this trip?" Tim asked with a laugh.

"Same river, same caves and we saved the big bucks," I said reassuring everyone as I climbed on the old school bus.

I decided to arrange for our shore excursions locally to save money. On this particular one, I had saved us fifty dollars each and as there were six of us it added up quickly and our tour offered lunch and Carnival's did not.

We rattled and creaked our way toward our destination. About an hour later, the Partridge Family bus was parked just to the left of the European Air Conditioned busses. Everyone was directed to the changing area where we all put on our swim suits. I came out in time to see the Carnival Tour people head up the trail. They were wearing Miner's helmets with attached lights, zippered ski vests, and carrying new vinyl river rat tubes.

Next to our bus was a truck with all of our gear. I was handed a bungee cord with a flashlight attached to it for my head, a little kid's size orange life jacket and an old truck inner tube with six patches on it and an eight inch inflation stem that looked very menacing. I looked around at our party and my gear was about average. My wife was giving me one of those looks. My brother Tim was laughing.

"As long as it holds air, I'm good," my daughter Claire said. She stood proudly next to me and gave me a little nod.

Evelyn, my sister in law, started to laugh and the tension was broken.

With that we headed up the trail toward our adventure.   Claire walked beside me.

"If it doesn't hold air, I'm taking yours," she laughed but she wasn't smiling.

After about a quarter mile, we arrived at the river. Our guide explained that we had to cross it to start the trek up to the caves. Every group had to cross it here.   It was about forty feet across and there was a rope spanning it. As I had gotten us into this, I put the inner tube over my shoulder and grabbed the rope and entered the river. Carefully I managed across and turned back to my family triumphantly. Cheryl was clearly pissed and glaring at me. In front of her was my daughter, Alex, who was sporting a fresh black eye and abrasion on her cheek and all of her gear was floating down the river with our guide in hot pursuit.

"What the hell?" I asked.

While waiting for the guide to return, I was told Alex had not held onto the rope as directed and was swept off her feet. Cheryl had managed to grab her by the hair and hold her until help arrived. Cheryl was sure it was my fault but I could not make that connection.

Well, everyone was annoyed as we started our jungle tour. It had rained heavily the previous night so the trail was muddy and slippery. It was warming up and getting humid. The brochure promised a leisurely trek through the fauna and flora of a tropical rain forest. I guess that's one way to describe it.

We were walking to the fourth of seven caves. The plan was to enter the river at the beginning of the fourth cave and tube the fourth, third, second, and first cave then run the river back to where the rope was.

After a while, the guide stopped as we were pretty spread out. As we gathered, she started rubbing her hand against the back of a tree. Then she held it out to us. It was covered in termites.

"Have one, they taste like mint," she offered.

"No thanks, I had mine for breakfast," I replied.

Alex decided she would try them. Claire passed. Cheryl just glared at me.

"This had better not be the lunch you promised," she said.

Tim came along side and told us about his survival training in the Philippines. The short version was that he ate bugs and it was an easier hike than what we were doing now during our 'leisurely trek' toward the caves. I always appreciate my brother's help easing the tension between my wife and me. He was eating termites as we started walking again.

"Nice," was her sarcastic response.

As we neared the entrance to the fourth cave, we started bunching up with the other groups on the path. Our guide went ahead to see what was up. After a few minutes she returned.

"Come on, they closed the fourth cave because of rising water. We have to get to the third cave before it gets closed," she said and started running back in the direction we had just come.

So we all started running after her. The Carnival People were not running and we were passing them by the European busload. After about a five minute jog, we arrived at the entrance to the third cave.

Our guide was very directive and got us in our tubes. I was on the front; Claire was behind me with her feet under my arms. She was interlocked with Alex, then Cheryl, Evelyn and finally Tim.

"Let's go," the guide said getting in her tube while handing me a rope.

"Robert, lift up your butt so we can go!" Tim yelled from the other end of our inner tube chain.

I did not respond to everyone's laughing as we shot out into the river. We were told to turn on our lights and we entered the third cave. It was pitch black except where our weak head lights hit the walls and ceiling. The guide was directing our attention to different rock formations but it was clear we were going much faster than she was used to.

I was turning my head and light every time she directed me but I had no idea what she was describing. We rocketed out into daylight as we left the third cave. Then back into the darkness of the second cave.

The guide gave up trying to describe the formations and started pointing out the parts of the ceiling she was afraid we might hit. She was paddling mightily avoiding hazards. We were helping but not as much as she would have liked.

Daylight again, darkness again, we were in the first cave. This was a long cave and we were flying through it. As we could start to see daylight again, we could see the Carnival people exiting the river. The guide paddled us into a little eddy against the right side of the cave. The water was flowing back up stream and we slowed.

She told me to paddle toward where everyone was getting out of the river. She explained she felt the rest of the river was too dangerous. Reluctantly we started paddling to the left side of the river. Although I did not know it, Tim at the other end of our chain was paddling away from the exit with all his might.

We were stuck right in the middle of the river and the current hit us again with full force. The guide looked at my brother and yelled, "If you want to run the river then we will run the river!"

She turned her attention downstream. We were already speeding up. It was clear it was faster than we should be going. The guide was telling us to paddle left, right, back, forward and we were listening.

"Look out for the bamboo!" she yelled with concern in her voice. We slammed into the right bank of the river against the brush.

Then we turned sideways and were heading downriver in a line. She was frantically trying to get us in a row again when we hit a tree broadside. We could not make it to one side or the other together so I let go of Claire so they could stay together.

As they freed themselves from the tree, I was racing past them on the other side. Tim paddled twice toward the middle of the river and stuck out his hand. I caught it and we continued around the next bend. The rope was visible and there was a man standing in the river with his hands on his hips.

"That's the director of all the guides, listen carefully and do what I say," the guide yelled at us.

We complied with her directions and we came to a perfect stop in a line against the shore in front of the director and about fifty people.

I stood up and started to notice the people on the shore.

"They closed the river. We don't get to go. This sucks." People were grumbling.

I turned back to Cheryl and they noticed the three gashes on my back. Then they saw Alex's black eye and blood flowing down her face from a cut on the forehead. We were all visibly shaken and out of breath.

"Well, I guess they were only looking out for our safety," the crowd settled down and was now happy they had closed the river.

The director came up to the guide and commented that she did a better job than any of the guys. She was beaming with pride.

We looked at the river marker. The river had risen nearly three feet in the hour we were walking and tubing. Interestingly, it normally took an hour to run the river and we did it in eighteen minutes.

We gathered our stuff and started walking back to the parking area.

"I thought we were going to get out at the end of the last cave," I mentioned to my brother.

"I was paddling as hard as I could the other way," he laughed.

"What? why?" I asked.

"If we got out there, we would have had to walk all the way back. There was no way I was volunteering to do that," he smiled.

We changed and boarded the bus. The return trip was abuzz with the recap of the dangers. They served lunch and jungle juice, 1 part Everclear to two parts Kool-Aid, on the ride back.

When we got back to the Cruise Terminal, I tipped our guide pretty heavily.

"That was a big tip," Tim commented.

"Did you see how she ran to get us on the river before it was closed? She was looking out for us," I said.

"You're an idiot. If they closed the river, they would have had to refund all of our money."

I just shrugged my shoulders which reminded me of the gashes on my back.

"I can't wait to see how you saved us money in Honduras," he said and let out a big laugh.

Similar to our bus! (Above) Calmer waters. (Below)

CHAPTER **34**

Cheating Death In The Jungles Of Central America

Cheryl: "This was our first Zip line adventure and to date, by far the best. I will admit to goading Robert terribly since I thought he was trying to be funny. I didn't realize he was actually terrified. And well, Robert deserves it most of the time." Circa 2010.

"Let me guess, these European busses aren't for us?" Tim said with a smile referring to our Belize trip the previous day.

"Funny, we have to leave the terminal to catch our ride," I replied.

The eight of us walked past the busses and up the hill through the shopping mall. I led them through the cab section and stopped at the road to look at my directions. They clearly stated we had to leave the terminal and go past the security gate. So off we went to the left and up another hill. Others not in our little group started following us. I guess it looked like I knew where I was going. I hoped they were right.

At the top of the hill, the road turned to the right and there was a security gate. Things were looking up. When we reached the gate, there was nothing outside the check point. The others looked at me and into my soul for any hint that I was worried I was going the wrong way. I just acted casual. I went over to the guard and asked where the meeting place was. He pointed down the road.

There were no sidewalks and the Carnival busses were blowing past us.

"Remind me to book my own excursions next time," Tim laughed.

"Carnival had a maximum weight of two hundred twenty five pounds; think you could have made that?" I asked.

"Think you could?" Tim replied.

"Yeah, are we booked on the Carnival trip?" I answered looking over my glasses. Then we both laughed. I had booked the trip directly saving nearly $400 and more importantly the local company had a two hundred fifty pound maximum weight. As long as they did not have an accurate scale, Tim and I were probably safe.

When we rounded the next corner, the meeting place became visible. Acting casual paid off. Our group arrived at the departure point intact. We were led to the waiting area. It was a wet grassy embankment behind the road barrier. I could say it was posh but that would be quite a stretch even for me. There was another family waiting there to go zip lining as well.

"Really?" Cheryl asked. She was none too thrilled about sitting on the damp ground.

Before I could formulate a response, Claire and Alex started yelling at each other and drew Cheryl's attention.

I called Claire over to me to separate her from her sister. She was next to me when I asked, "Out late last night? You look a little tired."

"Yeah, really late, I did not get in until almost 11:00pm."

I was going to say something but then I decided I should talk to the person in charge and explain we had brought along two extra people. I wanted to be sure it was okay. She was happy about it and confirmed them.

I went over to explain to Melissa and Arash everything was fine. This trip was about the time of their first anniversary.

When it was time to leave, a ten passenger van pulled up. This would have been fine as there were originally six of us and another family of four. But with the addition of Arash and Melissa, we were now twelve. I kind of expected the transportation would have accommodated the two extra when they confirmed them.

Miraculously, the ten passenger van became a twelve passenger van when the driver folded out two tin seats. We were shoved into the van, doors were closed and off we went.

I was in the front of the van with my Aunt Mary Jo sitting on a tin seat between the driver and me. Mary Jo started talking to the driver. It started out innocent enough but soon turned a little sketchy. I could not tell if she was having fun with the guy or trying to pick him up.

If I could not tell, the driver was really having troubles. It was kind of funny in an uncomfortable way. Mary Jo was all a chatting away and he was trying to follow along and politely respond.

After about forty five minutes, we arrived at our destination. We could not wait to exit the van's cramped quarters. We were offered lockers for our stuff alongside a patio which overlooked the hillside and the Caribbean below. It was a spectacular sight. I rented a couple of lockers and we put away all of our things.

A guide called us and we followed. He stopped in front of the guy who took the money and we settled up; then onto a lower deck where we were fitted with our gear. The guides were very professional and skilled at getting people into the harnesses quickly. Finally one turned his attention to me. He handed me a helmet then helped me into the harness. He started tightening the thigh straps.

"Don't touch my junk!" I yelled sarcastically. This was about the time the guy in Los Angeles had yelled that at a TSA employee. I thought it was funny. The guide just looked at me like I was an idiot. I know as I have seen the look before. When the harness was tightened the guide left.

"Who'd want to touch your junk?" Cheryl asked.

"You!" I said with confidence.

She just gave me the look.

Then the guide came back with another harness. It was kind of like a man bra. He put it on me and attached another carabiner. Cheryl just started laughing I was only comforted by the fact Tim was wearing one too. I put on the helmet and gloves that were provided. I walked over to where Melissa and Cheryl were.

"We ran into Claire at 2:00 a.m. by the pool," Melissa told Cheryl.

"Really?" Cheryl replied, "She told Robert she was in by 11:00pm."

Melissa just laughed. We laughed too. Claire was eighteen and old enough to not have a bedtime. The fact she had to lie about it was funny to us.

When we were all geared up, we took a photo and then walked down the steps to the first departure point.

I was genuinely afraid. The online description looked really cool. But now that I was in the gear looking off over a cliff reality was cruel. Whose idea was this, anyway? Oh, yeah, it was mine and since I had got us all into this I felt obligated to put on a brave face and lead by example.

I volunteered to go after the other family's small children went. My harness was attached to the cable and my man bra was hooked to the pulley. I was shown how to use the padded leather glove as a brake by pulling down on the cable. I confirmed I understood and they pushed me off the platform.

The slope of the first run was gradual. I did not go very fast and I was never more than ten feet off the ground. As I approached the next platform, I pulled down on the cable with my padded glove and slowed. When I came to a stop over the platform, I was helped by a guide with detaching from the cable.

That wasn't so bad.

It was a small platform so I was directed to the second zip line as Mary Jo was arriving behind me. Before I knew it I was attached to the second cable. Since I was watching Mary's arrival, I was not really paying attention to the second zip line until I was shoved off the safety of the platform. I realize I am fifty feet above the top of the trees below and flying across the valley between the two hills. What the hell? Do they even have OSHA in Honduras? Brake! That's the ticket. I grabbed the cable with the padded glove and started pulling. I wasn't slowing but my hand was getting hot. Good thing, it was kind of cold as we were in the Tropics!?

I was approaching the next platform at a terrifying speed. I was pulling down with all my adrenaline induced might. It was working. I was slowing down. My hand was getting hotter and my glove was starting to smoke. As I neared the platform, the guide was telling me to stop braking. Yeah right! Then I triumphantly came to a stop.

With great relief I looked around. I was fifty feet short of the platform and was just hanging there in mid air. Okay, well that was not where I was supposed to stop.

The guide looked annoyed as he hooked up to the cable. He moved hand over hand out to me and pulled me back to the platform. He was about to say something when Mary Jo approached and stopped about the same place I had.

He was shaking his head while detaching me from the cable then went out and retrieved my aunt.

Then everyone else flew into the platform without a problem. Show offs.

It was hot and humid and I was sweating profusely. The guide asked if anyone wanted to hang upside down.

"Hell no," I said to Cheryl.

She just smiled and yelled, "I want to!" She pushed me out of the way precariously close to the edge of the tree house.

One of the guides hooked to the cable first then Cheryl was connected next to him. In a flash they were shoved and took off across the valley. The guide held Cheryl's legs and she bent backwards until she was hanging upside down as they flew down the cable.

I was feeling a little awkward as the family was taking off from the platform in front of me without any fear and I was hugging the tree in the center of the platform. So I decided to put my fear aside once again. I let go of the tree, adjusted my man bra and approached the departure spot.

"You want to hang upside down?" the guide asked.

"I'll give you twenty dollars if you never ask me that again," I answered holding out a twenty.

He took it, smiled and gave me a little wink. Then I was attached and shoved to probable death.

While traversing the cable and in between prayers, I started to realize the zip line probably was fairly safe; compared to the platforms.

The platforms were made of wood nailed together like Randy Hamilton and I used to do in the vacant lot down the street from our houses in Kenmore when we were ten. The railing was made out of half inch galvanized pipe that was nailed at the base to the platform. Nailed?

As I slowed to land, I saw people sitting on the railing. Really?

I was detached from the cable and went to the center of the platform and hugged the tree. I could not wait to hit the next zip line. My family confused this eagerness with me having fun. I just wanted off this third world hazard before it collapsed.

We zigzagged back and forth across the valley. We took some pictures. Cheryl started hanging upside down by herself. I guess she figured she was probably going to die anyway so she might as well have fun.

When I arrived at the last platform, I threw my gear off and gave the guide another forty bucks. My life was worth it!

We rode the comfortable flat bed truck back up the hillside. The driver was careful to hit every bump and dip in the road on the way up. It was a good thing I had tipped prior to the ride back.

"Mom, let's do this again!" Claire said.

Cheryl was actually thinking about it. Are you kidding me? Fate should not be tempted twice in one day especially in the jungles of Central America.

"No!" I commanded.

Both Cheryl and Claire looked at me with disdain but turned their attention to the gift shop and left me standing there.

Tim came up. "That was fun but it is hard to get an adrenalin rush after flying fighter planes at twice the speed of sound."

"Did you have to stop the plane with a padded leather glove?""

He just laughed and slapped me on the shoulder.

"Let's go look at the pictures they're selling," he said and we followed after the gals.

Note: Zip lining back and forth from the top of a hill down to the bottom was much more fun than my next zip lining adventure in Cancun. There we had to climb stairs at each platform to the next zip line. I thought I was going to die! The highest platform was 170 feet off the ground. Cheryl actually wanted to do it again!?

Family Picture before the Zip lining began.

Cheryl

Tim and Claire

CHAPTER **35**

Scuba Diving In Roatan

Circa 2011.

We disembarked the ship and started the trek toward our tour operator. As our operator was not affiliated with Carnival, we had to leave the cruise terminal to meet them.   We had done this the year before, so I knew the way. While passing the Carnival Tour Operators, we collected other passengers looking for their budget tour operators and I led the way.   I wanted to get them singing as we went over the river and up the hill but no one was interested. Once we crested the hill and could see the makeshift assembly point less than another mile away their spirits lifted.

The collection area was much more organized this time and we were quickly directed to the van taxiing us to our scuba adventure. We had originally planned a dune buggy excursion through the middle of the island but it was cancelled due to a robbery at the operator's facility. I booked the scuba trip as a last minute replacement. The kids were excited. Cheryl reluctantly agreed. Other than the fact Cheryl does not like salt water or breathing through her mouth, she was fine.

The driver commenced giving us all kinds of information as we traversed the island. She was friendly and knowledgeable. As we pulled up to the beach, the driver said, "The water is very beautiful here but one must be very careful as we have lost many of our loved ones out there."

Cheryl snapped her head around glaring at me, "Really?"

"Scuba diving?" I asked the driver demonstrating I was clearly annoyed at her comment.

"What? Oh no, fishing," she replied after realizing what she had just said, "scuba diving is very safe here."

Cheryl continued glaring at me and Claire laughed.

We walked the beach to the dive shack at 7:55am local time. Our excursion was scheduled for 8:00am. The shack was locked. No one arrived until 8:30. When the instructors finally got there, they sat us in the dive hut and put in the required forty minute safety video. The video was well done and refreshed a lot of my knowledge as I had been scuba certified many years before. Halfway through the video, the image froze. Walter, our dive instructor, rebooted the computer and started the video over. Apparently, there was no way to advance the video to past where it had frozen.

"We are trusting our lives to him and he can't even run a DVD player?" Cheryl asked once again visibly annoyed or still annoyed depending on your perspective. I was thinking still annoyed. Claire laughed again.

I just smiled trying to soothe her. Cheryl started what looked like a panic attack or maybe a nervous breakdown, either way I went back to watching the video and hoped she would pull it together.

After the video, we were handed medical waivers. There was a list of ailments that we were asked if we ever had. There was a "Yes" and "No" box. If you checked any of the "Yes" boxes, you could not go.

"Panic attacks?" Cheryl pointed out.

"Just put "no"," I told her.

"Fainting?" Cheryl glared.

"Check the "No"," I assisted.

"Irregular heartbeat?"

"Just check "No" in all the boxes," I told her figuring it would speed things up.

She scowled at me but checked all the "No" boxes.

We were fitted with the scuba gear. When we were satisfied with our gear, they loaded us onto a boat and took us a quarter mile down the beach and tied up in front of the most expensive resort in the area. I guess we were their advertisement.

One by one, we were placed into our gear and asked to kneel in the surf which was about three feet deep. Here we showed the instructor we were able to clear water from our mask. When it got to Cheryl's turn, Cheryl's mask was half filled with water and no amount of blowing air through her nose could clear it.

Walter went over to her and tightened her mask by pulling the strap as hard as he could. This smashed the mask into Cheryl's face but did not stop the leak. Walter got her a new mask while the other instructor continued with my daughters and me.

We demonstrated the skill of removing our regulator, finding it and replacing it in our mouths. Once satisfied, our instructor led us under water out toward the reef. The instructor was followed by Alex, Claire, and then me.

As we zigzagged through the coral, Claire kept following Alex too close. Alex would turn and in doing so, she would kick Claire in the face with her fins. Claire's mask or regulator would get knocked loose. She would just casually put it back on. Then she would look to me for support. What could I say, we were underwater!

After a while, we gathered on the bottom and were joined by Cheryl and Walter. The girls and I gave Cheryl the okay sign. She returned it.

Then Walter swam up to Cheryl and tapped her on the side of the head. Any sign of joy left her face and she glared at Walter. Apparently, he had been tapping the side of her head continuously while they toured the reef and she had reached her fun limit.

He gave her the ok sign. He waited for her to return the sign telling him she was ok.

She shook her head no then took her flat hand and pulled it across the front of her throat. I am not sure of the hand signals but the intent was clear. Cheryl was not ok. Walter tapped her on the head again and gave her the ok sign. Once again she gave what I interpreted as not ok. Finally, Walter had the other instructor take her to the surface. Walter apparently was reluctant to swim with her any longer. As the driver had told us, "many loved ones had been lost." I started to see how that might have come about.

The kids and I continued on our underwater tour of the reef. When we surfaced by the boat, Cheryl was happily swimming around enjoying the warm water under the sun.

When we were all on the boat, I turned to Cheryl and said, "I was so happy to see you down there. I am proud of you."

"Every time I started to relax and enjoy it, Walter would tap me on the side of the head. I just wanted to beat him with my tank at the end," she laughed. It was sort of a scary maniacal laugh. I moved away from her slowly while hoping she wouldn't notice. I noticed Walter was keeping a safe distance from her.

The boat trip back was full of Claire and Alex telling their mother what they had seen. They had enjoyed the scuba adventure. They had enjoyed all the sights. They were full of joy at the time spent underwater. I was glad we went. Cheryl had looked fabulous under water in her swimming suit. I hoped as the day went on she would warm to the experience.

We changed at the hut and tipped the instructors. Cheryl thought I had given them way too much. Her sneer told me that my hope for her mood improving was misplaced.

On the drive back to the ship, Claire asked for her half of the money back from the drive to New Orleans so she could buy souvenirs. Her mother looked at me.

"We didn't fight the whole way," Claire said proudly and smiled at Alex and her Mom.

When the van dropped us in front of the shops at the cruise terminal, I took them aside.

"This is for you and here is yours," I said handing fifty dollars to each of my daughters. "Now remember, you have to make it all the way home to get your other fifty dollars back," I reminded them.

The previous year we had taken the same cruise itinerary out of New Orleans. On the drive back to San Antonio, my two daughters fought extensively making the eight hour drive miserable for Cheryl and me. I vowed then never to take them with me again on a trip. As that vow did not last very long, I had to come up with plan B: The Bicker Tax. I had each daughter give me a hundred dollars prior to leaving San Antonio. Since we arrived in New Orleans without them fighting in the car, I returned half of the money to them. If they made the trip home after the cruise, I would give them the other half. If they fought in the car, I would keep the money. So either the drive would be pleasant or I would have one hundred dollars to go out for dinner and drinks on my kids. Either way, Cheryl and I won.

Diving

CHAPTER **36**

Hello

Cheryl: "This story is riddled with facts, as Robert would say. The beach is breathtakingly beautiful and I did indeed take a shower with a bird named Gizmo. Then Robert puts his spin on it. When the bird says "Hello" to him, where he can simply just turn around and walk out of the dressing room, Robert calls it menacing. When the bird has me cornered in the shower, beak three inches from my foot, head turned sideways in order to simultaneously judge the fear of this featherless creature and size up whether my ankle will take one bite or two, he ridicules me for being scared. He would have cried like a little girl had he been in the shower!" Circa 2013.

"You're starting to burn," I told my wife. She had been tanning on the Caribbean Beach for the last three hours. During which, I read a book while trying to keep my body parts under the umbrella I had rented.

"I can feel it," she responded and started to rise from her lounge chair, "St. Maarten is truly beautiful."

I nodded in agreement. The beach was fairly secluded and only a few other people were there. We started to collect our things to head back to the cruise ship.

"Do you see a shower anywhere?" she asked wanting to wash the salt water and sand off from swimming.

"I'll look. Hand me the cups, I will throw them away."

Once I had all our things and trash collected, I headed up to the beach bar. As I discarded the debris, I noticed the "Shower" sign on the wall behind the bar. I pointed it out to Cheryl. She grabbed her things and headed through the swinging doors into the shower area.

I went and found the "Little Boy's Room" and then came back to the bar. As there were three flat screen televisions on the wall and it was a Saturday in September, I started to watch the college football.

Cheryl was in the shower stall undressing when she noticed a shadow at the door.

"Hello," she heard.

"This stall is taken," she replied.

"Hello," once again.

"Occupodo," she called out hoping it was Spanish.

After the silence that followed, she undressed and climbed into the shower. While rinsing the shampoo from her hair, she looked down to see this huge parrot IN the shower with her.

It turned its head and looked at her, "Hello."

She screamed.

"Hello," it said turning towards her.

"Goodbye," she replied waving her hands in a shooing motion trying to gain her composure.

"Hello," it said.

"Goodbye," my wife suggested. I guess she thought reasoning with a parrot was the best approach.

In the minutes that followed, she tried dressing; calling for help, while keeping the bird at bay.

Occasionally, I heard what sounded like my wife calling out or talking to someone but over the sound of the football games I could not be certain. On the fourth such occurrence, I decided to investigate. Yes, the fourth or maybe the fifth, I did not want to rush into anything besides it was first and goal, second and goal, third and goal, touchdown, then extra point! After that I had time to see why my wife was screaming for help.

I walked through the swinging doors into the shower area. There were four shower stalls so I called out to my wife, "Cheryl?"

"I'm down here! The last stall," she said and her voice was shaking.

The stall door was open which I found rather odd. I turned into it and my wife was standing half dressed in the shower. She was visibly upset.

"Get that thing out of here!"

"What thing?" I asked and then looked down. At my feet, half under the changing bench was a huge parrot. Its beak was the size of my hand and its two talons were easily that big as well. From its red tail to beak was nearly three feet long.

"Mother Jones!" I exclaimed. I had a coworker named "Mando" who's favorite swearing combination is "Mother F-bombing Jones." As I swear too much I had started using it in the abbreviated form. "What do you want me to do with that?" I asked.

"Get RID OF IT!" she insisted.

"No really, what do you want me to do about this?"

The bird started coming out from underneath the bench. It turned its head sideways and looked at me with its left eye, "Hello?" it said. It was a menacing "Hello".

"Robert Louis Olwell you get that bird out of here!" she insisted.

Robert Louis Olwell? I hadn't been called that since my mother was about to discipline me. Wow, I'm really scared, "Yes dear," was the only response I could manage.

What happened next took a lot of courage on my part, I might add. I don't like insects. I hate spiders. I took my towel and blocked the parrot from coming out the rest of the way from under the bench and slowly guided it back under the bench so my wife could exit. My wife contends I was not very brave, actually she said I was screaming like a girl in ponytails wearing a skirt but as there are no independent witnesses who speak English that are willing to come forward and I am writing this story, her claims are totally unfounded. Really, they are.

When my wife reached me I moved back and the bird followed. She screeched and put her back pack down in between her and the parrot. I exited the showers most expediously while that stupid bird kept mocking me with its "Hello".

My wife went to the bar and sat on a stool trembling. The bird followed her and using its beak and talons started to climb the back of her stool. She got up and moved quite rapidly away.

The parrot reached the top of the stool and said, "Hello!"

One of the bartenders noticed the bird, "That's Gizmo. Be careful he follows people into the shower."

"Now they tell me! By the way, what took you so long?" she asked me.

"Oh, I didn't hear you the first three or four times you called for help," I answered casually.

"Then how did you know I called for help three or four times?" Her lips were pursed when she finished the question.

"What? Look out! The parrot's coming this way," I said grabbing her arm and rushing her toward a cab. I hoped it would effectively change the subject.

When we got back to our stateroom on the ship, Cheryl went in to finish her shower. I waited a few minutes, and then I snuck in and ripped back the shower curtain saying, "Hello."
"Good bye," she scowled, "I would have rather seen Gizmo than you, Pippy Longstockings!"
"I did not scream like a girl!" I may have answered a little too high pitched to be believable though.

St. Maarten Beach above. Gizmo the Parrot below.

Gizmo after following Cheryl out of the showers.

Cheryl and me.

Scott, Mike and Cheryl in Cancun

CHAPTER **37**

Ek Balam Gas

Scott: "Robert has foggy memories of this day so I feel I must correct the record! First, we were leaving on a long trip and we were all hungry. As far as I could tell the McDonalds was only open the first day we arrived, and we never saw it open again. As we left civilization we had multiple opportunities to get gas and food, and finally we stopped at the equivalent of a Mexican Am/Pm WITHOUT GAS! Now we were in Robert's element, tasty looking pastries filled with god knows what, Pepperoni type sticks of mystery meat, packages of sugar dusted surprise. We loaded up on empty calories and hit the road. Now driving with Cheryl is a thrill ride of its own, if you remember the old Star Trek in the intro where the ship warps up and all the stars become lines of light THAT is like driving with Cheryl. Oh and don't complain because she finds the ability to milk another 10 mph out of the 4 cylinder rental just to show you who's in charge. As we cruised along with the engine compartment glowing through the hood, I noticed there was a strange silence up front, "you guys are kind of quiet now?" as we had been giving Cheryl a lot of crap about the speed. Nope, everything's great, I sat up and started looking around, noticing the light on the dash, is that the low fuel light? Yup! How long has that been on? Awhile! How awhile? Awhile. Then came the sign, 90 km to next gas station. ARE YOU SHITTING ME!!!! Yes, Yes I lost it, we were in the middle of fricking nowhere, and there was nothing but a real nice highway and NOTHING! Yes ass raping crossed my mind! At this point I have to acknowledge Mike, if you know Mike, nothing rattles him. I don't know if he can internalize all mind bending stress or if he truly is at one with the cosmos but all he kept doing was sharing fun facts from the guide book. After miles of stress and venting there it was, on the horizon a structure, what looked like a huge arch, was it heaven? Was this the end? No, it was a toll station and there must be a gas station. As we pulled in there *was nothing but a snack bar and a group of Mexicans admiring our vehicle. "So, who's going to go inquire about gas?" Robert asked. "Really! You can get your butt out of the car and find gas," I told him. Robert begrudgingly climbed out and engaged the Mexicans. After about five minutes he waved us over for two gallons of gas for $20.00. All was right with the cosmos and on we went to Ek Balam."*

Cheryl: "A week in Cancun with Robert and his buddies? You betcha! Boring and uneventful, but I'll get a great tan. Or so I thought. Circa 2013.

"Let's go, we'll stop and get food on the way! Daylight's burning, and we'll beat the crowds," I said to Scott and Mike.

"We can stop at McDonald's," Cheryl added.

The four of us climbed into the rental car and left the Hotel Presidente in Cancun. A few miles down the island, we arrived at McDonald's. It wasn't open yet.

"Don't worry. We will eat once we get on the toll road," I promised the others.

In no time we were off the island and a few miles south where we turned onto the toll road that crossed from Cancun to the ruins of Chichen Itza and Ek Balam. We were going to Ek Balam. Tourists were still allowed to walk and climb on the ruins. At Chichen Itza, you could not.

We quickly settled down on the three hour drive. Mike was reading a guide book about the Yucatan. Scott was reading a magazine. Cheryl was driving and I was riding shotgun. The toll road was very nice with two lanes heading each direction. The opposite lanes were divided by a large median so in most places you could not see the opposite traffic through the jungle.

We had been on the toll road for about an hour when the gas light came on. We still had not seen a gas station or any restaurants. Cheryl pointed out the gas light to me.

A few miles later there was a sign in Spanish that I believed read: Gasoline 142Km. Well, that meant roughly ninety miles. We had been on the toll road for at least ninety miles. I figured we had about forty miles worth of gas at best and we were past the point of no return.

"We're going to run out of gas," I said quietly to Cheryl.

"You think! I figured that out about twenty miles ago. We haven't seen one stop, gas station or restaurant this whole time," she said.

Then we both laughed. To us, we just figured this would be another adventure. We were not sure how the guys in the back were going to take the news. We just pressed on as there was no reason to head back. Either way the situation looked grim.

About twenty miles farther, I was watching the gas gauge go below empty a little further. We passed a road sign that translated: Toll Booth 60Km. Confident the situation was dire and we were not going to make it forty more miles, I decided it was best to inform the guys in the back.

"Hey guys, we are going to run out of gas," I said casually.

"Okay," Mike replied and went back to reading his book.

"What?" Scott screeched after finally digesting what I had said.

"We are going to run out of gas," I said again.

"That's just great. We are going to be stuck out here in the jungle. The Federales are going to find us and I am going to be ass raped," he said frantically.

"Well if the Federales stop us, I am okay if you're volunteering to be ass raped to save the group,"

I laughed, "All in favor of Scott getting ass raped first, say aye."

"Aye," laughed Cheryl.

"Definitely aye," joined Mike.

"That's real funny guys. This is serious stuff. I was chased by Federales all across the jungle in Puerto Vallarta while horseback riding with Morgan. My guide told me we barely made it out alive and it was only because of him that we made it," Scott said adamantly.

"Your guide told you that? I hope you tipped him well," I laughed.

Cheryl smiled and nodded getting my drift.

"You bet I did. You don't know how dangerous it is travelling outside the United States," he said and instantly regretted it.

All three of us laughed at that one. Cheryl and I had travelled extensively around the world. This was Scott's third trip out of the U.S.. The one trip to Puerto Vallarta was the only time he hadn't been with us.

Meanwhile, another couple of miles had passed.

"Don't you think you should slow down to conserve fuel?" Scott asked.

"Nope, I want to be going fast when we run out of gas. This way we can coast farther," Cheryl said and Mike and I laughed with her.

"Guys, this is not funny. I don't know how you can laugh at a time like this. I am not going to be stranded out here in the middle of nowhere out of gas."

"Not much we can do about it now," I said.

"Well maybe we can make it," he said optimistically, "How far to the toll plaza?"

"Based on the last sign, forty miles," I calculated.

"At least the gas light hasn't come on yet," Scott observed.

"Actually the light is on," Cheryl confessed.

"How long ago did the gas light come on?" he asked after writing down the forty miles on a piece of paper; like algebra was going to save us.

"Sixty miles," I answered.

"Sixty miles what?" he asked a bit confused.

"Sixty miles ago the gas light came on," Cheryl answered.

He wrote the sixty on the paper and looked at it for a full minute, "We're going to run out of gas!"

"Yeah, we got that. I think that's what we have been discussing for the past ten minutes," Cheryl replied.

She looked at me and whispered, "Is he always like this?"

I just laughed and nodded. I looked back at Mike. He was just reading his guide book. He seemed perfectly content. Scott on the other hand was not handling this well at all. Meanwhile, another two miles had passed.

We were about twenty four miles from the toll booth based on the signage when we came in sight of it. Miraculously the signs were wrong and the car still was running. As we got closer, it became apparent that there was no gas station there.

"Guys, this is as far as we are going. We will solve the gas situation here. I know Scott kindly volunteered to take it in the ass for us, but we have a better chance here," I decided.

"I agree," Cheryl said.

"Funny!" Scott said.

"That is funny," Mike laughed.

Cheryl pulled up to the toll area and then parked to the left of it on the shoulder. I got out and looked over the lay of the land. I noticed a couple of guys in a nearby building and walked over.

I walked in, "Speak English?"

He shook his head no, and then asked, "Gasolina?"

I smiled and he laughed. He pointed to the other side of the toll area where there were a couple of landscapers. I walked across the highway to one of the guys in orange jumpsuits. I was hoping it wasn't prison garb. If it was, Scott may yet come in handy I was thinking.

"Hola, gasolina?" I asked. They probably thought I was a local with my Spanish.

He just nodded and put down his rake. He went out back of another building. I turned and gave the thumbs up to Cheryl and she drove to this side of the freeway. A couple of minutes later, the guy returned with a can and a hose. He proceeded to siphon two gallons of gas into our car. I gave him the requested twenty bucks figuring it was cheap under the circumstances.

"Want a drink?" I asked Cheryl.

She replied that she wanted a Coke so I went to a little stand and bought a couple of drinks. I got back in the car. We paid the toll and headed onto Ek Balam. A few minutes later, Scott announced that I was buying lunch for the group.

"Since you were willing to get raped for us, I'll buy your lunch."

Everyone laughed except Scott.

Gasolina?

Cheryl and me at El Balam.

Carnival Triumph

CHAPTER **38**

Audrey's Cruise

Circa 2013.

"You know, Audrey hasn't been on a cruise and we have taken Claire and Alex on three. Maybe we could send Audrey and Claire on a five day cruise out of Galveston for their Christmas present," I suggested to Cheryl.

"How much will that cost?" Cheryl replied.

She would have never asked that if she didn't like the idea.

"Well if they go on the same date as us at the end of February it will be around $800 by the time we pay for an inside room, give them gas money and pay for tipping," I figured.

"They are not sailing with us. We have discussed it and the kids do not need travel with us anymore. It is time we have a little time to ourselves without the kids," she insisted.

"There is a sailing on February 2nd that is the same price, how about that?" I asked.

"I am okay with that. Audrey deserves a nice trip too and we can watch the grandbaby," Cheryl smiled.

Prior to booking the trip and putting down nonrefundable payments, I called Claire. I asked her to talk to Audrey and see if this is something she wanted to do.

"Yes definitely," Claire said excitedly when she called back.

I handed the phone to Cheryl. Both Audrey and Claire discussed the plans with their mother. Cheryl seemed pleased they were so excited.

"Tell them to confirm with their employers they can have the time off. I will not book the trip until they get back to me on that," I told my wife who passed on the information.

Several days later, Claire came by the house to tell me they both had permission to miss work during the dates of the trip.

I called up Carnival to book the trip. After all of Audrey's info was given to the booking agent, I started giving them Claire's info.

"Both of your kids need to be older than twenty-one years of age or one of them needs to be at least twenty-five," I was told. Audrey was old enough but Claire was only nineteen.

So much for plan A.

"Well, we can book them on our dates," I suggested.

"No! We are not taking them with us! Figure something else out," Cheryl said flatly.

So much for plan B.

I called Norwegian Cruise Lines. They only require that one person in the room be over twenty-one provided the other was at least eighteen. However, they did not have five day sailings out of Galveston. They only offered week long cruises. This would cost $1500, nearly twice our original estimate.

Cancel plan C.

"What if you go with them as a triple?" I suggested, "A third person sharing the same stateroom is only another $150. You could spend some quality time with the girls."

"I am open to that but I don't want to take a cruise three weeks before I take the same cruise with you," she said.

"Okay, there is a January 10th sailing for about the same price," I showed her on the computer.

"I can work with that," she confirmed.

I called and told the girls what was up and asked them to confirm they could get the time off.

The next day, Claire called to say neither could get that time off.

Great! Cancel plan D.

"We can add them to our date or you can take them on the February 2nd date," I told my wife as I was out of other ideas.

"Fine, I will take them on the 2nd," Cheryl finally agreed.

I called the cruise company and booked the trip. I then called and told the girls. Everyone was happy with plan E.

As a little something special, I booked Audrey and Claire a Scuba Adventure in Cozumel.

Cheryl and the girls arrived in Galveston the night before the cruise. The next morning after breakfast, Audrey saw the ship for the first time.

"Oh my god, it is so huge!" Audrey smiled.

"I know and I will show you all of it," Claire assured her.

After boarding, the three went to their stateroom to drop off their carry ons.

"Come on!" Claire said after tossing her things on Audrey's bed.

Cheryl turned around and they were gone. Cheryl laughed to herself and was happy at their excitement. Forty minutes later after looking all over the ship, Cheryl had lost a little of her amusement. She sat down at the pool bar and ordered a drink.

A twenty five year old guy sat down next to her, "Hey pretty lady, can I buy you a drink?"

Cheryl looked around to be sure he was talking to her, "No thanks."

"Come on, I'll show you a good time!" he promised.

"Check please!" she called to the bartender and took her drink and quickly departed.

Cheryl finally caught up with the girls at dinner time. At the dinner table, Cheryl explained the rules, "You need to meet me a half hour before dinner in the lounge adjoining this restaurant. We will enjoy a nice chat and then we will have dinner together. We will see Progresso and Cozumel together. Other than that you are on your own."

"Okay, I checked and there are lawn chairs on the little deck in front of our cabin so you are all set," Claire said.

"Thanks for the beverage stickers. It is cool to be able to get a soda any time we want," Audrey added.

After dinner, the girls went out to explore more of the ship. Much later that night, they came sneaking into the cabin. Cheryl pretended not to notice.

Cheryl was the first up. She went up to the Lido deck and had breakfast. Then she went to the gym and worked out. After working out, she cooled off while watching Good Morning America on the pool side big screen. Around noon, she headed back to the cabin to change.

"Turn off the light," Claire groaned when Cheryl opened the door.

"It is noon," Cheryl laughed and turned on all the lights in the room.

Claire covered her face with a pillow and Audrey rolled over, "Noon? Come on Claire, we have things to do."

By the time, Cheryl showered and changed into her swimsuit, the girls were gone again. Cheryl exited the cabin and went out on the deck at the end of the hallway. There was a small deck area with a few lawn chairs and she was all alone. On the last cruise, Claire and I had scoped out the deck area and planned the stateroom to be as close as possible. Cheryl enjoyed a quiet afternoon of sunning alone on her secluded spot.

The girls met her at the lounge before dinner.

"What are we going to do tomorrow?" Claire asked.

"I think we should just get off the ship and explore Progresso," Cheryl suggested, "I will go by the excursion desk and get some suggestions after dinner."

At the excursions desk, Cheryl was informed that the ship docks basically in the middle of nowhere. It was suggested that she sign up for a Merida City tour. So she did.

In Merida, they were shown the church and city hall. Claire and Audrey slept during most of the tour. At the third tourist shop, Cheryl insisted that they get taken somewhere to eat. The guide got Cheryl to a restaurant just in time.

The next day the ship arrived in Cozumel. When Cheryl and the girls got off the ship, they took a cab to the address of the Scuba Adventure. The cab dropped them off in a parking lot. There they were met by a pickup truck with a Scuba Adventure decal. Cheryl was unimpressed but decided to go with it. While the girls were getting their safety briefing in the parking lot, Cheryl took a few minutes to shop.

The dive instructor offered the girls a wetsuit at an additional charge of ten bucks each.

"We don't need a wet suit. The water is warm here," Claire told her sister.

"Right on, we don't need wetsuits," Audrey said. Neither had asked Cheryl before deciding.

Most of the others in the adventure turned down the wetsuits as well.

When all the training was completed and the gear was fitted, everyone was placed into cabs and driven up the beach highway. The cabs stopped and everyone got out. There was no real beach access or beach for that matter. Everyone just climbed over the guard rail and stepped down a few rocks to the water.

The girls got in the water and donned their gear. After a few minutes, they followed their instructor and submerged beneath the blue waters of the Caribbean. Cheryl really did not have any alternative but to find a comfortable rock to sit on.

About ninety minutes later, Cheryl was dehydrated and sunburned from the sun and reflection of the sun off the Caribbean. She had not brought any water with her. She did not know the scuba was not near a tourist beach. She did not want to leave her valuables unattended to get in the water either.

The girls surfaced. Their lips were blue and they were shivering. Both were ecstatic but cold. They now realized the water was colder thirty feet beneath the waves than at the surface.

"They should have provided wetsuits," Cheryl said while toweling them off and trying to warm them.

"They offered but Claire said we didn't need them," Audrey replied blaming Claire.

Claire shot her a look but was too cold to say anything.

The three of them hopped a cab back to the terminal. There they went in bar and ordered drinks.

The final day at sea was relaxing and the trip was a huge success.

Note: For the record, the cruise ship was the Carnival Triumph. Cheryl and the girls were on the sailing just before the ship broke down in the middle of the Caribbean for four days, on its next sailing! Carnival has not been able to connect the breakdown to Audrey and Claire yet but Cheryl still wonders.

As I was scheduled with Cheryl and friends later that month on the Triumph, we had to make other plans.

When Claire told me the story about turning down the wetsuits, I started laughing as I knew better.

Claire, Cheryl and Audrey.

Claire and Audrey before they realized the value of a wetsuit.

PART V

DAD'S CASES AND MISC. STORIES

Dad loved to tell stories. He often recounted cases from his legal practice. I have included my recollection of two of my favorites. The names have been changed not to protect the innocent but because I don't recall them. I believe the main events to be true as Dad told them many times.

Dad, Grandma, Uncle Mike and Uncle Bill 1975

Tim says Dad really needed a haircut. Luckily for Dad, there was still a chance of an inheritance.

As previously mentioned, Tim gave me a haircut when he thought I needed it. He also gave Tom a haircut before a wrestling match at Kenmore Junior High when the referee said Tom's hair was too long. Tom was so mad he pinned his opponent. It was Tom's only victory that year!

CHAPTER **39**

The Coast Guard Case

Circa 1974.

The Captain of the Coast Guard Cutter returned to his ship after spending the weekend with his family. After a briefing and a quick tour of the ship, he entered his cabin to stow his gear. Something wasn't right in his cabin. Upon further inspection, he found a pair of panties in his bed.

He called the men together and asked what had occurred over the weekend.

"Hello, Dave Olwell speaking," my Dad answered.

"Mr. Olwell, this is Captain Cooke of the Bellingham JAG office. We have had a Captain accuse his entire crew of gross misconduct. As is their right, several of the crewmen have asked for civilian representation. Your name was given to us by the Bar Association. May we assign you as counsel to one of the Seamen?" Captain Cooke said.

"Absolutely. When will I be needed?" Dad asked.

"The case is pretty straightforward. It seems the crew had a party aboard the Coast Guard Cutter when the Captain was off for the weekend. The sticking points are there were underage girls and underage drinking aboard. The Court Martial is scheduled in four weeks and you will be assigned a client tomorrow and you may have all the access you require," the Captain informed him.

"Okay, call me tomorrow with the Seaman's name and schedule a meeting with him for Friday at 9:00am," Dad said.

"Yes sir and thank you sir," the Captain said and ended the conversation.

"Seaman Scott, I am Dave Olwell. I was assigned as your civilian representation. I am a Seattle based lawyer," Dad said placing his yellow tablet on the table and sitting down across from a very nervous young man.

"Pleased to meet you sir," the Seaman said.

"Dave," Dad said.

"Sir?"

"It's Dave. You do not need to call me sir," Dad smiled, "You have been charged with Gross Misconduct, Contributing to the delinquency of Minors, Conduct unbecoming a Seaman, etc. etc. Basically, they say you were involved in a party aboard your cutter where underage girls were present and alcohol was served."

Seaman Scott just looked at him.

"Seaman Scott, Mike, this is the part of the meeting where you tell me what happened. After that the meeting will adjust to what we are going to do about what happened. So what happened?"

"The exec picked up some gals from Bellingham High School. We brought them back and had a party aboard. Somehow a pair of panties ended up in the Captain's bed but I do not know how that happened. I am married so I didn't sleep with any of them," he explained sweating profusely and wringing his hands.

"Okay Mike, the Prosecution is seeking a year in the brig with reduced pay and lowering of grade," Dad explained, "We can shoot for a better outcome at the Court Martial or I can try to get a plea bargain."

"I have a new wife at home. She counts on my pay check. There is no way our marriage will last if I am locked up for a year," Mike fretted.

"Would you tell the court what you know for a lesser charge?" Dad asked.

"Sir, I will tell what happened in any event. My honor requires that," he said.

"Good for you," Dad said. He got up from the table ending the meeting.

"Captain, what is the best outcome we can expect?" Dad asked.

"They want me to get a year for each of the crew but I think I can sell six months," the Captain offered.

"Here is what I need: thirty days in the brig, no loss of pay and no reduction of grade," Dad said.

"Is that all?" Captain Cooke laughed.

"My client was there and partied but he had no contact with any of the gals aboard. He is a newlywed. He doesn't want to lose his wife over this," Dad explained.

"If I can confirm that and he is willing to testify to what happened at the others' court martial, I might be able to get that to work," Captain Cooke said, "I'll be in touch."

Over the next couple of days, Captain Cooke was able to determine that none of the other seamen could place Scott with any of the girls. He called my Dad, "Dave, You got your deal: Thirty days, no loss of pay and no loss of grade. Yours is the best deal because you were the only one to ask for such a sweet one and you were the first to deal. This agreement is contingent on confidentiality. I don't want the other counselors to find out what you got."

"Thanks Captain. You have my word," Dad said.

"Okay, then you don't mind signing the document I had expressed to your office verifying our agreement?" the Captain asked.

"No problem, I will sign it and return it the same day. May I include my bill? You can sign off on it and forward it to the proper paper pusher's office," Dad inquired.

"If it is reasonable," the Captain said seriously.

"It will be. Thanks."

"May I help you?" Dad asked.

"Hi Mr. Olwell, I am Karina Scott," she said.

"How can I assist you Ms. Scott?"

"Mrs., I am Mike Scott's wife. Thank you for helping my husband. All the other crew were sentenced to at least six months in the brig. All lost pay and grade. I really can't thank you enough," she smiled.

"You are most welcome, the fact your husband did not fool around with any of the gals really helped his case," Dad offered.

"I need your help now," she stated.

"What can I do for you?"

"I have VD," she whispered.

"I'm not sure I can really help you with that," Dad said.

"You don't understand," she said raising her voice a little.

"I know what VD is," Dad assured her.

"I'm sure you do. No, that didn't come out right. But no, you don't understand. I slept with all the guards so they would treat Mike well when he is in the brig," she said now with tears.

"You gave all the guards watching your husband VD? They will kill him!" Dad exclaimed taking off his glasses and rubbing his face.

"Now you understand, I need your help!"

"Okay, go take care of yourself. I will deal with this," Dad promised.

"Don't tell Mike!"

"I won't," Dad said in a reassuring voice.

"Captain Scott, Dave Olwell here. Can you set a meeting with the Brig Commander and me for tomorrow morning?" Dad requested.

"I can make that happen. His name is Ensign Stark. I'll set it for 10 a.m. If there is some problem, I will call. Otherwise, see you tomorrow," the Captain said and then hung up the phone.

"Hi Ensign Stark," Dad said and introduced himself.

"Mr. Olwell, this is Chief Petty Officer Lionel. What can we do for you?" the Ensign asked.

"Here is a request for a change of disposition and a list of all the free off base clinics within thirty miles but outside of a ten mile radius,"Dad said handing him the documents.

"What's this about?" the Ensign asked without looking at the papers.

Dad explained the situation and the real concern about the safety of Seaman Scott. He went on to explain, "The clinic information is for the guards. I am sure some of the guards are married. They can't go to a base clinic as soon everyone will find out. When can my client be moved to a different brig?"

"You can't tell the United States Coast Guard what to do! Do you really think I am going to move a prisoner just because you tell me to?" the Ensign asked.

Before my Dad could reply, the Chief Petty Officer said, "Thank you Mr. Olwell. We appreciate the thoughtfulness of the clinic information. Seaman Scott will be on a bus to the Seattle brig this afternoon. Thank you for your discretion. Anything else we can do for you?"

The Ensign started to speak but stopped when the Chief lifted his hand.

"No, Thank you Chief, Ensign," Dad said and left. He knew how to take yes for an answer.

"Hi Captain, did you get my billing?" Dad asked.

Captain Cooke looked up and smiled, "Dave, I have it right here."

"Great I need to make an adjustment," Dad said and went on to tell him the story.

"I wish my wife was that concerned about my well being," the Captain laughed.

"Really?"

"Well, not that way I mean, I'll adjust your bill," he said and waved my Dad out of the office.

Forty five minutes later, Dad was sitting on the ferry upper level drinking coffee thinking how wonderful it was to be able to bill the US Coast Guard for his time aboard the ferry on such a nice day. The water of the Puget Sound was silver and Mount Rainier was in full view. It was a great way to make a living he thought to himself. He picked up his paper and started the crossword puzzle using a pen from his jacket pocket.

Dad and Dave

CHAPTER **40**

Doug Wheels Case

Circa 1976.

"We need you to get right on this," Steve from Oregon Auto Insurance said.

"Has the underwriter looked at it yet?" Dad asked. Oregon Auto was one of his biggest clients and Dad wanted to know their thoughts on the case before he formed his own.

"Yes, the policy is for $250,000. The underwriter has put it all in reserve."

"Really? I will look into this and get back with you next week," Dad said and hung up the phone. It was unusual for the underwriter to immediately put the entire policy amount in reserve so quickly. What could have caused that?

The insurance company's policy holder was driving to work in Bremerton. He was heading down a hill from the west toward Puget Sound. The sun was reflecting off the Sound and completely blinded him. His car struck a guy in a wheelchair in the cross walk. The policy holder called for an ambulance but unfortunately the guy died.

The interesting question in this case was: what was the value of a homeless guy in a wheelchair's life? Usually it was hammered out between attorneys. In this case however, the guy was Doug Schmidt. Doug was well known and liked in Bremerton. His nickname was Doug Wheels. In the past year, he had fallen in love and married a homeless gal named Cathy. Their wedding was talked about on the front page of the Bremerton newspaper. He was almost a local celebrity.

The Underwriter placing the $250,000 in reserve meant the Insurance Company thought that was what their liability would actually be. They were protected by the policy limit but their client might be on the hook for a larger judgment. Dad's job was to see that didn't happen.

Cathy's attorney, Jeff Klein, was unwilling to settle. Dad had tried several times to come to a number that was satisfactory. Klein figured a jury from Bremerton would be more generous than any of Dad's settlement offers. The case was expedited in the Bremerton courts which reinforced Klein's premise that a big payday was coming. Klein wanted a big payoff to increase his fee and the ensuing publicity the verdict would bring.

In the weeks before the trial, Dad arranged for expert testimony to prove the sun from Puget Sound was blinding. He arranged for the witnesses to be present. They would explain his client's concern and attempts to help Doug after the impact. Then Dad would do his best to negate the wife's sorrow in his end of trial summation. He was not very confident of the possible outcome.

While going over the documents, Dad came across a bill from a Funeral Home. He didn't like loose ends so he called.

"Hi, this is Dave Olwell. I am the attorney representing the driver that hit Doug Schmidt. Do you need your invoice number?" Dad asked.

"No Mr. Olwell, my name is Sarah Jacobs. I am familiar with the file. How can I help you?" she asked.

"I received a copy of your bill, has it been paid?" he asked.

"No, actually the remains have never been picked up," she said. She then went on to recall the conversation she had with the widow.

"Listen, I will see that a check is cut today. Would you be willing to testify in the upcoming trial to that conversation?" Dad asked hopefully. It was hard to compel a witness in a civil trial.

"I would like to," Sarah replied and the short telephone conversation ended.

The trial lasted about a week with expert testimony of the life of the homeless, the value of that life, his life expectancy, and how long Cathy might live. They had come up with a figure way over the policy limit before Cathy was called to the stand. Her attorney asked her to describe her marriage.

"Doug was the light of my life. We were both struggling alone on the streets. Then we met and our lives had meaning and love. I miss him so much. I lay awake at nights feeling so empty. How could this happen? How could someone just run him down like a dog in the street?" Cathy said stopping only to sob, "I'm sorry, but you don't understand the love we shared. I will never feel that way again. It is so unfair. Someone should have to pay for my pain. I have so much pain." Then she started crying uncontrollably.

"I have no further questions," Klein said handing her a Kleenex.

"Mr. Olwell?" the Judge asked.

"No questions at this time, but I reserve the right to call her at a later time if needed," Dad said.

"So noted."

"We have no further witnesses," Klein announced.

"Mr. Olwell, you may proceed and present your side of the case." The judge waited to see what Dad could possibly do to save his client.

"Your honor, I would like to call Sarah Jacobs to the stand," Dad stood and said.

"Objection your honor, Sarah Jacobs is not on any witness list I have received from Mr. Olwell," Klein announced.

"Your honor, she is a rebuttal witness to Mrs. Schmidt's testimony," Dad explained.

"Your honor this is highly irregular, I don't know how a Funeral Director can shed light on the frame of mind of a grieving widow. This should not be allowed," Jeff Klein insisted. After a short discussion at the judge's desk, he indicated he had heard enough.

"Your objection is noted but overruled. Mr. Olwell, I am giving you a very short leash on this one. Make your point quickly," the Judge warned.

"Yes, your honor," Dad said.

The Bailiff called Sarah Jacobs to the stand and swore her in.

"Please state your name and employment for the record," Dad said.

"Sarah Jacobs, Funeral Director of the Jacobs Funeral Home here in Bremerton," she answered.

"Your facility took possession of Doug Schmidt's remains, is that true?" Dad asked.

"Yes we did," she replied.

"Did you have an opportunity to speak with Cathy Schmidt?" Dad asked.

"I talked to her on the phone on one occasion," Sarah answered.

"Do you recall that conversation?"

"Very clearly," Sarah Jacobs told the court.

"Will you please tell the court what happened on that phone call?"

"Well, I called Cathy Schmidt. I asked how she would like us to prepare the remains. She asked how much we charged. I told her we charged between $2500 and $6000 depending on her wishes. She got irate and said she wouldn't pay that much. She then said, and I remember it quite vividly because it was so shocking, that we could put Doug's body in a burlap sack and throw him in the middle of Puget Sound for all she cared. Then she hung up the phone. Mr. Schmidt's remains are still in our possession even though the bill was paid by OA Insurance," she recalled.

"I object!" Klein said with his face turning red.

"On what grounds Mr. Klein?" the Judge asked. Jeff stared at the judge and then looked at his client. He was in shock at this turn of events. There went his judgment and his post trial publicity in one witness. How was he going to recover?

"May I have a short recess to confer with my client?" Klein asked.

"It is close to the noon hour, we will break for lunch and court will resume at 1:30. Court is in recess." the Judge said and banged the gavel.

About twenty minutes later, Jeff Klein tracked down Dad in the coffee shop. Dad was having coffee and a pastrami sandwich on rye. It was lean meat and very tasty. He was smiling to himself as he ate in silence.

"Dave, you really screwed me with Jacobs," Jeff said shaking his head.

"Jeff, Cathy screwed herself," Dad told him sipping his coffee and using the napkin to wipe his mouth.

"We need to settle this," Jeff said hoping to recover something of his dignity.

"Now we need to settle?" Dad laughed a bit taking a big bite of his sandwich.

"I know. I have been dodging your settlement offers for months but give me a break will you?" Klein pleaded as he waited for Dad to finish chewing before his answer.

"Jeff, this situation is a tragedy for everyone involved. My original first offer was $60,000 as it was truly an accident and that's what we felt was fair. My highest offer was $100,000. Why don't we say the $100,000 offer still stands," Dad said, "I really don't think that jury will give her that much but it is fair."

"Thanks, Dave. I thought you would let me twist in the wind. I'll make Cathy understand it is more than fair. Give me a few minutes to talk to her," Jeff said and left the coffee shop.

Dad took another sip of coffee as he examined how to take his next bite of this excellent sandwich. It tasted even better after their conversation.

"I settled the case," Dave told Steve from OA Insurance later on the phone.

"That bad, huh?" Steve asked thinking the verdict had gone way against their insured.

"No, that good, $100,000," Dad said proudly.

"You're kidding? How did you pull that off?" Steve said with joy in his voice.

"Buy me a drink and I'll explain the whole thing," Dad responded.

"Dave, you don't drink!" Steve laughed.

"Okay, I got two tickets to the Sonics' game on Thursday. I will explain over dinner. You're buying," Dad laughed.

"Call me with the name of the restaurant. I can't wait to hear this. Thanks Dave, really great work." Steve realized that Dad had just saved his insurance company $150,000.00. He had come through again.

Note: Dad invited ten people for opening day of baseball season every year. I was invited most years but he always invited his contacts at Oregon Auto. They loved to bring up this case at dinner. I learned a lot about my dad's cases during these Mariners games.

I have previously shared this and other stories with several friends and family members. This was to allow them to share their thoughts in the form of intros at the beginning of the chapters.

The most frequent comment was that they didn't remember the events the same way I did. Usually some small detail was different from their memory.

For example, in **You Remind me of one of my Students***, Rudy comments that he was drinking a Tom Collins and I wrote it was a Screwdriver in the following story. I asked him how that really changes the story. He just pointed out I was wrong. I found it interesting he argued my description of the drink and not his attire that evening!*

The most common liberty I have taken when writing my stories deals with timing. I often combine several actual events that occurred at different points of time into the same story.

Rudy was my best friend from 6th grade on. Along with Jon Edwards, Dave Bardy, Steve Garren and Scott Beedell, Rudy is one of my important lifelong friends.

Aunt Mary Jo and me at Grandma Wink's 90th Birthday

CHAPTER 41

You Remind Me Of One Of My Students

Rudy: "I went to Hawaii twice with Robert. Both times we stayed with his aunt Mary Jo. She was awesome and the trips were amazing. I have different memories of some of the events in this trip like I drank a Tom Collins at the Spaghetti Factory not a Screwdriver but one fact is certain: I got the girl!"

Mary Jo adds: "I had a wonderful time entertaining Robert, Rudy and CJ as their tour guide. The encounter at the Spaghetti Factory had me laughing so hard that I thought I was going to pee myself. I am happy to be a part in this 'Great Event' in history." Circa 1982.

"Excuse me, Miss," I said getting the flight attendant's attention.

"What can I do for you?" she asked.

"My earphones don't work and neither do theirs," I explained pointing to my friends.

"Let me see what we can do," she said and went to the front of the plane and placed a call for maintenance.

A short time later, a guy in a Canadian Airlines jumpsuit came back to our seats and asked us to get up. He crammed his body into the aisle and started taking the seats apart. After a several minutes, he explained to the flight attendant that it could not be fixed in the few minutes we had before takeoff.

"I'm sorry gentleman, it doesn't look like we can fix it," she told us.

"That's okay," Rudy said.

"Yeah, no it isn't. We need to change seats then. I am not sitting on this plane without music or the ability to watch the movie. Do you expect me to listen to these idiots for five hours?" I asked rather firmly.

She scowled at me but then really looked at Rudy and CJ for the first time. She nodded at me and then walked back toward the front of the plane.

"What's the big deal?" C.J. asked.

"Why are you causing a problem?" Rudy added.

"Watch, listen and learn," I smiled at them.

The flight attendant returned, "Please gather your things and follow me."

We did as asked and followed her to the front of the 747. Rudy was worried we were getting thrown off the plane. He was relieved when she directed us to a stairway to the upper section of the plane behind the cockpit. There were five spacious rows of seats. She pointed to three empty seats.

"I hope these will be to your satisfaction," she offered with a forced smile.

"Thank you," was all I could come up with.

After we settled in, Rudy turned to me and said, "These are awesome."

"Pretty cool, huh," I smiled.

"I still don't know why you made a big deal out of it," C.J. commented.

"Robert's always working some angle, you'll learn," Rudy informed him.

"Listen, after Greg's parents told me there was a seatbelt law in Canada; I was stressed out the whole drive this morning. You know my car doesn't have seat belts. I figured we were going to get hassled at the border. Then all the speed limit signs are in kilometers. How fast is 100 Kph anyway? My car was so old it doesn't have seatbelts. If it doesn't have seat belts do you think it had a metric reading speedometer? I was sure I was going to get pulled over for speeding then busted for no seat belts. Even after we arrived at the airport, I still had to get you two idiots on the plane with all your things. Besides, without a movie and music, I would have to listen to you two the whole flight. I need a drink."

"Would you care for a refreshment?" our new flight attendant asked after overhearing me.

"Coke, please," I responded.

"Same," C.J. smiled.

"I'll have a brewski," Rudy said.

"Excuse me," the attendant said directing her attention to him.

"Oh sorry, a brewski eh?" he laughed thinking he had spoken Canadian.

She didn't laugh, "May I see some i.d., please?"

Rudy handed her his ID. "Nineteen," he said proudly.

"You're using a library card for id? What is a Mossyrock?" the attendant asked.

"What? Oh, here is my driver's license," Rudy said sheepishly.

"We have Labatt's, Heineken, or Budweiser," she said shaking her head and returning his driver's license.

"Heineken," he replied.

She gave him the beer and went on to help others.

After that, we settled in. C.J. and I were talking after the movie ended and Rudy was heckling the college-aged guys in the row behind us. He was saying, "Eh" after every sentence. They were really starting to get annoyed. Then he started making fun of Canadian Football. After a brief exchange which ended with Rudy saying, "In the NFL, we have four downs because in America we can count past three."

I decided I better intercede, "Sorry guys, you remember when you had your first beer?"

They laughed and the tension was broken.

I knew they would laugh because others had laughed when Dave Bardy, my college roommate had said that about me.

I grabbed Rudy and took him forward by the bathroom right behind the cockpit.

"Quit mocking everyone, I want to get off this plane in one piece," I scolded.

"Hey, look the cockpit," Rudy said completely ignoring me and walked right into the cockpit. "Can I get you guys a beer? They're giving them away for free out here."

"I think we are good," the Pilot laughed.

Rudy said 'hello' and started asking all kinds of questions. We had seen quite a few passengers peek in the cockpit for a moment then quickly be removed by the flight attendant. She came to grab us when I said, "My brother is a fighter pilot in the air force."

With that, the copilot waved off the attendant and we proceeded to chat for about a half an hour. Things were going great until the pilot asked, "What plane does your brother fly?"

"The F-111," I replied proudly.

"The Canadian Air force doesn't fly the F-111," he said.

"Oh, he is in the U.S. Air force, we are from Seattle," I clarified.

With that the whole demeanor in the cockpit changed. We were kicked out. Too bad for them, I was about to offer them a free beer. We were dismissed to allow Canadians in. The rest of the flight was pretty uneventful.

We were met in Honolulu by my aunt Mary Jo. We loaded up the car and headed to Kailua.

After a few days of acclimating to the weather and the people, I decided to show off my prowess with the womenfolk. Rudy, CJ and I arrived at Kailua beach. It was within walking distance from my Aunt's house. The beach was empty except one gal on a beach blanket. I gave Rudy and CJ a nod and headed her way.

"The beach is a little crowded today, mind if I sit here?" I asked.

She looked at the empty beach, reached up and lowered her sunglasses and looked at me and said, "Go ahead," then raised her glasses back up.

We chatted for a few minutes. I had her laughing a bit which was always a good sign. Rudy and CJ came over and sat near. I gave them a nod indicating I had everything under control with this woman.

"You remind me of one my students," she casually commented.

"Really? What do you teach?" I asked, knowing she was interested in me and this was starting to get somewhere. I smiled at Rudy and gave him a little smile.

"Special Ed," she said.

Well after that, things went all downhill. I couldn't make a move with Rudy and CJ laughing out loud how I was like her students.

She tried to fix the damage stating that was not how she meant it but the damage was done. Finally, I couldn't stand it anymore and said goodbye and sulked off.

That evening, we decided to take the family out to dinner to say thank you for letting us stay with them. Mary Jo decided on the Spaghetti Factory in Honolulu. When we arrived, we were told there was a thirty minute wait. In the lobby, a waitress asked Mary Jo if she would like a drink.

"I'll have a screwdriver," my aunt replied.

"Me too," Rudy proclaimed.

C.J. and I ordered Cokes and the waitress went off.

"You don't even know what a screwdriver is," I confronted Rudy.

"No, I don't, but I will in a minute," Rudy smiled.

The drinks arrived and I paid for them. Mary Jo was impressed that I actually had a wallet and said as much.

Rudy was drinking his screwdriver through the stir stick. I commented that that was stupid looking.

"What? Did you learn the proper screwdriver drinking technique in Special ED?" Rudy said sarcastically.

"You're a jackass," I told him and looked to CJ for support. He wasn't paying attention and he too was drinking through his stir stick.

"What is that about Special Ed?" Mary Jo asked. CJ recounted my women chasing and they all had a good laugh at my expense.

Rudy elbowed me and brought my attention to a couple of gals who arrived in the lobby. One was stunning, a 10, and the other was okay, a 7. I turned to talk to Rudy but he was already approaching the girls. He stopped in front of the stunner, took a long drink through his stir stick and then said, "Hi, my name is Rudy. What's your friend's name?"

The really cute girl looked like she was slapped. The other gal beamed.

"My name is Eileen," she said for herself.

The cute gal decided to redeem herself by getting a guy for herself. She looked at CJ and me; then wandered off to find one.

We were seated for dinner. Rudy ordered another screwdriver. When dinner arrived, Rudy ordered a third.

"You better slowdown there Cowboy," Mary Jo said.

"Cowboy?" I asked. Then I looked at Rudy. He was wearing blue jeans one size too small. He was wearing a blue tank top; two sizes too small. He needed a haircut and he hadn't shaved in about eight weeks. You could tell because his twenty facial hairs were getting long. On top of his head was a cowboy hat of sorts. You know the floppy leather hat you see in old Cowboy movies on the donkey or in this case the ass.

Anyway, halfway through dinner, Rudy got up from the table and went over to Eileen's table.

"Hi, you want to go dancing?" he asked Eileen.

Eileen looked at her parents and the cute gal for guidance.

"You're old enough to decide for yourself," her Dad said.

She smiled at her friend, placed her napkin on the table and got up and left with Rudy.

Mary Jo just lifted her drink to him as he looked back leaving the restaurant.

CJ started to say something.

"Just don't," I said and he laughed.

The next morning, I noticed Rudy wasn't in the house. Mary Jo was taking us to Hanauma Bay so I grabbed some things and headed out front. We found Rudy sleeping in the back seat of her Toyota.

"The door was locked so I slept in here," he said.

"Dude, we left the back door open," I said and we all laughed.

On the drive to the bay, Rudy described his evening. After dancing and necking, he realized he had missed the last metro bus from Honolulu. He caught a ride on the Marine Base Liberty Bus.

We all thought that was pretty funny based on his long hair and outfit.

The rest of the week was a blur. We bought Mary Jo a six pack of Heineken before we left. It was our little thank you for the hospitality.

After the flight back to Vancouver, we dropped Rudy off and C.J. and I were soon back at WSU.

"Then she said she taught Special Ed," CJ said and all my dorm mates burst out laughing.

"Really, she said that?" Dave Bardy asked me.

"Yes," I said with a sigh. I just went in my room and shut the door. I tried to ignore their amusement. But it had been pretty funny. Too bad it was at my expense once again.

My cousin, Ben Morrow, and me.

The **Teasing Mom** story illustrates the fun Olwells have when we get together. Our mother is extremely tolerant of our good natured kidding. Dad was outwardly funny and Mom's humor was much more clever.

Occasionally, one of us would upset her. With seven kids, if each of us upset her once a week, was she ever not upset? We knew if we could make her laugh it would be okay.

In the picture above, Aunt Mary Jo is a brunette. I am fifty years old and I have never seen her without blonde hair. She must have dyed her hair brunette for Mom's wedding. Yeah, that must be it. (the top row: third from left) I guess I am Teasing Auntie, too.

CHAPTER **42**

Teasing Mom

Mom comments: " 'TEASING MOM' IS CERTAINLY RIGHT! You *make my life sound like one happy round of booze, cigarettes and sex!"* *(Actually I was only referring to her 20s.)* "To say nothing of 'sucking in *my lips!' Ha! Even though you're 50, you still know how to raise the hair* *on the back of my neck. But just think about it, if you start planning* *now, you might be ready for my 90th Birthday! Oh, and I expect* *something BIG from you Robert so start saving!" Circa 1993.*

It had been a few years since all of the Olwell children had been together. Grandma Wink's 90th birthday was an event that brought everyone from across the country and around the world. We were gathered at the old family house looking out at Lake Washington in Kenmore. It was fun sitting on the back deck chatting together. We always sat at the back of the house to limit the disturbance to our neighbors. We had been loud enough as kids; we didn't need to cause our neighbors any heartburn as adults. I had just turned thirty and Allison was the only Olwell child still in her twenties.

After a lively discussion about all the summer jobs we had held around Kenmore, Tim asked, "Mom, what did you in your twenties?"

"In my twenties? Let me see," our mother said thoughtfully, "I spent my twenties pregnant, breast feeding and mainly changing cloth diapers." Back then, disposable diapers were unheard of and you had to have a diaper service or rinse the diapers out in a toilet and then wash them in a machine. Mom had a service for a brief time but mostly rinsed and washed them as part of her daily routine.

"Pregnant? Diapers?" Veronica laughed.

"Think about it, I had eight children in eleven years," Mom laughed.

"Wow, you must have been quite the player, Mom," I commented, "I didn't know Dad was such a stud."

"Excuse me?" she asked in a disapproving voice, reaching for her glass.

"Eight kids in eleven years? You and Dad must have been all over each other like a couple of rabbits," I laughed and was joined by my six siblings.

"I was asleep most of the time," Mom said sarcastically.

"Really, Dad must have been a considerate lover," I pointed out.

"Why would you say that?" Mom asked, then immediately regretted that she had.

"I think it would be considerate if he didn't even wake you during sex," I laughed again joined by my siblings. We all reached for our drinks as we waited for Mom's reaction. She was sucking in a deep breath.

Mom scowled then laughed. She threatened to go inside. Instead, she took a long pull on her favorite alcoholic beverage and bummed a cigarette from Dianne. When her children gathered like this, she always had a favorite adult beverage handy. She didn't smoke very much; Tim claims it is mostly when I was around.

"Careful, she will take your picture down," Tim warned.

When our mother was mad at one of us she wouldn't even want to look at us. So she would take that child's picture off her desk at work and put it in a drawer. Then one day she would get over her anger or disappointment and put your picture back up. Sometime, your picture would reappear just so another could be hidden. It was a small drawer. The way things were going all of our pictures might end up in the garbage can. Tim made the joke because Tom had told him that his own picture was currently absent. I'm not saying she was mad at Tom a lot but every picture frame on her desk was sun faded except his. I thought I should smooth things over with my sharp wit.

"Sorry Mom, I was just kidding --- except for the fact you and Dad must have been hitting it like rabbits for a decade," I said.

Mom picked up her drink and went in the house. The rest of my siblings had enough respect to let her go in the house before laughing.

A few minutes later, she returned with a fresh drink.

"Mom, what was your job after working at your father's cleaners?" Veronica asked. Our Grandfather Pete Wink owned "Wink the Cleaners" and his children took turn working at the cleaners or doing chores at home. They did a thriving dry cleaning and wash- dry-fold business in North Seattle.

"Let's see. I worked as a demo lady on weekends," she reflected.

"What is that?" Allison asked.

"You know, when you go into a grocery store and they have a representative in front of a display talking about and sometimes giving away a product to improve sales," she clarified.

"Okay, what did you demo?" Veronica asked.

"I worked for Phillip Morris," she said, "They would send in a couple of pallets of cigarettes to the store."

"Cigarettes?" Tim asked.

"Yes, it was a good deal. I would make an arrangement that if I sold the entire product that I would be paid for Friday, Saturday, and Sunday. The store management never thought I could and would agree. Then I would try and get all the cigarettes sold by Saturday afternoon. Then I would get paid for Sunday and not have to work it. I was pretty successful at getting most Sundays off. It was really motivating getting paid for not working."

"Wasn't selling cigarettes enough of a motivation for you?" I asked.

Once again my siblings laughed except Dianne, who was the only one smoking at the time. Tom was in the process of lighting up a Marlboro and smiled.

"I should have dropped you on your head," she said lovingly.

"You did drop him on his head," Dianne pointed out while spilling her ash on her shirt as she laughed, reminiscent of Grandpa Brick and his cigarettes.

"Dianne!?" Mom exclaimed.

"You brought him home from the hospital and placed the baby carrier on the kitchen table and it fell off, remember?" Dianne reminded.

"So Robert is Mom's fault? All these years, she has been blaming Dad for him," Tim said shaking his head in disapproval.

"Wait a minute!" Mom said trying to keep things under control.

"You dropped me on my head?" I asked in my fake pathetic voice.

"Not often enough!" she rebounded.

My siblings laughed. Tim wondered out loud if Mom had smoked while pregnant with me. She certainly had been a drinker during her entire twenties as there was not the federal advice against it during pregnancy back in the early 60's.

Mom announced she had to start food prep for dinner and went into the kitchen where she was closer to her adult beverage counter and farther from me. Conversation drifted to High School days and who had spent the most time in the Vice Principal's office. Dianne was sure she was the winner. Tom told us he was better at avoiding the Vice Principal than we were. David was aghast that we thought principal visits were prized possessions. Veronica claimed she never even met a Principal at Inglemoor. The conversation went on long into the night. Tim later claimed that Mom didn't rejoin the group until I left to visit friends.

Twanoh State Park

Dianne, John Milot, Dave, Dad and Tim 1960

CHAPTER **43**

Twanoh State Park

Tim adds: "I remember Dad telling this story years later. His version ended with " 'I wouldn't have been banned for life if your Mom had handled the attendant better, Geez.' " Plenty of facts; the trip occurred, the individuals were all there, Dad and Mr. Hare were drunk, and Allison ran around naked whenever she could. I think she still does."

Mom says: "Well, the facts are sort of crooked. Carol Hare and I left Seattle with 9 kids on Thursday afternoon.   Your Dad and Steve Hare were supposed to come up that evening however, they didn't make it. In fact they didn't make it on Friday either.

As it started to pour down rain Thursday night, Friday was a mess with 9 kids in the Apache tent trailer. Clothes were hung up to dry everywhere and I was literally frying your tennis shoes to dry them and then shooing you all out into the rain to play again.

So, Mrs. Hare and I had had enough and decided to leave. Only the station wagon had a flat tire, so not only couldn't we leave but we couldn't even call the fathers to YELL at them. We couldn't change the tire. A nice man offered to help but the spare also was flat. Your Dad had neglected to have it fixed.

Mrs. Hare was a chocoholic and by this time she was literally popping chocolate into her mouth as fast as she could, two at a time.

Then, when the fathers came of course the sun came out and they offered to watch you kids so that Carol and I could go to Belfair to have the tire fixed and shop. We decided since we had taken their car that we should play "Daddy" and be irresponsible. We stopped and had a beer and laughed all the way home, we were so pleased with ourselves! HA!

The rest it true! When we returned to the park, they were passed out snoring and you kids were running wild. I didn't know about the banning, that must have happened on another trip after your father and I were divorced!" Circa 1998 and 1967.

"We're here!" I declared to the children as Cheryl turned the Explorer off the highway and entered Twanoh State Park.

The kids became alert as Cheryl cautiously maneuvered our trailer over the speed bumps. She put the car in park. After exiting the car, she went into the office.

A few minutes later, an old lady in uniform came out of the office and looked closely and strangely at me and then at Claire. She shook her head then returned to the office.

"What was that all about?" I asked Cheryl when she opened the car door to get back in.

"I was going to ask you the same thing," she replied in all seriousness.

"What happened in there?" I asked.

"I went in and filled out the registration card. The lady was real pleasant. We were chatting when she asked me to spell our last name. When I did, she stiffened. Then she asked me if I was related to David and Connie Olwell. When I told her they were your parents, she got up and came out and looked at you," Cheryl explained.

"She looked like she was trying to recognize me. She nodded her head once she saw Claire," I recalled.

"Well, she came back in and put me on notice she would be watching us. She told me to tell you this had better not be a repeat of your last visit. She also said that Claire is definitely an Olwell."

"Last visit? I haven't been here since I was around six years old. Is she old enough to remember thirty years ago?" I asked.

"Must be. What happened on that trip?" my wife asked.

"We are almost there, Carol," my mother said casually from the driver's seat of the sedan.

"It sure is nice going on one of these camping trips in a leisurely fashion. I still can't believe you made the boys bring the kids up yesterday and set up camp," she said.

"It was fun shopping this morning, wasn't it? Anyway, I am sick and tired of our husbands sending us with the kids on Friday to set up. Then they come rolling in half drunk out of their minds at two or three a.m. and then sleeping in all afternoon on Saturday while we tend to the kids. I figured this would teach them how hard it is to take care of the

Robert L. Olwell

kids on a camping trip. Besides the kids so look forward to spending time with their father. He works such long hours during the week. Our husbands will appreciate us more," Mom told her.

"Yes, they will. We sure showed them. Hey, what's that?" Carol asked pointing down the road.

My mother looked up in time to see my three year old sister, Allison, running across the highway naked. She slowed the car then looked at Carol who returned her worried look. All the kids were chasing each other around the park. As our car slowed for the speed bumps, the lady at the park office scowled at them.

After parking the car, they came upon Veronica and me.

"I am done watching her, it's your turn!" Veronica told me.

"I don't want to! You keep watching her," I yelled.

"It's your turn to WATCH HER!" Veronica yelled back.

"Watch who?" my mother interrupted.

We were both startled.

"Hi, Mom. Allison, I am tired of watching her, it's Bobby's turn," Veronica announced.

"You're watching her? Where is your sister?" Mom asked and she wasn't looking very happy.

My sister and I looked at each other then all around and neither of us could see her. We just shrugged our shoulders.

"She is across the street at the wading pool. Take her some clothes, go get her dressed and bring her back here," Mother demanded.

We did not have to be asked twice, this time. We decided we had better take our time. Mom and Carol went and looked in the trailer. Dad and Mr. Hare were passed out and there were beer cans everywhere. This did not sit too well with the wives. Then Mother looked at the case of beer and started picking up the cans.

"You're not going to clean up after them are you?" Carol asked.

My Mom just directed her attention to the case when she was done then to the ashtray where Dad's lighter was. Carol seemed to understand.

"David, Toby, Dianne come here NOW!" Mom yelled.

With that all the kids started returning to the camp site including Veronica, Allison and me. Mom just held out her hand to David and Toby.

"What?" David asked innocently.

241

Mom turned his attention to the twenty four spaces in the case of beer. There were six full cans and fourteen empty cans. She looked at the four vacant spaces then back at my eldest brother and his friend.

David just walked over to his tent and pulled out three of the missing beers.

"There are four missing," Mom said placing the beer on the table and returning her hands to her hips. "Well?"

Timmy stepped forward and handed her an empty can and smiled.

Mom sighed and didn't return the smile as she took the can.

"You're eleven years old! Did you really drink that?" Carol asked Timmy.

"Not all in one sip like Mr. Hare, I tried but it took me three," Timmy said. He looked disappointed in himself while recounting it. "If you give me a few more for practice, I am sure I can drink it in one sip."

Carol did not like what he had said one bit but she just looked distressed at my Mom.

"Dianne!" Mother said next and held her hand out to my sister.

Dianne looked around and slowly down at the ground. Then reached her hand into the pocket of her jacket and pulled out Dad's cigarettes. She placed the pack in Mom's hand.

Mom left her hand out. After an uneasy pause, Dianne pulled some more cigarettes out of the other pocket.

"We'll discuss the beer and cigarettes later. Why was your three year old sister crossing the street by herself?" Mom asked.

David looked at Dianne. She looked at Tim. He pointed to Tom. Tom glared at Veronica who said, "Dianne was supposed to watch her."

Dianne looked miffed at that. She turned on her younger sister then composed herself.

"She used the crosswalk didn't she?" Dianne asked hopefully.

My mother pursed her lips and inhaled deeply. That was enough of a response.

"You kids clean this area up! Right now," Carol directed saving us and Mom's sanity.

We all started talking.

"SHHH! You will wake up Dad and Mr. Hare," Dianne warned us.

"You kids make all the noise you want. I'll deal with your father," Mom said.

While we were cleaning up, Carol and Mom sat down in the lawn chairs. Mom reached for two of the beers David had returned to her. She opened one and handed it to Carol. Then she opened the other.

"It's one o'clock. A little early for that isn't it?" Carol said.

"Really?" Mom asked.

Carol looked back toward the trailer and all of us kids cleaning up the campground. Allison was naked again. She shook her head and took a long drink of the beer.

A short while later, Tim came by and said, "The park lady wants to see you in the office. She wants to know when we are leaving."

Mom just took another drink of her beer and walked slowly toward the office.

Later there was plenty of yelling coming from the travel trailer. I didn't understand a lot of it. But I did hear my mother say, "Banned for life," and Dad saying, "Sorry," a lot.

"How was I supposed to know the lady would still be alive, still working and still remember the family?" I asked after recounting the events.

"You picked the park," Cheryl said.

"Let's just set up camp. I'm not my father and you're definitely not my mother," I laughed.

"What's that supposed to mean?" she asked and she wasn't laughing.

"I mean who would send ten kids camping with two guys who drank way too much? Please, what was she thinking?"

"Wow, what was she thinking?"

After setting up the trailer, I told the kids to go look for the sign that said "No Olwells". I told them to look high in the trees as they had probably grown taller since the late 1960's. That kept them busy for a while.

Note: I loved camping in the tent trailer as a kid. I have really good memories with the family on those occasions. My kids experienced similar enjoyment when Cheryl and I purchased our own tent trailer when they were younger. Cheryl wanted to go camping and sleep in a tent on the ground, hence the tent trailer: Marital compromise!

Mom, Tim and Evelyn

CHAPTER **44**

Tim Visits

Tim: "The night of hanging around with our high school buddies is still a great memory. We didn't sit around recalling old times, we made a new adventure that is now the basis of this story. All of the guys mentioned in this story I still consider friends, even if I haven't seen them in years. This rendition is remarkably accurate." Circa 1988.

"Awesome, I'll be there in an hour," I said, hanging up the phone.

I turned to my wife and explained my brother, Tim, and his wife were in town for the weekend. I was heading out to my Mom's house to meet up with him. Then we were going to hook up with our brother Tom. Although invited, she knew better than to participate. She did suggest I invite my brother and sister in law over for lunch or dinner the following day.

On the drive from Everett to Kenmore, I tried to remember the last time Tim was in town. I think it was before he left for London in 1981. Since then, I had gone to and graduated from WSU and had married. I was also bigger; Tim had always tested how big I was by knocking me down. He had not tried it since I blindsided him with a kidney punch during our visit for his 1980 graduation in Colorado. The fact that I punched him in his van in the middle of the intersection didn't stop Tim from placing the van in park and knocking me around for a few minutes. That really impressed his date who was sitting in the passenger seat. Never the less, I made a mental note to be vigilant.

"Hello!" I said walking in the folks' house in Kenmore.

Mom came out of the kitchen and shushed me as Tim was on the phone with our brother Dave. I entered the kitchen and sat down at the kitchen table.

"Her usual self," Tim said on the phone. He then burst out laughing and said, "Who knows but I'm not going to ask."

He then passed the phone around and we all chatted with Dave for a few moments while our stepfather kept asking for money for the long distant call. After a short visit, we headed out to meet the guys.

We arrived at The Lake Forest Tavern after collecting Tom and Bill Taylor at Bill's house in Canyon Park. Tim and I went and ordered a beer while they claimed an unused pool table. I reluctantly agreed to team up with Tim. I was reluctant because I sucked at pool. We chatted and played pool for awhile. When Doug Clapper arrived, Tim bought him a beer and I gave him my rotation in the pool game.

Tim was in the middle of a shot when a couple of guys started hanging around us. Then one of them placed quarters on the table after seeing him miss the easy shot. By placing the quarters on the table, they were signifying the right to play the winner of the current game. Tim and Tom were annoyed as we were just playing for fun and to pass the time.

On his next turn, Tim purposely pocketed the eight ball out of turn. This made Tom and Bill the winners. I went and sat at the bar. Tim told them to do their best but to do it slowly.

As the game progressed, every time one of the other team set a beer down, Tim walked by and exchanged his empty glass for it. Tim would drink their beer to create another empty glass. It took a while for the other guys to figure out what was going on. Any idiot would realize eventually that if you put down a full beer and pick up an empty beer, something was going on. The final straw was when one of the guys was handed a new beer by the bartender, set it down to reach into his pocket for money, paid the bartender and then picked up an empty glass. The look on his face was priceless.

He turned to Tim who was enjoying the beer. His face started turning red.

"Thanks for the beer," Tim said.

He looked like he was going to say or do something. His friend stepped between him and my brother.

"Dude, I was just screwing with you. Go sit down and I'll send over a pitcher," Tim said in a jovial fashion.

They went back to their table.

"Should I send them an empty pitcher?" Tim asked me and started laughing. "Hey bartender, I need a pitcher of the cheapest beer you sell for my new friends."

He sent it over and we sat at the bar for a minute.

"Too bad Dave's not here," Tim sighed.

"Yeah it is. Hey what was all that laughing on the phone at Mom's?"

"He asked me if Mom was crazy because Dad was drunk or if Dad was drunk because Mom was crazy?" he laughed.

"Wow," I replied, "Hey Tom, why did the drunk cross the road? To get away from his wife." Well, Tim and I thought it was funny. Tom just smiled and went back to playing pool.

Tim passed a note to the bartender who was pretty good looking. She gave a small smile and a nod.

"Okay everyone to the bar," Tim said loud enough to be heard by all, "$2 each and the winner gets it all."

"What's the bet?" Tom asked approaching the bar with cue stick still in hand.

"Whoever guesses the color of the bartender's panties wins. Who wants to go first? How about you, Robert?" Tim asked directing the chaos.

I placed my hands to my temples. "My ex-ray vision says she's not a natural blonde." Well the bar erupted and the bartender scowled at me. I placed my $2 on the bar and guessed, "Pink."

The guesses went around the bar. "White, Red, Purple, Blue, None, Black, Beige, Green," until every color was exhausted. There was about $30 in the pile when everyone who wanted to participate had their guess.

"Who guessed Black?" the bartender asked.

To everyone's surprise but mine, as the note now made sense, Tim let out a yell. The guys patted him on the shoulder and lifted their glasses to him. Shortly, everyone went back to what they were doing.

"Give me my $2 back," I demanded laughing.

Tim looked at me and knew. He gave me $2 and split the rest of the money with the bartender. He gave me a smile and a nod.

A few minutes later, Tim refilled Bill's glass from a pitcher.

"I got the next pitcher," Bill offered.

Tim looked as if he got an idea. He smiled and headed to the bar.

"Okay, you pour a pitcher of whatever beer you have. If we can guess what type of beer it is, we get it for free. If we can't, we'll pay double," Tim proposed to the bartender.

She smiled and agreed. We went over to gather up the guys while she filled a secret pitcher. She saw there were five of us and poured five glasses. Everyone picked up their glass and examined it.

"What do you think?" Tim asked me.

"Me? I don't drink beer. What are the draft choices?"

"Bud, Bud Light, Miller, Rainier and Red Hook," she listed.

"It's not Red Hook, we play their team in Lacrosse and they always bring a keg. The color is wrong and it's not heavy enough. After that, I have no idea," I told the guys.

"Robert narrowed it down to four. Okay, what do you guys think?" Tim asked turning to Tom, Bill and Doug.

They sipped and huddled and came up with Rainier.

Tim turned to me, leaned in and whispered it was Bud. Then he turned to the bartender and declared, "We think it is Rainier."

"Sorry guys it was Bud, that will be $16," she declared with a broad smile.

"Damn, pay the lady," Tim said patting Bill on the shoulder, "I tried to get it for you for free." Tim then picked up the pitcher and walked away.

Bill was trying to figure out what happened as he gave the bartender the money.

The rest of the evening was pretty uneventful except for Bill walking up to a table of two guys and gals and asking the gals if they wanted to dance with a real man. That was a little dicey for a few moments.

Uneventful except for having the bouncer chase us through the parking lot trying to get the bar's glasses back from Bill and Doug. Tim gave the glasses back before they called the police. Tim commented it may have been nice to see Jay Lyons again.

Uneventful except for showing up at Doug's house to bbq steaks at 2 a.m. and interacting with Doug's pissed off wife. The fact we were lighting the barbeque in the kitchen had nothing to do with her anger. She must have had a bad day.

Uneventful except for Bill getting arrested at Hagen's taking a pee behind the store while we were buying steaks. Tim and Tom bailed him out in no time.

Yeah, it was pretty uneventful.

The next afternoon, Tim and Ev arrived at my house for a late lunch. After introductions to my wife, Tim and Ev sat down in the family room adjoining the kitchen. I was chopping some carrots when my wife grabbed my forearm and squeezed it hard.

I turned to her. She leaned in, "He's eating the potpourri!"

"Tim, that's potpourri," I said as he took another handful of the dried flowers and spices used to scent the air.

"Whatever it is, it isn't very good," Tim said.

Note: To this day, Tim still doesn't understand what potpourri is for but at least I haven't seen him eat it since. He continues to blame me for not having finger food out for him. In retrospect, I should not have said anything and let him continue to eat the potpourri. His breath was fresh that day.

McDonald's Barbie Happy Meal Toy.

CHAPTER **45**

Christmas Tree

Circa 1996.

"But we need a tree!" Bonnie continued.

"I didn't budget for lobby decorations. I always make my numbers," I explained again.

"What can I spend then?" Bonnie persisted, "Our lobby needs to look good for Christmas."

"Forty dollars is all I have in petty cash," I said looking in the safe.

"I will make that work," she smiled.

"Fine, but you know our budget," I finally conceded.

With that she was gone. She knew how to take yes for an answer. Bonnie was our hostess at the Mill Creek McDonald's. She had been keeping me on track since I came to this restaurant as a Second Assistant Manager and continued as I returned as the Manager. I smiled to myself and went back to work.

"Did you see that tree? It must have cost a fortune," Justin asked.

He laughed as I snapped my head up. He knew we had no budget for a big tree as McDonald's was all about controlling the pennies. I came around the corner from the office and saw the tree. It was an eight foot Douglas Fir and it was magnificent.

"Before you say anything," Bonnie started, "if you let me use our old Happy Meal Toys as ornaments I will stay in budget. My neighbor runs the Christmas Tree lot and gave me a deal."

"Okay, it is a nice tree," I said and went about preparing for the lunch crowd.

After lunch, I commented on how nice the tree looked in passing. Bonnie was pleased with the acknowledgement.

About four or five days later, my area supervisor came in. "What the hell is that?" she exclaimed.

"What?" I asked. It was odd to hear her talk like that.

"That!" she said pointing at our tree in the lobby.

"Looks good doesn't it?" I asked.

"Look at it!" she said then glared at me, "Look at it!"

So for the first time I really looked at our tree. I thought it looked pretty good. The tree was nice. The lights were nice. The garland matched the lobby décor. The ornaments. Then it dawned on me. You see, the last Happy Meal toy was Barbie. The only Barbies we had left were Black. Therefore, we had a tree in our lobby with a bunch of black people hanging from it. Not quite the symbolism McDonald's was going for.

"Hey Bonnie, go into the office and get the Whiteout!" I yelled to my hostess.

The supervisor snapped her head around at me.

"It's a joke. We'll fix the tree!" I assured her.

She assured me that we would.

Alex, Audrey and Claire 1995

CHAPTER **46**

Santa Didn't Come

Cheryl: " If you've read any of Robert's stories, you know that he has a two fact rule. The unfortunate part is that this story is all true. The fortunate part is that the children were all young enough to have no actual recollection of these events. Robert did miraculously recover from this "Ohhhh crrraaaaapppp" moment." Circa 1994.

Anyone with kids can understand the thrill spending Christmas Eve and Christmas Day driving around the state in your car from house to house to ensure the grandparents are not disappointed. My Mom, my Dad, her Dad, and her Mom all expected a visit. The car would be used extensively on these days. I have often felt we should have placed our Christmas tree in the back of the car! At least, we would have seen it more! It is interesting that our parents were never sympathetic to this plight.

Of course, they never bring up the fact that drinking a half rack of Lucky Beer in the car was okay when they were hauling me and my singing brothers and sisters around to visit their parents and friends. As a matter of fact, now that my mother has a home in Palm Springs, I think she was a little disappointed we did not drive the 1200 miles to see her Christmas morning.

After the normal friends and family tour on Christmas Eve in 1995, my wife and I arrived home late. We were exhausted. I always find it tiring to watch my brother, Tom, cook all day to feed me.

We put our daughters to bed and collapsed onto ours. I was even too tired to beg for that thing married people do. Oops, I meant my wife was too tired to beg me for it, yeah, that's what I meant.

I was awakened early on Christmas morning to the angelic voice of my five-year-old daughter Audrey speaking to my two-year-old daughter Claire.

"Look, Claire, Santa didn't come!" she said with disappointment.

We meant to get up early and put out the presents but overslept. It is difficult to feel good about yourself as a parent when you hear this from your children. As a matter of fact, you feel a little bit disgraceful.

"Nice!" Cheryl scowled at me. I guess it is the Dad's responsibility to put out the presents in our house.

"I'll fix this," I declared and out of the bed I jumped, "Time for your baths."

"Santa didn't come!" they whispered so softly it twisted the knife in my back.

"Come on, girls, let's get the bath running," Cheryl said herding them to the bathroom.

"Santa called and said he was running late!" It was a good save I thought and heck, lying to five, two and one year olds was pretty easy. Into the tub they were all squirreled. Yes, all three! It was a claw foot tub. They fit easily.

While they were bathing, into the attic above the bathroom I went. I jumped up and down. I yelled, "Ho, Ho, Ho!" with enthusiasm.

During my attic Santa impersonation, my wife put out the presents.

As the girls came out of the bathroom in their slippers and bathrobe their smiles lit up the room when they saw their presents had arrived.

Cheryl and I were amazed to find that Santa had come while the girls were bathing. I was shocked and speechless.

It was a good save, but trust me, you do not ever want to hear your children say, "Santa didn't come!"

Note: An unintended consequence was that our daughters expected presents after they took baths ever since. I took a bath only to avoid the consequences of not taking a bath!

CHAPTER **47**

Fine!

Cheryl: "This story is 100% true. Grandma always initiated, Gordy always yelled...then asked us to pick them up later than we had planned. According to Grandma, the girls where always 'Good as Gold.' Thank goodness for short stays, short term memory loss and very few grandchildren in the area. The girls lived for these weekends with all of the Grandparents and Robert and I could not be more thankful. As for Claire and her 'moods,' as my husband so lovingly calls them, they are not something she has yet outgrown. Just let her sleep. For your own good or back away slowly."

Tim: "All my sisters learned to cook from my mom. Enough said..." Circa 1996.

Most of the other grandchildren lived out of state and were older. My folks saw them infrequently but as often as possible under the circumstances. As Claire and Alex were born in Seattle and lived in proximity to my folks, they spent a lot of wonderful time together.

"Hello" I said answering the phone.
"Hi dear, we can watch the girls this weekend," Mom offered.
Before I could respond, my stepdad, Gordy, in the background was saying, "No way, Connie! We don't want those brats! Tell their parents to watch them."
So began the ritual, Mom would offer and Gordy would create false outrage. Cheryl and I figured out it was false outrage after the third or fourth time. Until then it was pretty disconcerting!
"How about dropping them off Friday at 6:00pm?" Mom continued.

"Then tell Robert to pick them up at 6:00am on Saturday," Gordy went on.

"Mom, if it is going to be a bother? Wait, you called me and asked for the girls," I replied.

"No bother, six then?" she asked.

"We'll see you then," I said.

Just before I hung up the phone, I heard Gordy yell, "Oh God! Not again! Connie, you're killing me."

On Friday evening, Cheryl and I dropped the girls off at the Kenmore house. They raced into see Grandma. After a brief exchange with Mom and dropping off their overnight bag, Cheryl and I headed out. Gordy met us on the front porch. This too became a ritual.

"What are your plans?" he asked.

"We are going to the hockey game this evening," I told him.

He handed me twenty dollars and said, "Have fun. When are you picking up the girls?"

"I don't know? How about 11:00am on Sunday?"

"No hurry, how about 3:00pm?" he suggested.

"Okay, thanks and we will see you on Sunday," I waved and off we went.

Weekends with Grandma were planned out. My mother spent a lot of time and energy coming up with an event schedule. The kids didn't just show up and sit in front of the television at her house. They were busy, busy, busy! There was swimming, shopping, visiting museums, dress up and baking.

Baking: Oh my god! My mother loved to bake with the girls but it was the one thing she never planned for. Grandpa did the shopping but was unaware of Grandma's baking plans so ingredients were always missing. Not a problem for my mom, she would just substitute. No eggs for the cake? Mayonnaise will work. Not enough flour? Krusteaze Pancake Mix will work. No sugar? A couple of Sweet and Low will do the trick.

Then once the 'cake' was baked, the decorating would begin. Two layers of the cake are uneven? A couple of crackers in between and voila; it is level. Frosting? Without sugar? No problem for my mother, she would just substitute.

I would arrive to pick them up and the kitchen would be a disaster. The girls would be covered in what I thought was flour but who knows what it may have been on this day, probably Comet. With glee on their faces, the girls would announce that they made me a cake. Me a cake? Never Grandma a cake or Grandpa a cake! Always me! I think my mom may be passive aggressive.

Then they would display the masterpiece.

Like my stepfather, I wasn't born yesterday! I had lived through my mother's cooking before, barely on several occasions. There was no way in hell that I was eating that cake.

"It looks really good but I am on a diet," I offered. It was not too credible as I was holding a coke and a bag of potato chips.

"They worked so hard on this. You must have a slice," Mom said trying the guilt trip.

For a brief instant, I considered eating some. Fortunately, in a moment of panic, I started scanning the kitchen counters; Sweet and Low, Mayonnaise, Krusteaze, Saltines, and Molasses. I looked at the sweet faces of my children and said, "I am not eating that!"

"Come on Dad, it is your duty to eat a piece of cake for your girls," Gordy said.

"I will have some right after you," I replied turning the tables on him.

"Oh god!" he said and left the scene of the crime.

Crime? Not yet, but had I ate any of that cake it may have turned into one!

I needed a graceful out. If you know any Olwells, you know that is not our strong suit!

"It is too good looking to eat without showing your mother first! Box it up and we will take it home," I announced.

Everyone was satisfied but it meant I had to stop and buy a cake from Safeway on the way home! Fortunately, the girls never seemed to notice the cake had changed in the hour drive home.

Then there were the times I would arrive to find a test of wills going on between my daughter, Claire, and her grandpa. She was three! She would be sitting at the kitchen table with food in front of her. She would have her hands folded across her chest. He would be across from her leaning back against the sink with his hands folded across his chest. Both would be scowling at each other.

"OOOOhhhhhh.....they are so mad at each other," Mom would say.

"If you don't eat it for breakfast, I will serve it for lunch," Grandpa declared.

"Fine!" Claire said.

"Fine!" Grandpa replied. A few moments later, he added, "If you don't eat it for lunch, I will serve it for dinner."

"Fine!" Claire said staring directly at him.

"Fine!" Grandpa responded again then added, "If you don't eat it for dinner, I will send it home with your father and he will serve it to you for breakfast tomorrow."

"Fine!" Claire said again without breaking eye contact with him.

"Fine!" Grandpa said.

While I was trying to figure out how I was just pulled into this, Alex would announce how good the food was. Then she would ask for more. She was thoroughly delighted to see her older sister in trouble.

After a few minutes, Grandpa would leave the kitchen. Then Grandma would try to make things okay, "Just take one bite."

Claire finally was coaxed into a bite. Her disgusted look said it all as she chewed.

"Okay!" Grandma said and discarded the rest in the trash. She would tell Grandpa how Claire gave in and ate it.

Claire looked to me for support. I did not know what to say. At least when Grandpa cooked, he followed the recipe!

I would get the kids stuff loaded into the car and wait for Claire to get around to hugging Grandpa, signifying the end of hostilities. Then off we went home until the next time.

My favorite was arriving on Sunday afternoon to Grandma and the girls all asleep on Grandma's bed still dressed all in scarves and jewels from the days Broadway production or piano recital. It was a refreshing reprieve from baked goods to eat or test of wills to break up.

My Mom would always claim, "They were as "Good as Gold!" I think she meant 24 karat on some occasions and electroplated on others!

Note: My father and stepmom would not take grief from Claire. She could be a hellion if she did not get enough sleep. I am not excusing her behavior. I am just pointing out the correlation between Claire being awful and not getting enough sleep. On more than one occasion, dad drove Claire home early when she was in one of her moods. He would keep Alex for the planned duration of the stay. After a couple of early weekends, Claire learned to go take a nap after she was warned.

The quality time my children spent with my parents was beneficial to all - including me. I needed a break from those kids!

CHAPTER **48**

McDonald's With Scott

Scott remarked: "The McDonald's years were dark ones, forgotten, mostly because I have to admit at one point I did work for Robert, or at least I led him to believe so." Circa 1996.

I was sitting in the lobby of the Lynnwood McDonald's when Scott came in. As the General Manager, I was usually required to open on Mondays to complete the weekly recap. This was no exception. I was reviewing the numbers, when Scott sat down with a beverage. He reached for the clipboard to plan for the closing shift. He was the First Assistant. We reviewed the weekly numbers.

"How was your weekend?" I asked.

"Great! I really needed a few days to unwind," he replied, "Hazel called in sick tonight? That's unusual."

"Yea, she will be out for the rest of the week. It was pretty funny. She was hit by a car on the way to work Saturday morning," I started.

"She got hit by a car and you think that is funny? That's strange even for you," he said and took a drink.

"No it is not funny that she got hit by a car. It is funny that when the aid car picked her up, she insisted that they drive her here to tell us she would not be in before she would let them take her to the hospital," I told him.

"You're kidding! How is she?" he asked.

"Fortunately just some bruising," I started when a customer was heard at the counter.

"Can I see a manager?" the guy said pretty loudly.

I started to get up. Scott just lifted a hand and said, "I got this one. Finish your drink."

He walked over to the teenager and introduced himself, "Hi, I'm Scott. I am a manager. What can I do for you?"

"You're a manager?" the kid asked.

"Yes, I still am," Scott answered.

"Good, I have a complaint. I was here yesterday. I ordered four McChicken value meals with Cokes. When I opened the bag, there were four Quarterpounders," he said with his hands folded across his chest.

"Why didn't you bring them back, we would have fixed it," Scott asked.

"We were on our way to Bothell and I didn't have time," the kid responded.

"Well, did you eat it?" Scott inquired.

"No, the fries were way too salty and the drinks were all Sprites and we ordered Cokes."

"Okay, if you didn't eat it. Give me back the bag of food and I will replace it."

"I can't. I was so mad I threw the bag out the window of my car."

"Well, I don't have to do anything but I really want to take care of you. So if you want to give me your name and address I will send you a coupon for free burger," Scott said and pulled a pen from his pocket and leaned down on the counter to write the response.

"You don't have to do that. My three friends are in the car and you can just replace the food now," the guy insisted.

"How convenient! But you don't understand, I am not giving you a coupon to replace four meals. I am giving you a coupon for one sandwich. So what is your address?" he asked again.

"You don't have to send anything. We are right here. Just give us the food!" he said loudly.

"I really don't have to do anything but again I really want to take care of you. Please give me your name and address so I can send you that coupon," Scott said calmly.

"I'm not leaving without four meals. You will give them to me right now!"

"No!"

"Well I am going to stand here and tell every customer who walks through those doors what a lousy restaurant this is and how you suck," the kid threatened.

"Go ahead and while you are doing that I will just call the police and have them drag your butt out of here," Scott replied calmly.

"Do you need to use a phone?" a lady customer in line who was witnessing the interaction offered.

The teen looked at Scott and at the lady then turned and stormed out of the restaurant. Scott thanked the lady and came over to the table again.

"Nicely done," I laughed.

"Thanks, you get the next one," he laughed.

A few hours later, as I was preparing to leave for the day, I walked up to the counter. A man came in the door and had the look like he needed something. I came out from behind the counter after setting down my coat.

"May I help you?" I asked.

"Yes, I just went through the drive thru and I think I was shorted five dollars change," he said and pointed to his car just outside the front doors.

"I'm sorry if that happened. If you have a moment, I will pull the register and count it. If it is over five dollars, I will gladly give it to you with my apologies," I explained.

"What if it isn't off by five dollars?" he asked.

"Well, first things first, if the register is not off we will deal with that then," I told him.

Then his car started moving. He was alarmed and ran out the building. He had left the car running with his kid in the car. The child had somehow placed the car in gear. It rolled across the parking lot and rammed the side of the adjacent building. I ran with him to the crash site. He turned the smoking car off. The child was shaken up but not injured. His car's bumper was pushed back into the radiator.

"Dude, I have no idea about the register but here," I said handing him five dollars out of my own wallet.

He didn't say much and took the money. After the tow truck took him and the car away, I told Scott that if the drive thru till was off by five dollars it was mine.

The next day, there was an envelope with the five dollars on my desk.

Note: As a First Assistant Manager, I was asked to cover the Mountlake Terrace McDonald's Manager's maternity leave. I met Scott during my coverage there. We did not get along. It wasn't after I was promoted to Manager and he was transferred in as my First Assistant, did we start to build a lasting friendship. After his stint with me, he was promoted to Manager at Harbor Pointe. He did an exceptional job there.

Alex

CHAPTER **49**

Alex Invites A Few Beatings

*Cheryl: "Since no one reading this book was present at the birth
of our youngest child Alex, I will let you in on a little secret. She is from
an alternate universe. The response that I have developed over the past
19 years when it comes to Alex looks something like this: My eyes
closed, shoulders hunched forward, head bowed slightly shaking side to
side in utter disbelief and a slight laugh to myself (or maybe God….who
must have given me this child in order to teach me patience and
understanding), then a modest shrug accompanied by a "Yep, that's my
Alex." I don't know how I am ever surprised at either her actions or
what comes out of her mouth. She is after all, an Olwell." Circa 2006.*

It was Wednesday afternoon around 4:20 when I started looking
out the front window for the kid's bus. The phone rang.

"Hi Dad, Alex is not on the bus," Claire said.

"When you get home, we'll go pick her up," I sighed. After I got
off the phone, I started to recount the number of times my youngest
daughter missed the bus home from junior high. If only I could get
them to serve food on the bus, she would never miss it again.

When Claire arrived home, I grabbed my keys to leave when the
phone rang.

"Mr. Olwell, this is the counselor at Spring Branch Middle
School."

"I'm on my way to pick her up," I interrupted and with that
Claire and I drove the twelve miles to get Alex.

When we arrived at the school, Alex was not in front waiting. I
sent Claire to get her. After about five minutes, Claire returned empty
handed. I was a little annoyed when I got out of my car and went
looking. The school's entrance was locked. After someone exited, I
went into the office with Claire in tow.

The counselor introduced herself and asked to me to join her in a conference room. She instructed Claire to wait outside. Alex was sitting at the table.

"Alex told several of her classmates that she was afraid to go home because her sister beats her. The classmates told her teacher who brought it to our attention," the counselor blindsided me with.

"Beats her?" I said with a look which could best be described as incredulous.

"When allegations of abuse are brought to our attention, we must investigate before we can release the child to go home."

"Beats her?" I was really at a loss. First, I was thinking about the beating I was going to give her when I got her out of this meeting. Then I thought that may not help the situation. Second, I was thinking about all the times I showed up to school battle scarred from the hands of my siblings growing up. Usually the teacher looked real concerned at me and said, "I hoped you learned your lesson." Implying I probably deserved it. That was their investigation and usually was followed by a note to my parents thanking them for disciplining me.

But I had to say something appropriate now to get this meeting over and me out of this situation.

"I have six older brothers and sisters and I know what a beating is, so I can assure you that Alex is not being beaten by her sister." I was satisfied with that response but it seemed the counselor found it lacking.

"We checked her for bruises and did not find anything," she informed me.

"Ya think?" I replied.

I started wondering if they were going to check her the following day, I was starting to think she needed a beating.

Then the principal came in and discussed what a great kid Alex was and the rest I just failed to pay attention to. I was looking at Alex who had a concerned look with a sheepish smirk on her face.

"Their mother will be home tomorrow, I'll let her deal with this," I said. I took Alex and excused ourselves from the office.

On the drive home, I started to think how my Dad would have handled this situation with the school. He would have told the school officials, "You are absolutely right to be concerned, I'll go home and get her clothes for you right now. She likes spaghetti." That would have been about right.

I was pretty angry on the drive home. I finally announce to my daughters, "Claire don't touch your sister. Alex, the next time you accuse someone of beating you, there had better have been a beating that took place."

When we arrived home, I sent Alex to her room.

By the way, it seems this all stemmed from Claire slapping Alex at the bus stop before school for some reason neither girl could remember.

Cheryl called after Alex went to her room; the counselor had called her before calling me. Since she was in New Mexico, they had to call me.

I explained the situation to my wife. I was feeling pretty good about my handling of the situation as I had neither smacked the kids nor said anything too inappropriate to the school.

Cheryl announced she was mad that I sent Alex to her room and Claire was not sent to hers. I assured Cheryl she could handle it anyway she wanted when she returned home. She may have made a sucking sound on the other end of the phone but I may have been imagining it. (My mother makes that noise when she is mad.)

About a week later, my brother Tim came over. While he was chatting with Audrey on the front porch, I noticed a tarantula on the house about ten feet away. I pointed it out. Audrey let out a scream and ran across the yard. When my brother started to corral the spider, I joined her standing across the yard. He put it in a box and took it across the street just as the school bus arrived.

The school kids including Claire and Alex did not believe there was a tarantula in the box. They went to investigate. A thirteen year old boy reached into the box, picked up the tarantula, and proceeded to let all the kids pet it.

I started feeling a little ridiculous for standing as far away as possible. But I was confident in my masculinity, and was sure it would not suffer from me screaming like a girl.

The next day Cheryl arrived at the school to pick up the girls for a dentist appointment.

The counselor met Cheryl in the office.

"There was an incident," the counselor started then explained.

Alex left her backpack in the front yard overnight where she set it down to look at the tarantula. It was full of opened food. Then she grabbed it on the way to the bus. In her first class of the morning she opened her back pack and all kinds of bugs spewed out of it. So many so, that the kids ran out of the room screaming, a response that I totally approve of, and exterminators had to be called to fumigate the room.

Cheryl was standing in the office with all the staff and teachers glaring at her. She was confident they were not going to vote for her as mother of the year.

"Too bad her first class wasn't Science, she might have received extra credit," I responded that evening.

Cheryl turned to me and asked, "Do you think they'll check her for bruises tomorrow?"

This is how I remember the dog!

CHAPTER **50**

Repairing Cujo's Air Conditioning

Mando: "I would like to think that I have had a hand in showing Robert a lot of the "dos and don'ts" in the HVAC business. My favorite saying for weeks was, "I wouldn't touch that if I was you!" That being said, I thought I had covered everything. With man's best friend, I told him, "Watch for raised hackles. Pay attention to their tail. Walk slowly and no sudden movements." Like a skipping record, I thought I hammered those points home. At least he listened to me about getting a rabies vaccination, I think. The foaming at the mouth with irregular and wild behavior appeared to be his usual demeanor; just good old Robert and another story for the book." Circa 2013.

"I've got a call," the dispatcher announced.

It was 4:45pm on Friday afternoon and we were all scheduled off at 5:00pm. Mark and Mando looked the other way and no one responded. The dispatcher looked annoyed.

"Give me a set of keys and I'll go," I announced. I needed the practice.

Mando handed over the keys to his rig and off I went.

I used the navigation system on my phone for directions. I arrived twenty five minutes later.

I knocked on the door. The woman of the house answered.

"Let me get my husband," she said.

"Hello," he said.

"Hi, I'm Robert from Blanco A.C.. I am here to look at your system," I said cheerfully.

"I called and cancelled the service request hours ago," he informed me.

"Well, okay then, I am sorry to bother you," I said with the normal goodbyes and headed off.

When I got back to the highway, I pulled over and called the office. I was told not to worry about it as another call had come in. After hanging up, they texted me the address. It was in a city sixty miles north of where I was. I noticed my phone was dying. I went to my bag in the back of the truck and grabbed my charger. In doing so, the cigarette lighter plug fell apart.

I decided to just drive north and I would figure it out. Several times, I tried to use the navigation system to locate the customer. The address was not recognized and the phone was beeping indicating the battery was dying. An hour later, I pulled into a convenience store where I purchased a soda and an overpriced phone charger.

Again I tried to use the nav system after I plugged my phone into the charger. No luck, so I called the contact number and got an answering machine. From 6:30 – 7:20 p.m., I tried to figure out the address and continued calling the contact number. I also placed several calls to Mando for guidance. I was pretty frustrated by the time Mando called me back at 7:30 p.m. He tracked down the directions for me and off I headed.

Fortunately, I was not too far away. I arrived and introduced myself to the homeowner Jim. I explained that I had been trying to get in touch for directions. He asked what number I was using.

"Oh, that is my wife's cell number. She is in Colorado," he laughed.

"Okay, so what is going on with your air conditioner?" I asked.

"The house is ninety degrees and the air inside is blowing warm."

"Okay, let's find out what was going on," I said confidently.

I walked over to the outside unit, the condenser. It was off. I turned on the breaker at the quick disconnect located nearby. It just made a humming sound. I turned the breaker back off.

I checked the capacitor and was somewhat surprised to find it was within tolerances; so much for an easy fix. I checked the condenser fan motor- it tested that it was shorted. I looked on the truck and saw that I had a replacement. I gave Jim a quote and he authorized the replacement.

I took the fan housing off, replaced the fan motor, and replaced the fan housing. I then removed and replaced the capacitor as it is always replaced with a new motor. When this was completed, I turned the breaker back on and the fan came on. The compressor did not.

I turned the breaker back off and tested the compressor. The common wire was open. This suggested that the compressor had overheated and the thermal switch activated to save the compressor.

Bad fan motor, hot compressor that makes sense I thought. I just needed to cool the compressor. I looked at it and it had a thermal blanket on it. Great, I removed the fan housing again. I took off the thermal blanket and the compressor was very hot to the touch. I went and got the garden house and rinsed the compressor for fifteen minutes. When I figured it had been long enough, I tested the compressor wires again and the common wire was closed as the thermal switch had reset.

I reinstalled the fan housing. I reconnected all the wiring. Then, I confidently threw the circuit breaker. The fan and the compressor turned on and the system started cooling the house. I was feeling pretty good about life when I noticed the thermal blanket.

I turned the unit back off. I removed the fan housing- it is easier the third time by the way. I replaced the thermal blanket. I reinstalled the fan housing. I turned the breaker back on and the system came to life.

I put away all my tools and wrote up the invoice.

Jim thanked me and I got in my truck and headed out. At the end of the driveway, the gate was closed. I got out to open the gate.

Then the dog bit me.

I looked down shocked.

"Did he bite you?" the homeowner yelled.

"Yes!" I said still stunned.

He grabbed his dog and dragged it to the backyard. Then he suggested we look at it. There were two puncture wounds on my calf just below the knee.

"I will get some disinfectant," he said in between apologies and went into the house.

He came out a few moments later, he returned with a bottle of Hydrogen Peroxide.

I was talking to his son as he used the peroxide.

"MOTHER JONES!" I yelled and looked down at my now throbbing leg. I swear too much so I have been saying "Mother Jones" instead of a fouler version.

Jim had placed the bottle on the puncture and squeezed the bottle and peroxide into my leg. Then it all bubbled and shot back out of my leg.

I decided that was enough first aid and said good bye.

It was about 9:00pm when I headed south. I was tired and bleeding but I had solved global warming, at this house at least.

Note: The guys at work wanted me to add the story about when I fell through a cattle guard nearly breaking my leg. It seems it was much funnier to them than it was to me. Maybe in the next book!

As you can see, I have been blessed with a wonderful family and wonderful friends that continue to supply endless story material.